A GREAT CONVENIENCY

A MARITIME HISTORY OF THE PASSAIC RIVER, HACKENSACK RIVER, AND NEWARK BAY

Kevin K. Olsen M.A.

American History Imprints
Franklin, Tennessee
www.Americanhistoryimprints.com

ISBN 10: 0-9753667-7-7
ISBN 13: 978-0-9753667-7-6

First Edition April 2008

Library of Congress Control Number: 2008928359

Printed in the United States of American on acid-free paper

This book is dedicated to my wife Barbara who made many sacrifices for it. A few that come to mind are the time that she gave up an afternoon of vacation while I worked in the Mariner's Museum Library, the times she put up with huge piles of research notes, and late nights at the library. On more than one occasion, she found slips of paper in my wallet with a woman's name and phone number, but they were all librarians, curators, or historians.

With love for Barbara.

Acknowledgments

No work of non-fiction is the product of a single person and it is traditional to begin by acknowledging those people who have made substantial contributions. This list should begin with my grandfather who brought me as a young boy to the site of Acquackanonck bridge and told me the story of how it was cut down during the Revolution to prevent its use by the British. From that day on, I had a love of local history.

In alphabetical order, here are just a few of the many people who generously contributed to the making of this book:

Ralph Colfax, George Sellmer, Sue Deeks, and Claire Tholl, of the North Jersey Highlands Historical Society.

Dr. Robert Cray of Montclair State University for valuable encouragement.

Thomas Fitzpatrick for supplying original artwork.

Jack Goudsward, archaeologist, who explored the Hackensack River with me and shared the story of the Cressy with me.

Al John, historian and boating enthusiast, who, among other things, recorded the story of the Cressy back when nobody thought it was of any importance.

Edward J. Lenik, archaeologist, who taught me to how to write about history.

Stephen Marshall, Esq., provided many of the illustrations from his collection and also provided materials related to Newark Bay and the Passaic River.

Larry Robertson, historian and Hackensack River tour guide who made many helpful suggestions for revisions and additions.

The Bergen County Historical Society, The Hackensack Meadowlands Environmental Center, The Pascack Historical Society, the Roebling Chapter of the Society for Industrial Archaeology, and the Wayne Township Museum all let me make use of their material. I received invaluable feedback, suggestions, and made contact with many individuals who later helped me tell this story.

David Kane, publisher, and Stanford Griffith, book designer, for their dedication and devotion to the project.

Table of Contents

Foreword

Ships and seafaring have always held a powerful hold on the human imagination. Helen of Troy had the face that "launched a thousand ships." Emily Dicknson when searching for a metaphor to describe the joys of reading said that there was "no frigate like a book." Films, novels, travelogues and history books all celebrate the romance of the sea and the allure of far away lands.

Surrounded by water on three sides, New Jersey boasts a rich seafaring history. Yet the ships that sailed from our local seaports seldom ventured more than a few hundred miles up or down the coast or farther than the West Indies. Even so, their story is important, because in their humble way, they helped to build the place that so many of us call home.

What's in a River's Name?

The names of the many rivers in the mid-Atlantic states caused confusion to early mariners. Their names were often changed on charts and other maritime documents to more accurately reflect geographical locations. The Hudson River was also known as the North River so as to distinguish it from the Delaware, or South River, even though the two rivers were more than one-hundred miles apart. The East River, technically not a river but a tidal reach, was so named because it ran along the east shore of Manhattan Island and separated it from Long Island. In New Jersey, because it was the second river encountered when traveling westward from New York Harbor, the Passaic River became known as the Second River. Perhaps because they were economically less important, the Hackensack and Raritan Rivers in the same state never seem to have been widely known by any other names.

According to Donald Becker's *Indian Place Names in New Jersey*, at the time of European contact, the group of Lenape Indians living on the river were known as the "Achensachys" or "Ackinsachys." These names were anglicized to "Hackensack." They appear to be derived the Lenape words for "hook" and "mouth of a river." The "hook" in this case is thought to be the tip of the peninsula between Newark Bay and the Hudson River. Other translators have taken the name to mean "tidal water" or a "stream that unites with another on low ground." This is certainly an accurate description of the tip of the peninsula between the Hackensack and Passaic rivers.

Most of the sources quoted by Becker agree that the name "Passaic" is derived from the Lenape word for 'valley." Another explanation comes from the Algonquin word "pach," meaning "to split or divide." Most Algonquin dialects use this word to describe the forks or branches of a tree. When the ending "-ic" is added to this word the meaning becomes "where it divides." In this case the division might be referring to the cleft in the rocks by the Great Falls of the Passaic River.

Newark Bay was named the Het Achter Cull or "Back Bay" by the Dutch to distinguish from the main harbor at New Amsterdam. The English took to calling it the After Col and the name was further corrupted to Arthur Cull or After Kull.

Chapter 1

Economics and Eras

During the period when Europeans lived in what is today northern New Jersey, the region's navigable rivers played an important part of the lives of cities and towns along their banks, as well as in the hinterlands beyond. Despite the abundance of various cargoes, ship types, mariners, and maritime activities, the patterns of trade have remained relatively stable, and we can divide the region's maritime history into distinct, though not mutually exclusive, eras.

The first step toward understanding patterns of trade is to have an understandable representation of the important concepts involved. As this story progresses, ships and cargoes will come and go but underlying themes will remain. The economic model and the historical eras that are presented in this chapter broadly define the activities that have taken place over time.

Economics is the basis for all trade patterns. For our purposes, think of a hub and spoke model, where New York City forms the hub of an extensive water (later road and rail) transportation system. The spokes are made up of the streams and rivers, feeding goods to the commercial center and facilitating the shipment of other products back to the outlying areas. Until the relatively recent disappearance of truck farms as a consequence of development, much of New York's food was grown nearby in "The Garden State". To a lesser, but no less important extent, New York's manufacturers and merchants were also the customers of the region's extractive industries which provided fur, firewood, iron, lumber, and various building supplies. Until the outlying region developed independent distribution channels, New York merchants supplied most of the manufactured goods. Thus the movement of goods down the spokes of our theoretical hub proceeded in both directions.

New York, however, is not merely the hub of a series of feeder streams; it is one of the nation's principle deepwater ports and the maritime crossroads for much of the eastern seaboard. To the north and east, Long Island Sound leads to New England. The Hudson River/Lake Champlain corridor opens up to Canada, Albany, the Erie Canal, and the Great Lakes. To the south, lower New York Harbor leads to the Intercoastal Waterway, which in turns runs south to the Chesapeake and eventually to the Gulf of Mexico. Directly south from the harbor entrance is the Atlantic Ocean and the world.

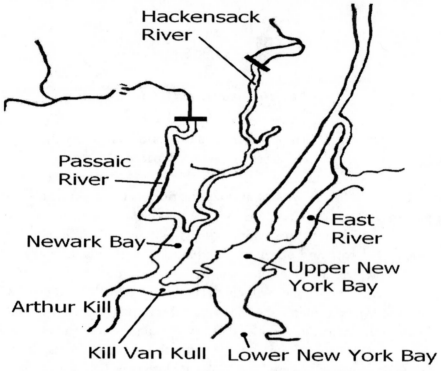

Courtesy Library of Congress

The second piece of our economic model consists of the landing, which was a kind of miniature seaport. These are the trading centers and trans-shipment points that developed along many navigable rivers. Unlike the major ports such as New York, Philadelphia or Boston, these ports served a relatively small geographic area. It is necessary to draw a contrast to today's smaller ports which almost always specialize in handling only one type of cargo, such as coal, grain or automobiles. Historically these lesser ports only specialized to the extent that the regional economy it served allowed specialization. Even so, these ports handled a much wider range of goods than their size would suggest. They eventually declined as a result of improved road and rail networks, but in their heyday they were truly diverse. Ships were built and repaired, crews were assembled and most importantly, reserves of capital were made available to carry on maritime trade. In general, the ship owners and officers were local people with family and economic ties to the region. We have to assume that the same held true for the ship's crews because written references to them are almost entirely lacking.

The ships sailing from the miniature ports were often engaged in trade along the hub-and-spokes with New York. Others made voyages to distant coastal ports such as Norfolk, Philadelphia, or Albany. Ships might carry general cargoes or be engaged in a specialized trade. Except for an occasional run to the West Indies, overseas trade was left to the larger, better financed vessels based in the larger harbors.

The third and final piece of our model is shipment of bulk cargoes. Normally we think of these as commodities that are shipped in large quantities, at slow speeds, with minimal subdivision into smaller containers. They can be heavy or light, liquid or solid, but bulk cargoes are invariably goods that are relatively inexpensive per unit of volume. It takes a quantity to fill any vessel to the point where a voyage is profitable. Although slow, ships are large and water transportation is cheap, so they are ideal for bulk loads. The more expensive goods are generally smaller and lighter and perhaps more perishable, and it pays to move them quickly. This is where railroads, wagons, or trucks outperform water transportation. As we shall see, one of the major recurring themes of this story will be a gradual shift from general to bulk cargoes.

Today we think of bulk carriers as specialized vessels. Modern ships are expensive, as are their crews, maintenance facilities, and ports where they are loaded and unloaded. It is faster and cheaper for a ship owner to build a dedicated vessel to handle one type of cargo rather than to incur the additional expense of refitting a generic vessel each time a different cargo is carried. Specialized loading and unloading equipment is incorporated into the ship's design and is used to minimize the time that the vessel is in port, i.e. not profitable. On shore, competition for vessels has prompted modern port authorities to install equally specialized equipment. Today we have many different bulk handling ports, oil terminals, coal terminals, and the like, but we have few ports that can accommodate more than one type of ship.

In the past, this was not the case. Since goods were packed into boxes, barrels, or sacks, no specialized equipment was needed to load or unload them. Any dockside crane or a gang of strong-backed men could perform the job. Since labor was cheap and capital was dear, the real cost was in the building of the ship, and few owners could afford to devote an entire vessel to one type of trade. There were notable exceptions to this rule, such as canal boats which were used primarily to move coal, and coasting vessels which were built for the lumber trade. In general however, a bulk cargo required only a large vessel, not a specialized one, and no dedicated port facilities were needed.

The eras of river navigation by Europeans can be defined by the relative importance of maritime trade in the regional economy. The trade patterns that existed when a riverside town was a settlement in the wilderness, almost totally dependent on water transportation, will be quite different from an era when the same town becomes an established village being served by a network of crude roads. They will change yet again when the town is linked to the outside world by railroads and paved highways. Although the share of water transportation as a percentage of the region's total economy becomes smaller over time, it continues to persist in importance and never really disappears entirely. As times change, people find new uses for the rivers.

Stage One — Fur and Pioneer Farms

It is clear that the first people to use the river were the Native Americans and that the first use of the river by Europeans was to trade with them for furs. New Amsterdam, founded in 1624 by the Dutch West India Company, was the principle base of operations as fur traders and explorers branched out along the rivers. Except for a few Indian trails, the river was the only means of transportation. This was the situation when the first European settlers arrived in what would later become Bergen County, and it persisted until there was sufficient population to justify the construction of a road network.

Stage Two — The Road Network Expands

When rudimentary roads began to reach out from the riverbanks, the landings where roads and rivers met became increasingly important. Merchants established their miniature seaports, or landings, at convenient points such as Acquackanonck Landing (now the east side of the city of Passaic) and Raritan Landing near New Brunswick. Several important commercial centers lined the Hackensack River - Old Bridge Landing, near the present day town of New Milford, New Bridge Landing, in River Edge, and several others in the city of Hackensack.

Eastern View of Acquackanonck.

When this 1844 engraving was made, Acquackanonk was a thriving shipping point at the Passaic River's head of navigation.

Local farmers and merchants shipped commodities into New York to either supply the growing city or to be stockpiled by New York merchants for overseas export. Manufactured goods, liquors, lumber, coal, and exotic foods were in turn brought back by returning boats. The merchants who operated the landings often sold these goods at their riverside stores, thus establishing important retail centers for the communities. Other goods were sent farther inland by a network of merchants and freight wagons.

This period lasted from the mid-1700s to the coming of the railroads. Trade patterns were not stable and they varied by economic conditions. For example, in the Hackensack Valley, passenger travel on river vessels succumbed in the mid-1700s to competition from stage coaches. In the Passaic River Valley, however, where both the railroads and the Industrial Revolution arrived sooner, passenger travel by steamboat was an important part of the regional transportation system.

Stage Three — The Industrial Revolution

The transportation network continued to expand throughout the 1800s, when steam ferries navigated the Hudson and railroads penetrated the river valleys. The importance of river transportation grew with the times. The rising population and growing cities needed cheap, dependable transportation. In particular, the lumber, fertilizer, and coal businesses relied on water transportation as a means of conveying goods. As the local farms continued to grow crops for the New York markets the demand for bulk transportation of wheat, flour, hay, and produce remained strong. As new distribution channels for consumer goods were developed, riverfront landings lost their appeal as commercial centers. Throughout this period there was also a gradual shifting to the carrying of bulk cargoes. This trend culminated in the late nineteenth and early twentieth centuries with the almost total replacement of sailing vessels by steam tugboats and barges, which were better fitted to facilitate such cargo transport.

Stage Four — Suburbia Ascendant

With the building of additional railroads after the Civil War, the pace of suburban expansion accelerated. On the Hackensack, the more industrialized reaches of the river south of the city proper continued to rely on water transportation, but the upper portions of the river needed it less and less. As farmers gave way to railroad commuters, there was no longer any need to move bulk cargoes of potatoes or grain. What the new residents wanted was recreation. Canoe clubs, boat clubs, and swimming beaches proliferated all along the Hackensack. Above the city of Paterson, a number of summer resorts and recreation areas developed on the Passaic and its tributaries. The growing population also needed water and the damming of the rivers for reservoirs had profound consequences on their flow and salinity.

Courtesy Waterworks Conservancy

A pair of kayakers paddle the Hackensack River near Oradell in this period photograph.

On both rivers, the increased population accelerated the shift to bulk cargoes. Barges with sand, cement, or gravel for building, and coal or fuel oil for heating became commonplace. By the 1930s, the effluent from factories and sewer systems was also common in the lower reaches of the rivers.

Prior to the early 1900s Newark's water-borne commerce was centered on the Passaic River and primarily served local industries. The shores of Newark Bay still consisted of low lying tidal marshes.

Stage Five — The Port Expands

By the late nineteenth century, the Port of New York had become severely congested with a mixture of ocean-going ships, coastal freighters, steamboats, ferry boats, and all types of small harbor craft. Large shipyards and major ocean freight terminals began spreading out into the nearby rivers, especially the Hackensack and Passaic. Newark Bay began evolving into the major port that it is today. Whereas in the past, these facilities would have only served regional needs, railroad connections now meant that these facilities could serve shippers anywhere in the country.

Stage Six — Ecological Awakening

For many years, the rivers were assaulted by siltation, pollution, and dumping. The passage of legislation at both the state and federal levels to control water pollution marked the beginning of ecological awareness. This was accelerated by the realization that the Hackensack Meadowland's sanitary landfills were rapidly reaching capacity. Steps had to be taken to close them and manage the area wisely, in an environmentally sensitive way. Maintenance dredging required in Port Newark to keep the channels open fueled debate over what to do about the pollutants in the dredge spoils and also broadened the scope of river clean up efforts. Canoe clubs, recreational boating and citizen activism for cleaner rivers mark this period, which continues to the present day. Commercial navigation is now limited to the southern reaches of the rivers and bay, and is carried on exclusively by barges.

Chapter 2

The Only Highway

It is certain we will never know for sure who the first Europeans were to sail on the Hackensack River. It has been suggested that it could have been Henrick Christiaensen and Adriaen Block, two Dutch captains making the first reconnaissance of the area that would later become New Netherlands. They no doubt explored the area since it was reported in 1613 that they had,

> by means of trading-boats visited every creek, bay, river and inlet
> in the neighborhood where a settlement was to be found.

The Dutch claim to the Hudson Valley and what would later become New York City dated back to 1609 when Henry Hudson explored the region. While Hudson's ship, the *Half Moon*, was anchored somewhere between Staten Island and the Navesink River, five men under the command of John Colman became the first Europeans to sail Newark Bay. They had been sent to gauge the depths of the water in the bay to ensure safe navigation. On their return trip they were attacked by Indians near its mouth. According to contemporary accounts, twenty-six Indians in two canoes made up the attacking party. Colman was killed and his body was later interred on Sandy Hook at what became Colman's Point.

The 1609 voyage was followed by other exploring voyages, similar to Christiaensen's and Block's. Finally, in 1624, the island of Manhattan was purchased from the Indians and a permanent settlement was established for the purpose of exploiting the natural riches of the area. In the river valleys, the principle trade was with the Indians for furs.

In New Amsterdam, the settlers quickly took advantage of the network of rivers and harbors to reach the Indians. Three important outposts were established west of the Hudson River. Paulus Hook, later to become Jersey City, was founded in 1630 on a site where several Indian trails converged on the

9

Hudson. This location later became the landing for the principle trans-Hudson ferries. Vriessendael, a plantation in present day Edgewater, was founded by sea captain and explorer David Pietersz DeVries in 1640. Pavonia was the first permanent settlement stretching over lands in what today is Hoboken and Jersey City. Although the settlement eventually failed, a trading post remained.

The first trading post on the Hackensack River was located on its east bank in present day Bogota. This post, Achter Col, which was the Dutch name for the Hackensack River, was founded about the same time as Vriessendael and likewise was destroyed by Indians in 1643 in reprisal for Dutch atrocities.

While a full account of the relationship between the Dutch settlers and the local natives is well beyond the scope of this book, it makes for fascinating reading and exciting scholarship. For the purposes of our story it is only essential to note that the earliest trading posts were situated on the rivers. The Dutch also traded directly from their boats. Beaver and otter furs, and bear, deer, and elk skins made up the major part of the trade. The colonists also depended on trade with the Indians for staples such as corn and tobacco. Indian wampum, made of finely cut and polished shells, was an accepted currency in the colony, even among the early settlers.

The fur trade was structured as a monopoly by the Dutch West India Company, but anyone who owned a boat and had some liquor was able to enter the trade and undercut them. In 1665, the company issued a now famous proclamation,

> nobody shall sell from any yacht, ship, boat, or canoe, cart or wagon... directly or indirectly any beer, wine, brandy or other strong waters to any Indian.

The proclamation was much easier to issue than to enforce. In any case it unintentionally reveals good information about the travel methods of the Dutch colonists. The yacht was not necessarily a pleasure boat, although some were built for that purpose. The term refers to a particular type of small Dutch craft. The small yachts that were used in New Netherlands would have had one mast like a modern sailboat, but there the resemblance ends. It's lines were sharp with a carved beakhead below the bowsprit. There would also be a raised quarter-deck near the stern, which was also embellished with elaborate carvings. Passenger accommodations were usually provided in the cabin near the stern. Two egg-shaped lee boards instead of a deep keel provided lateral resistance when tacking. A more technically precise description will be provided in a later chapter.

Author's sketch

A sloop typical of those in the New York region during the early 1700s.

The Dutch "sloep" [sic] was a boat type related to the yacht and was also common in the Dutch overseas colonies. They were less fine-lined and rarely exceeded sixty feet in length. They carried a fore and aft rig, which might vary by including a bowsprit or auxiliary sails. As they were designed to be rowed as well as sailed, they did not have leeboards. (Leeboards are thick boards or planks hung off the side of vessel. When lowered into the water they provide the lateral resistance necessary to allow sailing into the wind.)

The term ship usually refers to a vessel having three masts and rigged primarily with square sails. Although we tend to think of these as ocean-going vessels, smaller examples of this type could be easily used on the Hudson and Newark Bay.

Most canoes found in the New Amsterdam colony were dugouts. The Indians had constructed dugout canoes from tulip trees for centuries, because in this region birches did not grow large enough to use their bark for canoes. There is some evidence that bark canoes could have been brought into the colony via the northern outposts on the upper Delaware River. Local tradition however, is emphatic that the Dutch imported West Indian dugout canoes, sometimes equipped with sailing rigs.

In 1996, a West Indian dugout canoe, which had been found by a fisherman on the banks of the Pompton River in Pequannock Township, was brought to the attention of local archaeologists. The abandoned vessel had been patched with plywood and obviously had been used recently. Archaeologist Edward Lenik arranged to have the wood identified and radiocarbon dated.

The surprising result was that the wood used in the canoe comes from the

Courtesy Project Gutenberg

The British Revenue Cutter Wickham *was a typical sloop of the early 1800s. From* King's Cutters and Smugglers 1700-1855, *Edward Keble Chatterton, London, George Allen & Company, Ltd., 1912.*

ceiba tree. This tree only grows south of the Tropic of Cancer. The logs of this particular tree are large, light, easy to work with, and they float readily. Ceiba is the perfect material for building a canoe. Radiocarbon dating of the wood showed the salvaged canoe to be about 400 years old. The most plausible explanation was that the canoe was brought to New Jersey by Dutch or Spanish traders and used on the local rivers. Sometime later the canoe sank or was buried under low-oxygen conditions. There is no other way that the wood would have survived 400 years. Then in the twentieth century, perhaps as a result of the river's frequent flooding, the canoe refloated and was salvaged and reused.

As happened in so many places, where the fur traders first penetrated, the settlers soon followed. Before the late 1650s almost all white settlements on the west side of the Hudson were failures. It was difficult to induce colonists to leave a peaceful, prosperous, and tolerant Holland for an unknown overseas wilderness. Mismanagement and poor judgment on the part of the Dutch colonial government exacerbated tensions with the Indians. Twice, in 1643 and again in 1655, war broke out and the natives forced the colonists back across the Hudson. After the second war, Peter Stuyvesant, Director General of New Amsterdam, decided to guarantee the colonist's land deeds by negotiating a new land purchase from the Indians for all of the territory between the Hackensack and the Hudson.

This purchase initiated a second wave of European immigration that spread out along the river banks. This time they had come to stay. Bergen, which occupied the present-day site of Journal Square in Jersey City, was laid out in 1660. The first road in the region was also laid out from that settlement to the Hudson River ferry in 1660. Modern Lyndhurst, or as it was then called New Barbados Neck, was purchased by a Captain William Sanford on behalf of Nathaniel Kingsland in 1668, after the Indians accepted payment of 170 fathoms of black wampum and 200 of white. The area near the Hackensack's head of navigation, the modern towns of River Edge and New Milford, was first settled by French Huguenot David Demarest in 1677. Hackensack proper was established at the junction of a small creek and the river. A detailed study of settlement patterns in the 1600s, while fascinating, is well beyond the capacity of this work. The reader should remember that the only land travel possible at this time was via the Indian trails. Water travel was the principle economic link both within the colony and to the outside world. No roads existed in Bergen County until the early 1700s and no bridges spanned the Hackensack River until the 1720s. It was no romantic exaggeration when one historian said that early itinerant ministers reached their scattered congregations by "canoe, sloop and horseback."

In 1664, when Holland surrendered possession of her North American colonies to England, the settlement of East Jersey accelerated. The rivers were instrumental in providing a great boost to the colony. In 1684, Gaven Lawrie, the Deputy Governor of East Jersey, wrote to London,

> There is great conveniency for traveling from places through the Province in boats, from small canoe to vessels of 30, 40, or 50 ton and in some places 100.

One of the first settlements established under English rule was New Barbados, on the peninsula between the Hackensack and Passaic rivers and extending back into parts of Paramus and River Edge. English immigrants settled in what became known as the "English Neighborhood," present day Ridgefield, Leonia, and Englewood. In 1666, a groups of Puritans from Connecticut founded Newark. They chose an isolated spot on the west bank of the Passaic River, just north of the head of Newark Bay. From there additional settlements moved inland along the Passaic River.

Newark's location on the west bank of the Passaic isolated the town. To reach New York, a traveler had to take a ferry over the Passaic, cross the marshes to the Hackensack, and then take another ferry. The traveler then climbed over the hilly spine of Bergen Ridge. Finally he went down to the Hudson River and boarded a third ferry for the trip to Manhattan. (This is the same route a modern motorist takes crossing the Pulaski Skyway and the Holland Tunnel between Newark and New York. It is also the route of the Port Authority Trans-Hudson Railroad or PATH between Newark's Penn Station and lower Manhattan.)

In March of 1669, the town of Newark made an arrangement with John Rockwell, a boatman. He would settle in the town and maintain a boat for the use of the community and its citizens, "as long as the Lord shall enable him thereto." In turn, the town would temporarily suspend the payments due on the purchase of his land.

A month later, in April, the town made further efforts to encourage another boat owner. Azariah Bush was to be admitted to the town as a "Planter" and would be granted three or four acres for his home lot. In return for the favor, Bush was also to maintain a boat for the use of the town. Like other communities, Newark offered these incentives to encourage skilled craftsmen to settle there.

Settlement and exploration continued to advance up the Passaic River. Among the first Europeans to venture beyond the head of navigation and to Paterson's Great Falls were two Labadists, Jasper Dankers and Peter Sluyter, who were taken there by a group of Indians. The Labadists were a small religious sect who were searching for a home in the New World due to persecution in the old. Although they were favorably impressed by the region, the sect ultimately settled in New York.

The first European to actually see the falls was the explorer Jacques Cortelyou, who later described them to Hartman Michielson. Michielson had been born in Bergen, New Jersey. As an adult he went west to set up an Indian trading post. In 1678, Michielson purchased Menehenicke, (later Dundee) Island in the Passaic River from a Lenni-Lenape chief who had been given the European name of Captahen Peeters. Michielson's island was located just below the river's head of navigation.

The falls were a convenient site for the Indians because it was a short distance upstream to the site of their fish weir. The weir consisted of a line of stones and boulders placed across the river with a short gap left in the center. Water could flow over or through the stones but fish were forced to swim through the gap where traps could be placed.

Five years after establishing the trading post, Michielson was a principal organizer of the Acquackanonk Patent. At total of fourteen men formed a company that purchased 10,000 acres in what is today the central and lower portions of Passaic County. To encourage settlement, 100-acre lots were assigned by a random drawing; all of these lots lined the Passaic River. In time, the area around the head of navigation became the port for the region, Acquackanonck Landing. It was centered around the area that is today Gregory Avenue and River Road in the city of Passaic. The original Acquackanonck bridge was on the site of the present-day bridge between Gregory Avenue in Passaic and Main Avenue in Wallington.

Another example of how the early settlers depended on river transportation can be found further north, where in 1680 a group of 13 men joined in a company with John Pietersen Haring to purchase 16,000 acres from the Tappan Indians in what is today southeastern Rockland County and northern Bergen County. Politically, it was then considered part of East Jersey. The land was a well-watered wilderness lying between the Hudson and Hackensack rivers, although it did not actually extend all the way to the Hudson. Except for Indian trails and a few scattered areas that the natives had cleared, the area was completely untouched by man.

One of the reasons for selecting this site was to avoid the port duties that were imposed on all vessels trading at New York. By floating their produce, wheat, and timber down the Hackensack, they could trade in the "free" ports of Perth Amboy, Philadelphia, and Burlington, all well to the south.

Their plans were dashed when in March of 1684, the mayor and aldermen of New York City made a proposal to the governor of New York, Thomas Dongan. As the "unhappy" separation of New Jersey from New York diverted trade from the latter colony, Dongan should persuade the crown to allow New York to re-annex New Jersey. What had became known as the Tappan Patent became part of New York and trade was funneled down the Tappan Creek to the Hudson instead.

We can only make some educated guesses as to what type of boats would have been found at the riverside settlements. For longer voyages to New York, there would have been the yachts and sloops described earlier. For strictly local use it might have been possible to trade with the Indians for a dugout canoe or failing that to chop down a tree and craft one yourself. If lumber were available, another possibility would be to cut the canoe in half lengthwise and insert some planks to widen it. Even someone with no knowledge of boat building who had rudimentary carpentry skills could knock together a serviceable scow. More elaborate boats with finer lines could be built by more professional boat builders who were beginning to set up shop in the larger towns.

As a project for future research, the records of wills might be examined to determine the extent of boat ownership and the types of vessels among the riverfront colonists at this time in history.

Boats were not just for transportation. A great abundance of natural resources awaited the settlers in the river valleys and the Hackensack Meadowlands. In addition, there were a number of commercially important fisheries, animals available for trapping, and salt hay and cedar wood to be harvested. Wolves were so common that the colonial legislature offered bounties on their heads.

Aside from the rich farmland and the timber, the most important natural resource in the Bergen County area was the Hackensack Meadowlands. The area supplied the region with game, shellfish, animal fodder (in the form of salt hay), berries, pelts, and cedar wood. The most important of these resources was salt hay (a native grass that thrives in brackish estuaries), and to a lesser extent the last remaining stands of native cedar.

As background, the areas that comprise this important wetland as well as the Passaic River Valley's Great Swamp, were formed during the last Ice Age. About 18,000 years ago, as the glaciers moved south, they stopped advancing after reaching a line that ran across lower New York Bay and then westward through New Jersey. Where the glaciers stopped, a terminal moraine was formed. A terminal moraine is a geological term that describes the massive accumulation of rocks, soil, and debris that is pushed out as a glacier advances, marking the southernmost point of its advance.

This moraine plugged the outlets of the region's rivers, and lakes were created behind it. Both the Passaic and Hackensack rivers backed up into huge glacial lakes. Lake Hackensack was 15 miles across at its widest point. Although it was originally a freshwater lake, a rise in the sea level eventually gave Lake Hackensack a tidal ecology. Farther west and at higher elevations, Lake Passaic was not affected by the sea level change and it retained fresh water characteristics.

About 8,000 years ago, when the glacier receded, the dams broke and the rivers flowed freely again. The lowest lying portions of the former lake bottoms became the Great Swamp and the Hackensack Meadowlands. Eventually the latter region came to be dominated by an alder-oak forest underlain with sphagnum and drained by freshwater streams. About 800 years ago, cedar trees established themselves and displaced the alder-oak forest. By the time of European settlement, the cedars had largely died off and except for a few isolated patches were replaced by grasses adapted to the brackish water environment.

There is an old legend about the cedars that needs to be debunked. During the early days of settlement, the stands of cedar trees were said to be so thick that woodsmen were forced to wear miner's hats (with lamps) when they went to work in the forests. It makes a nice tall-tale, but in reality the trees had largely disappeared by the 1600s.

The historical records related to land purchases and patents show that the settlement of the area began in the mid to late 1600s. Nicholas Varlet and Nicholas Bayard were granted a patent by Peter Stuyvesant in 1663 for the 2,000 acre "Sekakas Plantation" on the east bank of the Hackensack River. Secaucus lies in one of the few elevated portions of the meadowlands region. This patent was followed by the New Barbados Patent in 1668 which granted 15,000 acres in Kearny, Lyndhurst, Rutherford, and North Arlington to a Captain William Sanford. Major Nathaniel Kingsland purchased 5,300 acres of upland and 10,000 acres of meadowland in 1668 and John Berry followed a year later with the purchase of land in what is today East Rutherford, Carlstadt, Moonachie, and Little Ferry.

Archaeologists and paleobotanists examined the pollen preserved in the Hackensack Meadowlands soils. Their studies have revealed that the earliest efforts at reclaiming the meadowlands appear to be attempts at draining the brackish waters so that freshwater English grasses would thrive. Scientists have still not identified the exact cereal and grass species that were introduced during this time period. Even though these attempts were unsuccessful, the regular mowing of salt hay would in time alter the vegetation. There is some evidence that species not normally found in the Meadowlands, such as ragweed and plants in the goosefoot family, were introduced into the region as a result of ground disturbance during the attempts to make it more agriculturally productive.

In 1751, the Swedish botanist Peter Kalm wrote that:

> The country was low on both sides of the river, and consisted of meadows. But there was no other hay to be got than such as commonly grows in swampy grounds; for as the tide comes up in this river, these low plains were sometimes overflowed when the water was high. Mosquitoes were prevalent in such conditions.

The more extensive drainage and land reclamation schemes would take place in the 1800s, lasting into the 1900s.

Chapter 3

Colonial and Early Federal Era Boats

Whether trading for furs or carrying crops to market, the basic requirements for a Hackensack River sailing vessel remain the same. A deep draft would not allow it to navigate in shallow and tidal waters, so a flat bottom would be ideally suited for sailing and enabling the boat to be grounded at low tide. (Even today sailboats with deep keels are seldom seen at area marinas.) Also, a fore-and-aft rig such as a lug or gaff is easier to handle and requires less effort to sail into the wind.

The ideal combination of all these features was a flat bottomed sailing barge called a periauger. Appearing in the New York area in the first half of the 1700s, these working vessels persisted until the mid 1800s.

Characterized by a level bottom, with a modest cargo capacity between 5 and 10 tons, they carried two masts and had a cat schooner rig. Although the larger ones built in the 1800s could be up to 75 feet long, the colonial periauger was about 30 feet in length.

In the purest examples of the type, the periauger's foremast was mounted in the bow and in some cases was canted forward. The mainmast was raked aft. A cat schooner, a related type of vessel, has no bowsprit or jib. This arrangement is well suited to working in crowded harbors. Since the foresail is mounted on a solid spar, the aerodynamics are improved and it can function as a jib. In addition, there is no bowsprit to restrict maneuvering.

Sadly, most descriptions we have of these boats are somewhat incomplete. A 1774 newspaper advertisement publicized a periauger for sale but the accompanying description only mentions that it "will carry upwards of five cords of wood." Using modern measurement, this gives a capacity of about 640 cubic feet, about equivalent to a large delivery van.

It is believed that the periauger originated from West Indian sailing canoes that were brought into New York. The name "periauger" is derived from "pirogue," which in turn may be derived from the Spanish "piragua", meaning a small dugout canoe. When larger vessels were needed one of two techniques could be employed. Planks could be added to the dugout's sides in order to make the hull deeper. Alternatively, the hollowed out log could be cut down the long axis to make two identical halves. The bottom planking would then be installed between them to make the boat as wide as desired. There is some evidence that the periaugers used on northern New Jersey's rivers were built this way. Of the two methods, this would provide a flatter hull and hence, a shallower draft. It would also require less complex cutting and fitting of planks. Eventually, the desire for still larger and wider hulls prompted builders to use more conventional construction methods to produce a greater variety of hull shapes.

According to Folsom's *The Municipalities of Essex County 1666-1924*, an area west of Newark was known as the "Camptown Navy Yard" because of the periaugers built there. Camptown was an earlier name for what is today part of the city of Irvington. The boats were built in the Vinegar Hill section between Irvington proper and South Orange and then launched into Bound Creek. The creek's current was much greater at the time and the completed boats could easily be floated into Newark Bay. In later years Bound Creek became the feeder stream for Weequahic Lake.

One of the best documented periaugers from this period, the *Sally and Betsey*, was launched at Camptown. She had been constructed for the merchant Caleb Camp. Camp's papers mention the boat as being built for himself in company with Obadiah Meeker and John Brant. According to the custom house license issued October 20, 1789, by the Collector of the Port of Perth Amboy, the *Sally and Betsey* had a capacity of 17 tons. Her owner was listed as "Caleb Camp of New Ark in the County of Essex." Camp posted a $200 bond and his vessel was "by Law exempted from Entering and Clearing at the Custom House, for the Space of one Year ... provided it "shall not be employed in any illicit Trade..." Customs documents from 1793, also issued at Perth Amboy, licensed the "Pettyauger called the Sally and Betsey," to Jabez Johnson of New Ark, master, for the "coasting trade."

Records for building the *Sally and Betsey* were kept in Camp's "pettiauger account" for the period March 1784 to August 1785. Building was commenced during nine days in March when 1,033 feet of plank and one large log for the top timbers were cut at Cheapside (near Newark.) Dragged to the saw mill by four horses, the rough timber was cut into boards, and then carted to the Navy yard on June 6 and 7. The keel was laid in June 1784 but then work ceased until after the fall harvest came in. An additional 199 feet of lumber arrived on October 25 and deck planking was later purchased in New York.

On December 1 Camp entered an item in his account for one half gallon of rum. In April of 1785 the periauger was nearing completion, and entries were made for sails, oars, boat hooks, caffs, and "one Crow Bar for to Make the anchor." On August 20 Camp made his last entry, cash paid to a Mr. Kingsland "for Caulking the deck." The total cost of the *Sally and Betsey's* 18-month long construction was 226 pounds, three shillings and five pence.

The *Sally and Betsey* was in service from 1785 until at least 1796. In that year "An Account of Money for the Raft" lists cargoes of rope purchased at Albany, fish at Newbury, sugar and eggs at Dobbs Ferry. At that time Camp was in partnership with Meeker and Brant, an arrangement that lasted until about 1788. The partnership may have dissolved when repairs to the *Sally and Betsey* began to become too expensive. In 1786 the mast had to be replaced two times, first by Josiah Tichenor, who charged 16 shillings, and then by Moses Baldwin, who also received payment for unspecified "repairs done the petiaugre." In 1795 Camp is listed as owning the periauger "in company with Messrs. Murry and Baldwin."

Wherever they were built, the periauger had many uses. They became the preferred vessel for Hudson River ferries and may have been used at the "Little Ferry" which gave the name to the town where it operated. The Hudson River periauger type ferries were often described as being scow shaped, with leeboards and a schooner rig. In one instance, they were described as having masts that could be lowered. There was considerable variation in the exact configuration of the sailing ferries. Some were constructed so as to allow vehicles to roll on and off. In this case the mast might be stepped on the gunwale. Others were built without provision for carrying vehicles cargo and passengers were loaded over the gunwales. Any vehicles making the crossing were also hoisted over the sides.

Of course, not all periaugers were used as ferries. They were frequently employed for other types of work. The flat bottom allowed the vessel to be brought very close to shore, so they became a popular boat for hauling crops or firewood from the riverside farms to market. There are also numerous records of periaugers used as short haul cargo vessels, harbor lighters, and sometimes even pleasure boats. During the 1820s the Navy even built a few gunboats utilizing the periauger rig. Deck arrangements were variable. Some were completely decked with a small cabin, while others had partial decks fore-and-aft, while still others appear to have been completely open. Individual variations extended to the hull shape. Many were built with scow shaped hulls (especially the sailing ferries and others used in sheltered waters) but others had a bow and stern which were somewhat sharply pointed. All accounts are in agreement that the hull was shallow draft, flat-bottomed, with leeboards substituting for a deep keel.

Original Artwork by Thomas Fitzpatrick, Ph.D.

The periagua had a number of different hull designs but all boats of this type had lee-boards and a schooner rig that lacked headsails.

The periauger was not designed to be an ocean-going vessel. Its main use was in the rivers and harbors, but some made short trips south along the New Jersey coast. The inquest into the death of Francis Ryerson gives us a glimpse into one such voyage. In July of 1745, the 60 year old Francis Ryerson was on the "Nysank" river in a periauger. Under a "full gale of wind", Ryerson's foot caught on a rope, sending him overboard, where he drowned. There were two witnesses at the inquest, Jurie Tomason and John Van Riper, so we can assume that there were at least three men aboard the vessel. The inquest was held at Second River in Essex County (near what is today Newark), although the most likely location of the "Nysank" river is the Navasink River in Monmouth County.

In a period painting of one of the sailing ferries used at the "little ferry", a single masted, gaff-rigged vessel is depicted. The hull is not shown in sufficient detail but it can be safely assumed to be a flat bottomed boat with lee boards. As mentioned earlier, some double-ended sailing ferries had their masts stepped amidships on the gunwale. The spars could be swung around to either side of the mast, depending on the direction of travel. There could be a single mast or two masts, one on each gunwale that could be joined at their tops. Spars would be shifted as needed. In either case, the vehicles could roll unencumbered on and off each end.

The Dutch yacht is one of the most important types in the history of small craft. Although not exclusively used for recreation, they were the first widely used pleasure boat in the modern world and are the direct ancestors of the luxury boats sailing today. Yachts were originally developed in Holland for working the shallow coastal waters and in time were brought to the New World by the Dutch. There the yacht further evolved into the Hudson River sloop, a vessel that would dominate commerce on that river for over a century.

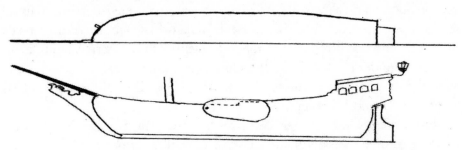

Author's sketch

The Dutch word "jacht" or "yacht" was used to describe many types of smaller vessels. Today the word is mostly used to describe the type of vessel in the sketch above. About 62 feet long this craft from the 1670s had a high stern, large bowsprit, and blunt bow. The leeboards hang from a position at the widest part of the hull.

Courtesy Project Guttenberg

Illustration from the mid-1800s shows the gaff-rigged sails, lee boards, and generous hull. From Man on the Ocean; A Book about Boats and Ships, *by R.M. Ballantyne, London: T. Nelson and Sons, 1874.*

Yachts could be rigged with up to three masts. Henry Hudson's *Half Moon* was an example of a ship-rigged three masted type. All yachts were distinguished by a narrow hull, little deadrise, fine lines at the bow and stern, modest tumblehome, and a flatter shear than other coastal vessels of the period. They also had more decorative work than other boats of the period and a prominent beakhead. Smaller yachts were equipped with leeboards. Fore and aft rigged types usually had two headsails on a bowsprit. The mainsail was on a long boom and short gaff. Auxiliary square sails were sometimes carried from a topmast, which later became the standard rig on government boats. Most yachts had passenger accommodations either in the stern cabin or in another cabin under the foredeck. The Dutch government and the Dutch Navy found the yacht to be a useful tender for large ships. They also used yachts as dispatch boats and for other official work.

From these Dutch vessels came the Hudson River Sloop. Sloops were the most common vessels in the colonial coastal, riverine and West Indian trade. Although larger ones were often armed, especially if sailing in the pirate infested West Indies, the coastal and riverine sloops generally were not. The sloops found on the Hudson River by the mid-1700s were characterized by a shallow-draft and a broad-beamed hull with a single gaff-rigged mainsail and two headsails. A topmast and topsail were often carried. Sloops working the Hudson River and around New York City did not draw more than six feet. Although these vessels were usually fully decked, smaller ones were often open, with three benches forming a "U" shaped seating area near the stern.

Many had a prominent stern cabin which could occupy as much as a quarter of the vessel's length, often sweeping up to a high transom. On a typical voyage five or six passengers could be accommodated in the stern cabin, which was well provided with windows for light and air.

Vessels built for work in rougher water had deeper hulls, but the rig was very similar as were the deck and cabin arrangements. The keel ran the length of the hull. Unlike modern sailboats, there was no centerboard or deep keel. We have no exact descriptions of the sloops used on the other local rivers but we can safely assume that they were not much different than those found on the Hudson River.

Other points of difference between the modern sailboat and the colonial sloop were found in the mast and rigging. The gaff rigged mainsail was carried on a mast that was raked aft. There was frequently a long bowsprit. The standing rigging (the ropes that hold the mast upright) on the colonial sloop was also much simpler than on the modern sloop. Ladder-like arrangements of ropes called ratlines not only held the mast in position, but also gave the crew access to the masthead. This was especially important if the sloop carried a topsail. The standing rigging on a modern sloop is made of wire. The complex arrangement of wire needed to support the mast reminded sailors of early radio towers and so became known as "Marconi" rigs, after the inventory of wireless telegraphy.

The great advantage of the sloop was in its small size and great maneuverability. While researching his book *For Want of Trade,* James Levitt found that prior to 1720, 90% of all vessels built in New Jersey were sloop rigged, which is not surprising given their ease of handling. The sloop's other advantage, which was important to merchants, was that its small size meant that it seldom sailed with any unused cargo space.

But having only one mast, the sail area of a sloop was limited. As mainsails increased in size to permit faster sailing, so did the problems handling them. A new type - the schooner - resulted from splitting the sail area between two or more masts. This preserved the best features of the sloop while dramatically increasing their capacity. Levitt concluded that after 1720, only 50% of the vessels in New Jersey were sloop rigged.

Original Artwork by Thomas Fitzpatrick, PhD.
The typical colonial sloop is shown in this drawing. The main sail is gaff-rigged and the mainmast carries a topsail. These vessels were used for trading along the coast. Many made voyages to New England, the southern states, and the Caribbean.

Schooners were the principle working vessels in the coasting trade. Surviving photographs and paintings of local ships almost invariably depict two-masted schooners. Larger schooners of three and four masts were too large for practical work on small streams.

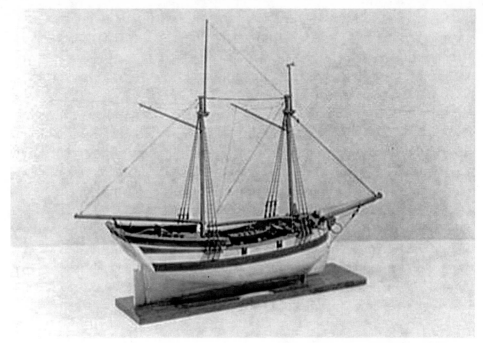

Courtesy Library of Congress

This model shows a typical coastal schooner of the colonial period. The hull is much fuller and the bow much blunter compared with modern sailing vessels. This model was on display for many years at the Seamen's Bank for Savings, 74 Wall St., New York City.

Some descriptions of local vessels built before the Revolution survive. Two Passaic River cat schooners were described in 1776,

> The dimensions about 45 feet in length, 14 feet breadth, 14½ feet depth, draw but very little water & one of them sails remarkably swift.

This account was found in correspondence between colonial officials who wanted to convert these vessels into small warships. We can use their proposed armament to estimate the ship's capacity, assuming of course that the military planners did not plan to overload them dangerously. Two six-pound cannon on each side and a six or nine-pound cannon in the bow was one possible configuration. Alternately, a three four-pound cannon along each side with a six-pounder in the bow would mean that the ship would be carrying at least 5700 pounds. Since there is no specific mention of the hull shape or construction so these vessels could have been large periaugers.

The single most complete description of a Hackensack River sloop was from the Bill of sale for the sloop *Union* of Hackensack. She was sold in

October of 1794 by the estate of Jost Zabriskie to George Zabriskie for "one hundred Twenty Pounds Current Money of the State of New York." The Bill of Sale describes George Zabriskie as a "Mariner of Hackesack in the County of Bergen in the State of New Jersey." The *Union* was built in Rochester, Massachusets, in 1783. She had a capacity of 22 tons, was 42' 7" long, 12' 9' wide, and the depth of the hull was 4' 7" deep. She had no "Gallery" and "no head."

The last two items in the description are somewhat confusing. The word "gallery" probably refers to either a group of windows at the stern that were part of an elaborately carved wooden structure or to a largely ornamental structure at the stern. On a ship a lavatory was known as the "head" since it was always at the ship's bow. Alternately, this could mean that the sloop had no bowsprit or headsails. It is clear that the *Union* did not have a deep draft which made her well suited to shallow river channels.

In general, little is known about 19th century shipbuilding on New Jersey rivers, and even less is known about 18th century shipbuilding, although we can be certain that some ships were built locally. There were a number of part-time shipwrights, mostly farmers and others whose work was seasonal. They sometimes built boats or even small ships during slow periods and hauled them to water when winter snows made sledging heavy loads easier. The small schooner *Enterprise* was one such vessel. Built in Camptown (present day Irvington) and hauled on wheels to the Passaic River when completed, she was used for smuggling between Canada and Maine during the War of 1812.

Little is known about the life span of colonial vessels. For many of New Jersey's colonial shipwrights, labor was readily available, but capital was lacking. Working on low budgets, and often pressed for time, many shipwrights did not properly season or match the timber. Records show that ships constantly leaked, from small sloops to even the largest Continental frigates. Between 1720 and 1740, the average age of New Jersey sloops and schooners was three and a half years. All analysis demonstrated, "continual introduction of growing numbers of newly built vessels into maritime commerce." At least a portion of the new construction was necessary to keep pace with losses from frequent failures in craftsmanship and seamanship.

In a Word, Square

All sails and to some extent all sailing vessels, fall into two broad categories, square rigged and fore-and-aft (shorthand for foreward and after rigged). Despite thousands of variations in mast arrangement and sail plan, the basic principles behind each type are really very simple.

Square rigged vessels are those whose sails are more or less rectangular. Their sails are perpendicular to the long axis of the hull. In a word, square. The main advantage of this rig is once the ship is on open water, winds pushing from behind drive the ship forward. The principle disadvantage is that the sails are not very efficient on a course to the windward. At best, a square rigged ship cannot manuver more than 20-30 degrees in the direction of the wind.

On the other hand, a fore-and-aft rigged vessel, such as a sloop, has sails that run from the mast, (forward) aft to the stern or back of the ship. This arrangement of sail is in reality an airfoil, which works on the same principle as an airplane's wing. As the breeze causes it to billow, the wind moves faster over the outside than on the inside. The differential in air velocities creates greater pressure on the inside of the sail than the outside, and this is what propels the ship along. The main advantage here is maneuverability, and a fore-and-aft rig can sail far more closely to the wind. But on the open sea the rig is far less efficient than one with the wind directly behind it. As a result, the fore-and-aft rig was principally used in the coastal trade.

Chapter 4

Where Road and River Meet

Water transportation and Indian trails were insufficient for a growing colony and settler's attention soon turned to building roads.

Unlike some later roads intended to transport European immigrants into new territory, the early thoroughfares in northern New Jersey linked existing settlements. In 1660, the first road was built to connect Bergen with the Hudson River Ferry at Communipaw. It was more than a score of years later, in 1682, that the General Assembly formally appointed Commissioners of Roads. Twenty more years passed before the first road would be built along the banks of the Hackensack River. Queen Anne's Road connected Little Ferry to Teaneck and originally terminated at the present Cedar Lane in Teaneck. Its later continuation is now known as Westfield Avenue. In 1718, a road connected the English Neighborhood with Weehawken.

With or without roads, the river front farm still had its wharf and perhaps even a small sloop. In an advertisement from February 1774 describing a farm for sale in Hackensack, amenities included a dock where a sloop bound for New York stopped once a week. Another example is found in an inventory of goods seized by the British from the Kuyper family farm during the Revolution. It lists two boats, a periauger with a capacity of two "cords" (of wood presumably) valued at 40 pounds, and another vessel of an unspecified type measuring 24 feet long and 3½ feet wide. Also included was "Half of one fish net near 100 fadam [sic]" valued at 1 pound, 15 shillings. As this net would be almost 600 feet long, it represented a substantial investment of labor. Obviously its owner was not a recreational angler.

Where the roads from the interior met the rivers, small ports known as "landings" developed. In our hub-and-spokes trade model, merchants in New York shipped finished goods to the landings and the landings in turn served as the feeder ports that sent goods to New York for resale or shipment elsewhere.

Local farmers exported their cash crops of corn, wheat, buckwheat, white cabbage, flax, tobacco, vegetables, and watermelons. Some of these cargoes, especially livestock, which did not need to be carried in wagons, came from as far away as the Delaware River Valley for shipment via Raritan Landing to New York. Often there would be a mill at the landing where flour could be loaded directly onto boats for the trip to market. Non-food items shipped from the landings included iron, lumber, firewood, and hay. A retail store could be found at many of the landings, taking advantage of the traffic in goods and customers. Most of these trans-shipment points grew up either at bridge sites or ferry sites where roads ran directly to the river. Another common site was at the limits of tidewater navigation.

The Earliest Bridges

The church at Schraelenburg built the Old Bridge over the Hackensack River, so that the geographically scattered congregation could gather more easily. It was the first bridge over the river and was located at Demarest Landing, today New Milford. Constructed sometime after 1724, it was destroyed towards the end of the Revolution, but over the years it was rebuilt in several styles all of which could open. The current steel and concrete highway bridge is the first fixed span on the site, having replaced a 1920s era bascule type lift bridge.

Author's collection

Hackensack was still a small village in 1780 as depicted in this 19th century wood cut.

The second bridge over the Hackensack was built by the Cole, Van Buskirk, Demarest, and Zabriskie families in 1744. The New Bridge, just above Hackensack and two miles below Old Bridge, also became an important shipping point on the river. The Bergen County freeholders' records show that it was the first drawbridge built prior to 1757. It was a slide drawbridge: the east end could be drawn back to allow boats to pass. Prior to the American Revolution, the New Bridge was the southernmost bridge over the Hackensack. During the war, both the bridge and the roads leading to it were of the highest strategic importance. A draw bridge over the Hackensack River, at Court Street in the village of Hackensack, was built in 1793. That same year, the legislature also authorized construction of a bridge over Overpeck Creek.

Roads, Ferries, Landings, and Economic Growth

At the northern extremity of the Hackensack's tidewater navigation, the Van Buskirk family operated a gristmill as well as a store. The area became known as Van Buskirk's Landing.

The most important landing on the Passaic River was undoubtedly Acquackanonck, in present day Passaic. Located at the head of navigation and about one mile upstream from a pre-Revolutionary bridge, the landing served much of the area drained by the Passaic River including what would eventually become Paterson and Wayne.

Newark's position at the eastern end of Essex County, at the terminus of many roads that extended both into the central part of the state and beyond to the Delaware, ensured that it would become an important trans-shipment point for freight.

Passengers often traveled overland to the Hudson after crossing the Passaic and Hackensack Rivers by ferries. The three principle ferries over the Hackensack and Passaic Rivers were located in the lower reaches where the streams were too wide for bridges. Brown's Ferry, located on the road from Newark to Paulus Hook was established in the mid 1760s. Douw's Ferry was located on the west bank of the Hackensack on the same road. Both of these ferries were made obsolete by a bridge built in the 1790s. The Little Ferry, which gave the town its name, was also established in the 1760s. Ironically, the ferry was based in what is now Ridgefield, on the east bank of the Hackensack, while the town of Little Ferry is on the west bank. The ferry crossing was immediately north of the mouth of Overpeck Creek. There are no known contemporary paintings or sketches that show the boats used on these ferries in any detail. Some historians believe that this ferry was made obsolete in

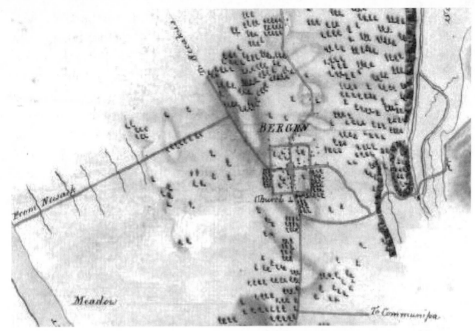

The surveyor John Hill made this sketch of the road from Paulus Hook and Hoboken to New Bridge in 1778. This map clearly shows the distinctive street plan of Bergen and the roads to the Hackensack ferries. There are two roads reaching west from the town to the ferries on the Hackensack. The roads extending to the east connected the town to the Hudson.

the early 1800s because the heavier wagons needed to use the bridges farther upriver. The modern town of Little Ferry was not created until 1894 when it was broken off from Lodi.

A description of the land around the Little Ferry comes from a newspaper advertisement published in March 1773:

> To be Sold or Lett, (And to be Entered upon the 20th of April next), A pleasant and well situated farm or plantation, on Hackensack River, and Overpeck Creek, in the county of Bergen, in New-Jersey, (now in the possession of Capt. Josiah Banks) three miles to the southward of the court-house, and not four miles from Bull's ferry on Hudson's river, to which there is a good road, and from whence small boats daily attend the New-York market. The farm contains 500 acres, by much the greatest part is valuable meadow; about 80 acres clear'd, which produces timothy grass and clover, and bears good crops of rye, Indian

corn, oats, and other grain; on the other part of the meadow may be cut 200 tons of good fresh grass. All the produce of the farm may be transported to New-York, Hackensack, or elsewhere; The boats from Hackensack daily pass by: It affords excellent pasture in the spring and summer season, and is very commodious for raising cattle. There is on it a good house, kitchen, and barn, placed so advantageously on an eminence as to command a view of the whole farm. A ferry over Hackensack River belongs to this tract of land, which at present is of the annual value of $360 from one side of the river only, and daily increases; and under the present situation of the said ferry, and lands adjacent, the profits from both sides may be appropriated to the sole use of the owner of this farm. The whole plantation may be inclosed with about 200 pannel fence. Several milch cows, oxen, and yound cattle, with farming utensils are also to be sold or lett with it. If any person is inclined to purchase or hire, they may apply to and agree with David Ogden, at Newark, who will give a good title for the same.

Newark did not have an uninterrupted road connection to the Hudson River ferries until after the American Revolution. One of the biggest bridge building projects of the early Federal Era began in 1790. The State Legislature decided that the "public good" would be served by a 64-foot-wide roadway from Paulus Hook to the Newark Courthouse. There would have to be two long bridges over the Hackensack and Passaic rivers. For this immense task, the road's financial backers hired Josiah Nottage, one of the nation's leading bridge builders. Nottage hired twenty carpenters, plus an unrecorded number of laborers, and by the summer of 1795 they had spanned both rivers - the Passaic with a bridge of 492 feet and the Hackensack with one of 930 feet. Both spans were toll bridges. Travelers paid "four cents for a man and horse; ten cents for a horse and chair; twenty-nine cents for coach or light wagon with two horses, and thirty-nine cents for vehicles with four horses." to cross the Passaic and slightly more to cross the Hackensack. To traverse the marshes between the two rivers, the road builders laid three or four layers of logs. These were covered by sod and earth dug from the sides of the road. The layers were finally topped by gravel. The immediate effect of the new road was to bring thousands of travelers through Newark and begin a transformation of the town into the major crossroads that it is today.

As the roads continued to extend into the iron-rich mountains of the

New Jersey Highlands, a trade pattern developed in which New York merchants shipped goods to the landings at Old and New Bridge for the iron mines and furnaces. Trans-shipped to wagons, they were then transported to the mountains of Northwest New Jersey. Thanks to the research of Mr. Jack Chard of the North Jersey Highlands Historical Society, we can read about the delays and frustrations encountered while trading between New York and the Highlands. Three brothers, Isaac, Josiah, and Jeremiah Pierson began building an ironworks in 1795 situated on the Ramapo River near the town of Suffern.

Supplies and tools for the venture were to be sent via the Hackensack and Hudson rivers. The letters between Josiah and his brothers Isaac and Jeremiah illustrate the process and its inherent frustrations. While Jeremiah and Isaac were setting up the ironworks on site, Josiah, on account of illness, stayed in New York City and shipped tools and supplies to them. Work began on the works in the spring of 1795. The first shipment went aboard the *Maria* (Captain De Noyelte) on May 25. It was followed by a shipment aboard Boskirk's boat to Boskirk's Landing, three miles above the town of Hackensack. More supplies were sent up to Boskirk's landing in September 1796 and via Demarest's boat in October of 1796, probably to New Milford. The letters mention frustrations such as a lack of horses at the landings and other causes of delay. For example, by December of 1796, both Hackensack boats had arrived, but the river was frozen. By December 23 Boskirk's boat with a load of planks was frozen up, but the Eleanor arrived at Haverstraw Landing (on the Hudson) with her cargo of prime mess pork. One can only imagine the problems that would have resulted if things turned out the other way around.

An ominous tone appeared in a letter of February 17, 1797, when Josiah reported that the boatman who had been sent for sand and clay had not yet returned. There was still no word on the 23rd of February. A storm prevented the boatman from getting enough material as late as the 19th of March. Boskirk's boat apparently survived the winter because she is next mentioned as carrying a load of planks for sashes in March of 1797.

Unfortunately, Josiah succumbed to tuberculosis in December of that year. He never saw the works that he had labored so hard to establish. When Jeremiah finally completed the project in the spring and summer of 1798 it had 31 heading, 65 hammer and nail cutting machines, and a rolling and slitting mill to manufacture barrel hoops and nail strips. Eventually the company employed its own sloop to bring supplies to Haverstraw Landing. Appropriately, she was named the *Josiah Pierson*.

The Hackensack River also served to transport iron for export. For example, the Sterling Ironworks shipped their wares on the river to New York. David Anderson is mentioned as a "Boteman, of New York, Say Old Bridge NJ, owner of a sloop used for shipping iron." This cargo became so common that Kinderkamack Road, running along the west bank northwards from Hackensack, was once known as the Iron Trail.

Even though the Hackensack afforded excellent communication with New York and beyond, passenger travel quickly turned to the roads leading to the popular Hudson River ferries. Even the crudest roads were safer and more reliable than the sailing vessels. Not only were the sailboats unsafe, they also required favorable winds and tides. In addition, winter weather made sailing miserable at best, dangerous at worst. In an age before the invention of such lifesaving devices as reliable life preservers, radio, and radar, mishaps on the water often proved fatal.

The first stagecoach from Hackensack at New Bridge to Paulus Hook on the Hudson was the "Flying Machine", which began service in 1763. The fare was "two shillings sixpence" and it ran twice a week. The owner, Andrew Van Buskirk, announced proudly that it was pulled by "four good horses" and the coach itself was a "commodious machine."

Other stage coaches making the trip from Hackensack to the Hudson River included the "New Caravan" of Verdine Ellsworth. There was also Isaac Vanderbeek's "New Wagon" that was reported to accommodate up to fifteen passengers, and Peter Demarest's wagon which was advertised as "new and well fitted with curtains."

One example of the type of accidents that road travel could avoid was the fate of William Christie (1776–1827), who four months after the death of his wife decided to move his eight children to New York City from their farm in Schraalenburgh (now Dumont.) He chartered a sloop in March of 1827 for the move, and the journey began auspiciously with the family propelled down the river by fresh spring breezes. But when the sloop reached the bend opposite Bogart's Dock in Hackensack, a sudden gust of wind swung the boom around, and William was struck in the back and knocked overboard. Although a celebrated swimmer, his injuries were too severe, and he instantly drowned.

In his autobiography, Benjamin Franklin recounts an experience he had while traveling from Boston to Philadelphia. He left New York City for the Amboys where he could catch the stagecoach for the trip across New Jersey. But the ferryboat he was on was caught in a storm, blown across New York Harbor, and was forced to take shelter off Staten Island for thirty hours.

Delays caused by winter weather and ice jams also resulted in additional shipping costs. The Society for Establishing Useful Manufacturers calculated the costs of transporting goods and material from Paterson to New York. In 1829, the figures demonstrated that winter transportation over the rutted and frozen roads cost Paterson merchants dearly. It was calculated that bringing cotton to Paterson from New York cost about two-thirds as much as shipping it to England from New York.

The same report revealed considerable savings for merchants who used water transportation. Even so, expenses of cartage to the docks, trans-shipment, and sailing were still formidable obstacles for business. The calculations show that the cost of moving freight from Paterson to New York were higher than the all-water transportation from that city to Albany! Worst of all, when heavy and bulky items were involved, e.g., coal and iron, the freight was about equal to importing those items from England.

What was happening was typical for most of New Jersey's rivers. The vessels in our story were owned locally and served local needs. While imported manufactured goods might be found at a riverside store, they were probably first brought to New York by another merchant. Similarly, a commodity like iron would be shipped to that city before being loaded on a larger ship for export.

Exactly as Gaven Lawrie had predicted in 1684, New Jersey's rivers gave a great boost to colonization. They allowed settlement to spread out with it capital and labor. Easy access to New York and Philadelphia shifted commercial activity to these cities. This made the Hackensack one of many "feeder" streams. For New Jersey, the effects of these trends prevented any viable deepwater ports from being established in the state. The diffusion of population ensured that there would be no concentration capable of supporting a major seaport and no reason to create one. The New Jersey hinterlands could not by themselves generate or consume enough cargoes to fill ocean-going ships. Until the creation of Port Newark and Port Elizabeth, the rivers of New Jersey consisted only of small shipping points tied to larger ports and the coastal trade. Complete discussion of the factors that led to the state's inability to create a major seaport and a full discussion of shipbuilding can be found in Levitt's 1981 book *For Want of Trade*.

The Hackensack River has a suitably modest tale of a lost treasure. In the fall of 1773, a traveler was returning home from Long Island with a large hoard of dollars. (There is no record of whether the money was paper, gold, or silver.) While crossing on the Hackensack ferry his horse took fright and leaped from the boat. His saddlebags were not fastened on properly and they were lost overboard, along with all the money. There is no record that the bags were ever retrieved or that anyone even looked for them.

In 1797, the area on the Hackensack's west bank at the tip of a triangle formed by Bayonne, Snake Hill, and Rutherford was briefly the scene of a pitched battle between pirates and police. A number of extremely popular and fanciful legends have grown out of this incident. The two most absurd of these has William Teach, *aka* Blackbeard, using the hill as a hiding place and the other story has Captain Kidd burying his treasure somewhere near Secaucus. The historical facts are much less fanciful.

Robberies frequently occurred in the Meadowlands as travelers crossed the Hackensack Meadows on the plank roads. But according to the former Union County historian, Daniel Van Winkle, in the years after the Revolution piracy in New York Bay became an extremely serious problem. Pirates would board ships at anchor and rob the vessels. There were even reports of kidnapping and sexual assault.

These "pirates" were not organized companies of men sailing their own ships complete with articles, officers, and cannon. They appeared to be no more than small gangs of wharf rats, minor criminals, and unemployed sailors.

These accounts would agree with the general pattern of piracy in the New World. During any colonial war, thousands of seamen were employed on warships and transport vessels. With the coming of peace, they found themselves unemployed, and as a consequence piracy would flourish for a time. While the civilian economy was still recovering from the war, corrupt merchants did not enquire too closely about the origins of suspicious cargoes, and port officials often turned a blind eye. Once the economy began to recover, and legitimate trade again became profitable, pressure was put on the Navy to hunt down pirates. A very small number of pirates retired and lived quietly until the next war. Other pirates accepted offers of clemency in return for their surrender. Most, like Blackbeard, were hanged.

According to one story, in 1797 the sheriffs in Old Bergen and New York Counties organized a raiding party of over 1,000 men and boys. They were recruited from lower Bergen Neck and the ships anchored in New York Harbor. Led by naval officers, and using small boats, they drove the pirates from the Hudson River, Staten Island, and Bayonne peninsula into the swamps. Quickly withdrawing west over the Hackensack, the pirates established a stronghold opposite Snake Hill, where they held out held for two days. On the third day, a wind blew from the south and the sheriffs' men set fire to the marshlands and woods. The fire spread northward from the tip of the Kearny Peninsula and as the pirates fled the flames many were captured or shot. Those that stumbled out of the meadows at Rutherford found the sheriffs waiting for them.

The 1797 battle was most likely the result of a particularly bad state of affairs and something of an isolated incident. Piracy was common enough on the seas but most historians make no mention of it as a problem on the local rivers. Writers who highlight the battle tend to lump it together with unrelated pirate activities and treat it as the climax of decades of piracy in the region. This author has always believed that small bands of pirates occasionally did operate in New York Harbor and the local rivers, and that they were a minor threat but never really a significant force. Just as today, people learn to avoid driving in certain high-crime areas and sailors of the 1700s no doubt did the same thing when they ventured out on the waters of the area.

Rumors still persist about a pirate treasure hidden somewhere in the Meadowlands. This is the result of the fictionalized biography of William Kidd, the notorious pirate. According to this account, in 1701, Captain Kidd burst into a New York Courtroom where one of his men was on trial. After holding the court hostage, Kidd and the pirates were said to have escaped across the Hudson and fled into the Hackensack Meadowlands. The reader should not rush off to search for Kidd's treasure. On May 23rd, 1701, Captain Kidd was being hanged in London, still protesting his innocence.

In 1863, draft riots raged throughout New York City. To raise men for the Union Army, the federal government passed a hugely unpopular conscription act. In July of that year, in a prime example of bad timing, the names of first draftees were posted simultaneously with the names of those killed and wounded at the Battle of Gettysburg. The worst riots in the history of New York followed, and according to historian John T. Cunningham, after order was restored many of the rioters escaped to the Meadowlands where a similar fire-raising tactic was employed to drive them from their hiding places.

Chapter 5

The American Revolution

It is worth reviewing the strategic and political situations that prevailed in the greater New York region throughout the Revolution as they have had a profound impact on this story. The Hudson River was the dividing line between the New England and mid-Atlantic colonies, and British control of it could split the colonies in half. It was also a highway into Canada and the Great Lakes. At its mouth, New York Harbor was the largest port in the colonies. So in one sense, the struggle for the Hudson was the struggle for the continent itself.

It began in the winter of 1776. The war had broken out in Boston in the spring and summer of 1775, and after several months of sporadic fighting and maneuvering the Americans succeeded in driving the British from that city. Their ships left Boston Harbor bound for Canada on March 17, 1776. George Washington may not have known their ultimate destination, but he knew they would eventually be back. He supposed, correctly, that their plan was to establish a base of operations in New York City, and on March 18, Washington conveyed troops there.

The British ships began arriving in New York Harbor on June 25. Three ships, one of which brought General William Howe from Halifax, arrived first. The plan to develop New York as a base of operations was already in place. Four days later, 45 ships arrived, and one day later another 82. The ships unloaded 9,300 soldiers onto Staten Island before they were joined by another force under the command of the General's brother, Admiral Richard Howe. The naval commander, Sir Peter Parker, descended on New York with nine warships, 30 transports and 2,500 men. On August 12, 28 more transports arrived with 2,600 British troops and 8,000 Hessian mercenaries. By the end of the summer of 1776, 32,000 soldiers, 10 ships-of-the line, 20 frigates, and hundreds of transport vessels opposed 19,000 untrained and poorly equipped

Americans.

The result was perhaps inevitable. In a series of battles, the Americans were first driven from Long Island, then from the tip of Manhattan, then from the northern end of the island and finally, in November 1776, they found themselves in retreat across New Jersey making for the relative safety of Pennsylvania.

All of the territory that is today New York City was held by the British for the entire war. Protected by the unassailable guns of the Royal Navy, the city became the major base of operations and a haven for thousands of Loyalist refugees from other colonies. The British established such military installations as supply depots, military prisons, and training facilities. They also re-opened the theaters that had been closed by the war and played the earliest games of golf in the Americas. Among the Loyalist refugees were printers who began publishing newspapers and hundreds of tradesmen who served the needs of the suddenly expanded city.

For others, New York was not a haven, but a hell. American prisoners of war were confined aboard demasted hulks in the harbor off Brooklyn, suffering some of the worst deprivations of any military captives in American history. There were many women among the Loyalists forced to take refuge behind British lines. Some toiled as laundresses, nurses, or domestic servants, but many were reduced to prostitution.

Meanwhile, the Americans established their own strongholds. Behind the first chains of mountains inland from the coast, they controlled a vast, crescent-shaped territory stretching from the Hudson River at West Point, to Philadelphia and south-eastern Pennsylvania. Within this area were the vital Highlands iron furnaces, secure lines of communication, military hospitals, supply bases, and the nation's infant manufacturing centers. Strategically placed forts guarded the important road junctions and mountain passes.

This arrangement eventually resulted in a stalemate. The Americans were unable to cross the Hudson and capture New York, but the British never had sufficient strength to drive the Americans from the mountains. This was especially true after France, Spain, and Holland entered the war and Britain began withdrawing troops from the American theater to defend the islands of their marine empire. The British position was made worse by the fact that they were at the end of a very long transatlantic supply line. Their ships could never hope to carry everything that they needed. Fortunately, there was rich country just across the Hudson.

As a result, the area between the two armies became a no-man's-land. It is very difficult to define the eastern edge of the American controlled territory, because it not only shifted with the fortunes of war, but was pierced in many places by enemy raiding parties. The infamous Loyalist partisans led by Claudius Smith even managed to operate a stone's throw from the American militia fortifications that guarded the Ramapo mountain passes and the vital ironworks at Ringwood, New Jersey.

While the Hackensack and Passaic River valleys were generally under American control, they were still vulnerable to British attack. The force of the American government was never sufficient to completely suppress the action of Loyalist partisans, spies, and those Americans who traded openly with the enemy.

The British only had two important posts on the west bank of the Hudson. One was a fort lying at the tip of Paulus Hook. The other was a log blockhouse constructed on top of the Palisades at Bull's Ferry (today the town of Guttenburg), manned by the Loyalists. Both posts will be discussed in greater detail later.

The most visible British force that operated in the area were the Loyalist partisan fighters known as the Refugees. When Loyalist property was confiscated in the name of liberty, many families were reluctantly forced to abandon their homes and flee to the enemy. Returning under arms, they raided the country in search of the food, forage, and firewood that were needed in New York. They also robbed and plundered their former neighbors. While it is true that some Refugees were motivated by sincere convictions, the record strongly suggests that the majority were inspired either by revenge or criminal inclination. We can assume that both sides had a number of Partisan fighters who were in reality simple criminals who found the war a convenient excuse for their actions.

The earliest American defensive plans for the Hackensack and Passaic rivers during the Revolutionary War involved the ferry crossings on the road from Paulus Hook to Newark. This section of road was also the eastern terminus of the main thoroughfare across New Jersey. George Washington had expressed a wish, in June of 1776, for flat-bottomed boats to help transport troops and supplies when operating on the Passaic and Hackensack rivers. On July 4, 1776, General Hugh Mercer ordered guards to be placed on the ferries. An engineer officer, after examining the area, reported that the Americans had failed to move all the cattle from Bergen Neck and as a result, Loyalist families were still able to supply the enemy. A Colonel Ford was dispatched to the site but he had fewer than 350 men and little hope of reinforcements. Mercer eventually stationed two captains with 122 men at the ferries.

Meanwhile, amid a flurry of plans, the Convention of the State of New

Photograph by Todd Braisted

This photograph of Loyalist reenactors at Fort Less Historic Park illustrates the problem of distinguishing friend from foe. A regular officer in a red coat reviews the motley collection of fighters dressed in everything from the heavy smocks used for farm work to the full uniforms issued to a few Loyalist units.

Jersey sent their own proposal to the Continental Congress for the defense of the Passaic and Hackensack River ferries. Because of the low lying terrain, the Convention felt that a defensive earthwork would be useless, as it would be vulnerable to attack from above. They proposed to refit two civilian vessels as small warships, but their plan came to nothing. The Committee of Newark presented another idea for the defense of Newark Bay. In July of 1776, they wrote to the New Jersey Provincial Congress and requested that four row-galleys or gondolas should either be built or bought, fitted with cannons, and sent to patrol the bay as far south as Perth Amboy. This plan also came to naught.

On August 9, 1776, recognizing their strategic importance, the Provincial Congress of New Jersey passed an ordinance which removed control of the ferries from private hands. Two commissioners, William Camp and Joseph Heddon Jr., were appointed to manage the operations. They were directed to provide at least four scows with sufficient crewmen at all times. They were also responsible for providing necessary supplies, including the ropes that guided the boats across the rivers. All military personnel or wagons were to be carried at one-third of the normal fare, but wagons belonging to the civilian contractors who were supplying the Army were not entitled to this special rate. Military control of the ferries lasted until the fall of New York to the British at the end of 1776.

One of the earliest American military operations on the Hackensack River was a routine supply mission. In late 1776, with the British Navy holding New York Harbor, American transports were blocked from sailing up the Hudson River. Accordingly, when General Philip Schuyler requested fresh meat for his troops at Lake George, he directed it to be sent via an alternate route up the Hackensack River. Peter Zabriskie received the 1,000 barrels of pork and transferred them overland to the Hudson River. Once upriver from the English ships, the Americans then carried the provisions by water to Albany. Sadly, there is no mention in the records of this plan worked, but from what is known about the disposition of the British forces, it was mostly likely successful.

The first vessel on the Hackensack River known to be sunk during the war was a schooner lost at New Bridge. It was during the Continental Army's retreat across New Jersey into Pennsylvania following the losses of Fort Washington (the last American outpost on Manhattan Island) and Fort Lee (the principle outpost on the west bank of the Hudson) in November of 1776. At that time the 14th Continental Regiment, known as the "Marblehead Regiment", was serving. Its members, who would soon prove themselves during the Crossing of the Delaware, included fishermen and sailors who were called upon whenever George Washington needed men who could handle boats. These men seized boats on both sides of the Hackensack River in order to hamper British pursuit of the retreating army. Once the army crossed the New Bridge, the decking was torn up as there was no powder available to blow up the bridge. As the Americans fled across New Bridge they decided that the schooner moored to the Zabriskie docks should not fall into British hands. Consequently she was quickly towed to mid-stream and scuttled. When the British vanguard reached the New Bridge, they had to pick their way across the wooden framework while snipers fired on them. Although earthworks were thrown up on Brower Hill and Teaneck Ridge, the Army continued moving west and these were soon abandoned.

Even though the British had for the moment driven the Continental Army from New Jersey, the situation was only temporary, and they found themselves surrounded by hostile forces, still dependent on transatlantic supply lines. To alleviate this, a navy consisting of small sailing vessels, ship's barges, and row galleys began raiding the countryside for grain, cattle, sheep, horses, fodder, and firewood. As early as the fall of 1776, when British troops were chasing the American Army across northern New Jersey and occupying New Bridge, Hackensack, and Acquackanonck, some of their supplies were

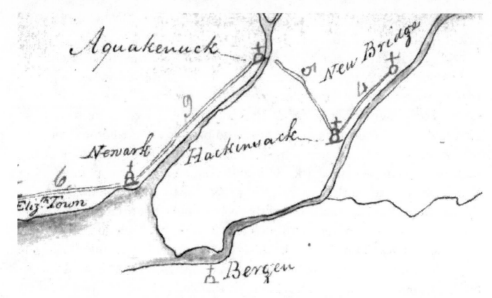

Courtesy Library of Congress

After the American retreat across New Jersey in the fall of 1776, the British Army took up positions along the major roads and river crossings. The map maker used small crosses to identify these places.

being moved by water. Even after the British withdrew, the riverfront landings and towns became the targets of enemy foraging parties. Boats raided Hackensack, New Bridge, Seacaucus, Elizabeth, Moonachie, and other towns. Raritan Landing was burned to the ground, and British row galleys even patrolled Newark Bay.

On a memorable day in 1779, Royal engineer Archibald Robinson noted in his diary that some 30 sloops had arrived in Manhattan from various points in New Jersey, Staten Island and Long Island. The sloop from New Jersey, Robinson laconically notes, "foraged Hackensack."

When the farm of Jacob Van Wagenen was raided by an English barge on the Hackensack, 12 head of cattle were carried off. When one of Van Wagenen's African American servants objected, he was hung from a tree but was cut down after promising to remain silent about the incident.

After the American retreat in the fall of 1776 the British were free to scavenge the area around Acquackanonck. Peter Garritse on Wesel Road had a number of household goods carried off, as well as a new set of "Pettiaguer" sails worth 25 pounds. Richard Ludlow, a merchant at Acquackanonck, had 20,000 barrel staves and ten cords of walnut wood stored on his dock. These were all carted off, as was his boat with all her sails. The boat was valued at 60 pounds. Another merchant shipper plundered at the Landing was Christopher Vanoorstrand.

Photograph by Susan Braisted

Reenactors from a Loyalist unit are shown drilling at New Bridge Landing State Park. Although some Loyalist units were issued distinctive uniforms, many of the men did not have regular uniforms and went to battle in civilian clothes. Others wore bits and pieces of British Army uniforms. This often made identifying friend from foe difficult during the partisan fighting in northern New Jersey.

He lost a boat valued at 225 pounds. His household lost two "negro men," two "negro women," a quantity of cider, water pots for bleaching, pans, trunks, corn, apples, sheep, hogs, potatoes, turnips, cabbage, and tobacco.

The correspondence of the American commanders is filled with observations about British movements in New Jersey by water.

On September 27, 1778, General Nathanael Greene wrote from his headquarters at Springfield, New Jersey, that the British had 11 or 12 vessels, "brigs, sloops, and row gallies" heading toward Crain's Ferry [sic]. (Crain's Ferry or Crane's Ferry was located near Elizabethtown Point.) Not being able to view the entire flotilla and assuming it was a major attack, Greene called out the militia. The ships turned and headed into Newark Bay and then up the Hackensack River. The ships had a twofold purpose. They were carrying supplies for the troops operating in Bergen County and were also deployed to help consolidate British control of the river. Greene wryly observed that, "They have in their power near one-half of Bergen County."

In May of 1780, George Washington wrote from headquarters in Morristown that British troop movements near New York, "seems to have resolved itself into a Forage in Bergen County, as several small Vessels have

45

Photograph by Todd Braisted

In 1997 Loyalist reenactment groups set up camp at New Bridge Landing. The uniforms, tents, and camp drills are identical to those that would have been seen when the British occupied the Landing in the early part of the war.

Photograph by Todd Braisted

The Loyalist reenactors are assembled for morning formation at the New Bridge Landing. This was not only an occasion for officers to inspect their troops but a chance to communicate important news and general orders.

Original Artwork by Thomas Fitzpatrick, Ph.D.
A reconstruction of a small British row galley of the American Revolution. Such vessels were commonly used for patrolling bays and rivers. Their ability to carry a heavy cannon in the bow gave them a substantial advantage when fighting against an enemy on shore.

gone up Hackensack River; some have also, I am informed, gone up the North River." He then warned the local commanders to be on their guard.

The main defense used against British raiding parties were the local militia companies. The principle ones were the Bergen County Militia commanded by Colonel Theunis Dey and the Outwater Militia, commanded by Captain Outwater. These units were similar in some respects to today's National Guard and reserves. They were citizen-soldiers mobilized either for short periods, or when the enemy was active in the area. When they were no longer needed, they were free to return to civilian life. Unlike many irregular troops, the militia units were under strict control of the state governments and were expected to fight alongside Continental troops when called upon to do so. In contrast to today's reservists and National Guardsmen, every able-bodied man was automatically considered a member of the militia.

The headquarters of the Bergen County Militia was at the home of Theunis Dey, now the Dey Mansion Museum in Wayne Township. Before the war Dey was a wealthy farmer who owned 600 acres. Active in the local political events and preparations leading up to the Revolution, when war broke out Dey was appointed a Colonel in command of the Bergen County Militia. Largely because of the role that the militia played in the war, George Washington chose the Dey Mansion as his headquarters in the summer and once again in the fall of 1780. Today the Dey Mansion Museum is operated by the Passaic County Department of Parks.

The military effectiveness of these militia units varied greatly. Because of the close British presence, the Bergen County Militia and Outwater's Militia were more seasoned than most and on many occasions achieved victories against the British. These units also performed valuable service guarding strategic roads and bridges, manning observation posts, building fortifications, and preventing Loyalists from aiding the enemy. As civil law deteriorated under wartime stresses, militia companies often provided the only effective police forces in many areas.

In the spring of 1781, a British gunboat arrived at Moonachie and "plundered the inhabitants and carried off about twenty head of cattle." Captain John Outwater collected his militia, routed the British and retook the cattle. During the action, Outwater lost a total of eight men - seven killed and one captured. Additional details of this engagement are unknown. In one account these British raiders were said to be Hessian troops. The account reported that as the British drove the cattle to the boat, they were pursued by angry farmers. When the Hessians arrived back at the river, they discovered that their gunboat (probably a warship's boat that was armed with a small cannon in the bow) was stranded by the receding tide. Several of the hapless raiders were killed by gunshots and others drowned while trying to escape across the river. More might have been killed or wounded had not the Americans' ammunition ran out. Since there is no mention of the gunboat being captured, we can assume that the perpetrators were finally able to drag their boat back into deeper water. Whatever the actual facts, this incident is important because it dramatically demonstrated that the ad-hoc militia units were able to fight with increased effectiveness and confidence as the war progressed.

Were Americans also raiding Bergen County? On April 7, 1777 the New-York Gazette reported that the crew of an "American" vessel raided a Secaucus farm and carried off "grain, horses, cows and sheep." The report does not say exactly where they took the plunder, except that they carried it across the river. Had the raiders been British, they might have been expected to move downstream, towards friendly territory. It may be that the newspaper meant "Loyalist Americans" and the farm belonged to a patriot. It is also possible that "patriots" were raiding the farm of a Loyalist. Unfortunately further specifics of the incident are lacking.

The British used a variety of small craft to exercise control over the waterways and support their foraging and intelligence operations. Of the three types most commonly mentioned - barges, sloops and galleys - the row galleys were the only ones specifically built as warships. They were generally short, shallow draft vessels with a long row of oars along the sides with one or two masts. They almost always carried a cannon in the bow. If the vessel were large enough, there might be another cannon in the stern or several positioned along the sides. Larger galleys had a raised stern and a small cabin. They might even carry a few swivel guns along the quarterdeck railings. Smaller galleys, also called gunboats, were completely open and only carried a cannon in the bow. Barges were long rowing-boats that were used primarily as ships boats and as water taxis in the larger ports. Although they could carry a sail on a collapsible mast, they were most often rowed.

In September of 1777, Sir Henry Clinton felt that a strike into New Jersey would "operate strongly in favor of the Grand Army, but be attended by other advantages." These "other advantages" no doubt meant the opportunity to forage the rich farms of eastern Bergen County. The strike began with some 200 Loyalists being sent up the Hudson to land near Tappan to begin driving cattle southwards. In addition, fifteen hundred men were landed at Fort Lee under the ample protection of the massive warship *HMS Rose*, built in England in 1757. Meanwhile the British collected some 1,250 men and sailed into Newark Bay and landed at Elizabeth. Afterwards, these boats and an additional galley moved up the Hackensack to Schuyler's Ferry to protect the troops who would arrive there after marching overland from Paulus Hook (Jersey City). Thanks to the excellent coordination of land and naval forces, the operation was a complete success.

When Elizabeth was again raided in March of 1779, local militia troops had advance warning and were able to assemble. Although the British withdrew after only a short time, parties of American troops were able to harass their column. Originally intending to reembark where they landed, they changed plans because the site was an exposed ferry dock in the salt marshes. Now the galleys went into action. They withdrew and began moving up Newark Bay while the troops moved along the water's edge. The galley and some gunboats covered the march and the troops were reembarked safely.

On November 15, 1780, a party of Loyalist Refugees landed near Newark and advanced on the town through the marshes. They took the precautions of placing a cannon on a hill overlookinng the town and stationing a gunboat to cover their advance over the marsh. After withdrawing from Newark, they were surrounded by American troops and strategically formed a defensive square. They then moved slowly and cautiously back to their boats. Again sea power came to their rescue as firepower from the gunboat kept the Americans from closing in and preventing their escape.

Some small boats were given to the Loyalist Refugees by the British, and these were used to raid the Newark Bay area. One of these was lost in August of 1781. According to a report published in Philadelphia, the Refugees held two American seamen prisoner aboard their boat. When the boat's crew went ashore on Sandy Hook, the prisoners promptly seized the vessel and fled to the southward, eventually bringing the confiscated boat to Philadelphia.

Another Refugee boat, *Old Ranger*, was captured near Egg Harbor in 1782. She was described as having seven swivel-guns, one three-pound cannon and a crew of 25 men. Her commander was a man named Tyran, but no details are given about him. Although there is no proof that the boats used in Newark Bay were all like the *Old Ranger*, the account does suggest that Loyalist naval forces were at least well equipped.

The most dramatic encounter with a British galley came, however, on an October night in 1780. Looking out at the shores of the Bergen peninsula, the crew of a galley on patrol in Newark Bay heard a man call out to them. He was in a great hurry as he strapped a valise to his shoulders and dashed through the marsh grass. Swimming out to the bay with the shouts of pursuers ringing behind him, the man finally reached the vessel and was taken on board. Little did the crew know that their new found American friend was really a spy on a dramatic secret mission. Details of John Champe's adventure are given in Appendix A.

As the British presence in New York grew, so did the need for supplies, especially beef and firewood. The Loyalist Refugees established a blockhouse on the west bank of the Hudson, atop the Palisades and overlooking Bull's Ferry. By the summer of 1780, the partisan raids launched from this post had become so effective that General Washington decided that something should be done. In July of that year, he had General Anthony Wayne lead a force of 1,800 men against the Refugees who were barricaded in the blockhouse. Despite cannon fire and repeated infantry charges, the defenders held their position. General Wayne was humiliated while the Loyalist leader of the Refugees, Captain Ward, became England's latest war hero.

Although General Wayne's attack failed, the Refugees abandoned the post and moved to Bergen Neck towards the beginning of fall. With winter coming on and British forces in need of firewood, the Refugees began stripping the neighborhood of trees. The post at Bergen Neck meant a longer transport to New York and the boats used to bring the firewood to the city were now vulnerable to American whaleboat attacks.

Whaleboats were open boats pointed at both ends that were developed for hunting whales on the open ocean. Fast and seaworthy, they could be either sailed or rowed. The American Army used them as reconnaissance vessels and transports. During the operations around Boston in 1775, whaleboat forces were extremely successful in capturing supplies from the enemy and striking at British positions on the Harbor Islands. Whaleboats were also the favorite means of transportation for American privateers and irregular forces. At night, they could silently glide up to an unsuspecting transport vessel and a boarding party could be over the side before the victim's crew had a chance to react.

A number of whaleboat raids originated from Newark and Elizabeth. On August 30, 1781, a party left from Newark and captured two British sloops lying near the refugee post on the Bergen Shore. They took eight prisoners, who were marched to Morristown, but no mention is made of the fate of the sloops themselves. On December 12, 1781, Captain Baker Hendricks led a party of men in whaleboats down Newark Bay. They boarded and stripped the "wood boats" and took one prisoner. A week later they raided Bergen Neck.

For proof of the military effectiveness of small boats and determined crews, we need look no farther than an attack that took place off Staten Island in May of 1782. A Captain Quigley and three men left Elizabeth in the evening. Crossing over to Staten Island in a small boat, they carried the vessel overland for a distance of about four miles. At about 2:00 am, they boarded a British brig (a two-masted square-rigged vessel) that was anchored near a twenty-gun warship and shore batteries. Captain Quigley and his men overpowered the three man British crew. They cut the ship's anchor cable and sailed it to Egg Harbor, New Jersey. The brig had been bound for Halifax and was carrying a rich cargo of salt, pepper, tobacco, china, and queen's ware before she was captured. The total value of the ship and cargo was estimated to be 4,000 pounds.

After the battle of Yorktown in 1781, the fighting was largely over. However, Raids by Loyalist partisans continued to plague the countryside and the presence of the enemy in New York revealed a previously secret activity. Boats belonging to people known as "London Traders" now "sailed openly" to Manhattan and returned with salt and other goods that had been unavailable during the long war years.

Continental soldier Abraham Vanderbeek was stationed on the river and ordered to watch for these boats. On one lucky day he spotted a boat and raced to inform his two comrades. Captain Outwater, returning with Vanderbeek and the two men, found the boat deserted except for 12 live sheep. They towed the boat upriver where Justice Jacob Terhune condemned the lively cargo as a prize of war.

The many English raids in the river must have drained the local people emotionally as well as economically. One writer in a Chatham newspaper may have unwittingly summed up the feelings of many weary residents when they watched for enemy vessels on the river:

> Last Sunday twenty six sail of vessels went up Hackensack river. Time will develop their intentions.

Chapter 6

Ships, Voyages, & Sailors in the Nineteenth Century

The most active period of river navigation began after the American Revolution and coincided with America's Industrial Revolution. Although New Jersey was a leader in the construction of roads, railroads, and canals, unprecedented economic growth fueled a demand for building materials, coal, fertilizers, and other cargoes that moved by water. There was a gradual shift from general to bulk cargoes being handled at the landings as better roads and railroads became available for transporting consumer goods and perishable farm products. The invention of the steam engine that could move ships on regular schedules gave passengers the opportunity both to commute and take excursions by steamboat. The growth of population created demands for fish, pelts, game birds, and shellfish.

It must be stressed, however, that all of these changes were gradual. For example, as late as the 1920s, more than fifty years after the first railroad came to Paterson, much of the city's lumber was still being unloaded at Acquackanonck Landing, but the stores at the landing selling consumer goods were a thing of the past.

Aside from fishing vessels, the smallest working boats were scows used by area farmers. Residents of the Mill Creek area of Old Bergen were reported to have used periaugers as market boats to carry produce to New York. And when flooding made roads impassable, their boats carried residents to church. Scows were used by farmers for moving heavy loads of loam and hay. There is mention of one man, a young English farmer of East Hackensack, who was drowned in May of 1858 when his scow carrying loam overturned. Some historians also make mention of farmers using these vessels to bring loads of grain to the tidal gristmills.

The use of water transportation was an important part of the local agricultural economy. The fertile Hackensack Valley was producing over

An artist's conception of the Passaic River in 1851. The scene is unidentified but is probably meant to depict Acquackanonck bridge. A schooner is moored at the wharf on the left side of the picture.

50,000 bushels of wheat, rye, and corn by 1850. According to a local jurist named Millard, who was quoted in a late 19th century county history, the sale of garden vegetables brought thousands of dollars every year to the Hackensack area during the mid-century period. However, it must be stressed that prior to the late 19th century the region's agriculture was a combination of market-driven and subsistence. Although cash crops were obviously important, farms were not highly specialized and many foodstuffs were produced purely for a family's own use.

Some of the cash crops were sent by road directly to the Hudson River ferries, where as early as 1828, steam ferries were operating on this run. This became a popular method of bringing crops to New York markets as witnessed by the 1858 statistics for the Bergen Turnpike toll road. During the strawberry harvest, on one Monday night, 170 wagons with 221,000 baskets of strawberries passed between 8 p.m. and 4 a.m. At about the same time 283 wagons brought the strawberry crop to New York via the Hoboken Ferry.

From the 1830s to well into the twentieth century, New Jersey railroads had a profitable relationship with New Jersey farmers. Beginning in 1842, the Paterson and Hudson River Railroad began running the 5:00 a.m. "strawberry train" for farmers who wanted to move their berries by rail. When the line was extended north into Suffern, strawberry growers in Mahwah, Allendale, Ramsey, and Saddle River began using the railroad too.

Cereals and Grains were very well suited to bulk transportation by water. At several points along the Hackensack River and its marshes, tidal mills were constructed. These gristmills included a dock at which boats could load the ground grain and take it to market. They were ingeniously powered by water trapped behind the mill dam by rising tides. The mill dam was constructed across the creek and built higher than the high-tide mark. At high tide, sluice gates were opened and water filled the creek area behind the dam. The sluices were then closed. When the tide fell, gates were opened and the flowing water powered the mill as it raced back downstream to the sea. At low tide, the cycle was repeated. Several creeks in the Hackensack Meadowlands are named for the tidal mills that lined their banks. The best known today is Mill Creek where a large shopping mall has replaced the earlier tidal mill.

The Van Buskirk family operated one such gristmill in what is today New Milford. One of the first families to settle in the area, they constructed a dam and a mill at the head of navigation. In time they also operated a store. During the second half of the 1800s the family even owned two schooners, the *Kate Lawrence* and the *General Grant*, to bring grain from New Milford to Paterson and New York. The *Kate Lawrence* was 58 feet long with a 21 foot beam. She sported an "almost" life sized female figurehead. *Kate Lawrence* was the maiden name of the owner's wife and she was the model for the figurehead.

The May 30, 1907, obituary of 70-year old Anderson Zabriskie of North Hackensack mentions that he and his father were the owners of the *Kate Lawrence*. This contradicts all accounts of the Van Buskirks being the owners of the ship. Either Anderson Zabriskie and his father bought the ship at one time from the Van Buskirks, or the obituary was in error and one or both of these men commanded the ship for other owners. Eugene Bird states that the *Kate Lawrence*'s first captain was Joe Whitehead. He was succeeded by an African American known only as Captain "Bob." Sadly Bird did not record which men commanded the ship during what years and how Anderson Zabriskie fits into this picture.

The *Kate Lawrence* burned and sank sometime between 1885 to 1889. She had been ice-bound in the upper Hackensack when the owners ordered the master to get her free. Her master, whose name does not appear in the records, was reported to be young and inexperienced. He was a recently promoted deckhand who had heard that pouring kerosene on the ice would help it melt. He did not realize that the kerosene was not supposed to be ignited.

Agricultural fertilizers such as lime, phosphates, and manure were brought to the landings by ship. Very little detailed information is available about these cargoes. Except for manure coming from New York city, the sources of these cargoes are unknown. An 1858 newspaper advertisement for the firm of Banta and Terhune announced that both building materials (sand and lime), red and white ash coal, coal, and fertilizers (super phosphate of lime) were for sale at their docks in Hackensack. Fertilizer shipments of another sort did attract much attention. The "manure schooners" were reported to have been the best known boats sailing on the Hackensack River. Local farms supplied New York's horses with hay and oats, and the horses in turn produced fertilizer. Area residents reported that manure boats could be smelled several minutes before they could be seen. One young man employed to help unload manure at New Bridge slipped and fell into the cargo. After the ship was unloaded, his mother would not allow him back into the house for three days!

Blacksmiths used coal for forge work, and as the 19th century progressed, more and more homes came to be heated by coal. Schooners, canal boats, and barges were all used to transport coal into the region from the mines of Virginia and Pennsylvania via rivers and canals. This traffic will be treated to a more detailed discussion in another chapter.

As the region's population grew, the demand for all sorts of cargoes increased, with building supplies and lumber being the most important. Certainly, this trade was well documented since there are many available period newspaper advertisements.

Utilizing newspaper advertisements from the Paterson Intelligencer, we can glimpse a typical coasting schooner's work. The *General Jackson* can be followed as she made her many trips up and down the east coast and back to Paterson Landing, on the Passaic River. There, her cargoes were sold at a store operated by Peter Jackson. A more complete portrait of both Paterson Landing, or Acquackanonck, and the Jackson's business will be found in Chapter 7.

In January of 1828, Peter Jackson was selling 2,000 bushels of blacksmith coal from the schooner. In March, Peter Jackson and Son offered Virginia lumber for sale - 40,000 3 foot-long and 10,000 2 foot-long shingles. In the same ad, they also offered the cargo of the *Invincible* from Albany - 1,350 planks and 3,100 boards. Apparently the shingles sold well because advertisements in August announced that the *General Jackson* had made a five day trip from Norfolk with 50,000 "company's" shingles. The ship and her master, Captain. Turner, then made a three day passage from Philadelphia with 62 tons of Lehigh Coal for the Jacksons. She arrived at Paterson Landing on August 26th, where the coal was offered at $10 per ton.

Another schooner that called at Jackson's on July 15th, 1828 was the *Hetty*

Jackson, loaded with boards, planks, joists, and siding. Lumber was not the only cargo offered for sale; coal (Lehigh, Schuylkill, and Virginia), flour, pork, mackerel, cider, gin, lime, chocolate, Jamaica rum, molasses, cognac, brandy, and "American brandy" could all be purchased at the Jackson's store.

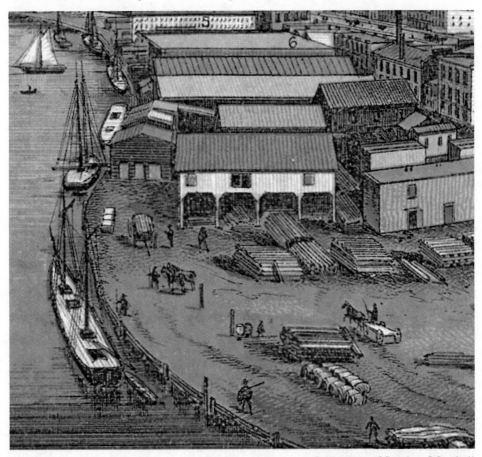

Collection of Stephan Marshall

Schooners are shown unloading logs at Ripley's saw Mill in Newark in this 1881 drawing. The Newark Gas Works (labeled building number 6) is just beyond the mill.

The most prominent merchants in the lumber business were the Anderson family of Hackensack. Throughout the nineteenth century, the Andersons sailed their own fleet of lumber schooners. Family members served as the masters of these ships and some of the ships were even built by the Andersons.

A typical Bergen County newspaper advertisement announced that D & I Anderson was selling 300,000 pieces of "superior" sawed ceiling laths "cheap." It was the cargo of the schooner *Rose In Bloom* which arrived in April of 1828. The Andersons also advertised shingles for sale later in May. A typical run for their schooners was between Hackensack and the Carolinas, bringing finished wood north to the family's stores.

Although their shipping operations were comparatively well documented in 1800s, the Andersons themselves remain a bit of an enigma. There are copies of two surviving letters written from Hackensack by John Anderson to his brother David. David Anderson was living in Virginia at the time where he acted as an agent for the family business. As mentioned, most of the lumber shipped by the Andersons came from southern ports in Virginia and Carolinas.

In his letter of March 17, 1833, John describes some of the troubles encountered by the *Harriet Ann* on the relatively short voyage between Hackensack and New York. The ship departed on the tenth of February just before a snowstorm began. She just made it to the Kill Van Kull where she took shelter for four days. Meanwhile, the Hackensack River was closed by ice and was shut until the thirteenth.

But the snow brought excellent sledding and brisk business, according to John's letter. All hands were safe when she returned to Hackensack where she was loaded with planks. The letter went on to describe the strategy for the upcoming voyage of the *William H.*, planning to use as ballast what was needed in New York. It is hard to decipher exactly what the letter says at this point, but apparently hay and shingles were also be carried, and then a load of pine was to be taken to Albany. There lumber bound for Hackensack was to be loaded.

A year later, another letter describes the preparations for building a new schooner. The Brown's yard laid down a keel, "a very handsome stick of white oak and straight as a line." Apparently locating suitable shipbuilding wood was something of a problem because he went on to say that "you have no idea of the scarcity of these trees until you undertake to search for them." He found two promising trees on some land he bought from Paulis Terhune, feeling that the seventy dollars an acre would be amply returned after harvesting just the two trees and selling the remainder.

In the same letter John describes the sudden failure of the Washington Banking Company where the family had its accounts. In a brief survey of the assets on hand, there is a list of all the shipmasters working for the Andersons - Captains Ward, John Halli, P.H. Voorhis, and A.H. Berry. Writing in the early 1900s, journalist and historian Eugene Bird also mentioned a Captain Patrick Brown who commanded the John Anderson, a boat in the lumber trade between the Carolinas and Hackensack no doubt owned by the Andersons.

Eugene Bird's 1915 article *Wind Jammers of the Hackensack* was for many years the standard work on the working ships of the Hackensack River. Sadly for generations of subsequent historians Bird did not provide any dates and left many of the relationships between the various ship owners, masters, and merchants unexplained.

Bird mentions several schooners in his article but explains nothing else about them. Among these are Barney Cole's *Onward* which carried coal, wood and lime. The *Caleb Wood* was commanded by Captain Tom Banta. The *Caleb Wood's* name was later changed to that of her owner, *Ira. W. Hoover.* Under the command of Captain Jospeh Kinzley the ship was employed in Chesapeake Bay trade. The *Two Sisters* was commanded by Captain Henry Berry and the *A. O. Zabriskie* by Captain Dave Parcells. Parcells was succeeded by Captain Henry Lozier.

The last significant cargoes to move by sail on the Hackensack River were bricks. There were several clay pits and brickyards along the river south of Hackensack, centered in the town of Little Ferry. The first to realize the value of the clay was Mrs. Elizabeth Sutliff Dufler, a freed black slave who in 1847 bought 10 acres along the river. She sold clay to potteries in Newark and Jersey City.

Large-scale brick manufacturing began in early 1867 when the Mehrof brothers — Nicholas, Philip, and Peter - purchased a brickyard near Little Ferry. The German-born brothers were the sons of Philip Mehrof, an architect originally from Darmstadt, Germany. Philip emigrated to America in the 1840s and brought his family followed soon afterwards. The Mehrof brothers found work in various brickyards in the region before striking out on their own. When they took over a brickyard in Little Ferry, it had already been in operation for five years, but under the brothers' direction it grew into one of the largest in the country. By 1882, it was producing over two million bricks annually and shipping them via a private fleet of schooners to New York, Newark, Paterson, and Providence.

Bergen County Historical Society

A schooner lies off a brickyard in Little Ferry in this 1904 photograph. The long sheds along the riverbanks are to protect bricks while they are drying. Bricks were the last significant cargo to move under sail on the Hackensack River.

Other brickyards were established in the early 1870s. According to a 1904 report by the New Jersey Geological Survey, there were ten brickyards located on the river between Little Ferry and Hackensack. Together they made up the second most extensive brick industry in the state, producing millions of common bricks annually. All of these yards were situated on the tidewater where they could take advantage of water transportation. As late as 1917, brick schooners were serving the Schmult's, Mehrof's and Gardener's yards.

In some areas the clay pits reached depths of sixty feet below the river's water level. One surviving photograph was taken at the bottom of a clay pit with the camera looking up the sails of a schooner. Another photograph in the report shows a two masted schooner near the waterfront sheds of one of the yards.

Of the 15 schooners known to be in the brick trade four were named for and presumably owned by members of the Mehrof family. These were the *Nicholas Mehrof*, *Philp Mehrof*, *Peter Mehrof*, and *Annie Mehrof* (formerly the *Stephan Underhill*). A brick trade schooner whose owners went unrecorded was named the *John Schmults*. Captain George Mehrof was noted for being one of the youngest masters in the Hackensack River brick trade. The oldest master and unofficial "Admiral" of the brick fleet was Joe Kinzley, Sr., who retired in 1915. There was also a Captain Walter Kinzley but the exact relationship of the two men went unrecorded. Joe Kinzley was the son of German immigrants who settled in the Hackensack Valley. Although the Kinzleys were farmers, he was reputed to be dissatisfied with farm life and he began his sailing career on the Hackensack River as soon as he was old enough. A complete list of the known brick schooners and masters is presented in Appendix D.

There were other cargoes that were small in volume but still important to the area economy. In 1832, the New York Chemical Manufacturing Company (which became Chemical Bank after an 1844 reorganization) sent "oil of vitriol" (sulfuric acid) to the Lodi Print Works via "schooner for Hackensack."

Schooners also brought fine lumber to a custom furniture factory at River Edge (Old Bridge) until the 1920s.

One of the more unusual cargoes during the 1800s was hard-shell clams for the making of wampum. During the 1840s and 1850s, northern Bergen County produced much of this trading material for fur traders in the Pacific northwest. To obtain the prized shells with "black hearts" it was necessary to travel by rowboat from New Milford to Rockaway, Long Island. Once the cargo had arrived back in New Milford, all of the wampum factory's neighbors were allowed to help themselves to the mollusk's meat, but were admonished to leave behind the shells. Later when the Washington Market in New York City

Journalist and historian Eugene Bird was the author of Wind Jammers of the Hackensack. *Published by the Bergen County Historical Society in 1915, for many years this monograph was the standard work on the Hackensack's working ships.*

Author's Collection

opened, the Cambell family contracted for the empty clam shells. Arriving by boat to the market, they would break the black hearts from the shell and put them in barrels. Returning with ten or twenty barrels worth, they would supply them to local women who ground and drilled them into beads on a piece-work basis. Contemporary observers note that the extra income from making wampum provided much needed extra cash for many local families.

All available surviving photographs, paintings, engravings, and drawings show that two-masted schooners were the only type of large sailing vessels used throughout the 1800s and into the 1900s on the upper Passaic and Hackensack rivers. Larger sailing vessels, such as three and four-masted schooners, could reach Newark and other ports on Newark Bay. Above these points they were impractical because of their deep draft and sail plans that were ill-suited to winding channels.

Of the eight schooners listed in a Lloyds Shipping register as having a home port in northern New Jersey, six hailed from Hackensack, and two from Newark. Two were built locally, the *David A. Berry*, built in 1858 in Acquackanonck and the *Henry Brown*, built in Hackensack in 1839 (she was rebuilt in 1864.) The *David A. Berry* was 108 feet long with a capacity of 205 tons. She was owned by her captain and various partners and was based in Newark. The 130 ton *Henry Brown* was not only built and ported in Hackensack, but was owned in part by the Loziers, a local family with many ties to the Hackensack River trade.

The third of the six Hackensack schooners was built in Baltimore in 1851, the 238 ton *John Haxall*. The 148 ton, 88 foot long *John Warren* and the 93 ton *Amelia* were both built on the Hudson River in the 1850s, and both listed Hackensack as their home port. Incidentally, the *John Warren* was commanded

Courtesy Bergen County Historical Society
This photograph of an unidentified schooner appeared in Eugene Bird's 1915 article,
Wind Jammers of the Hackensack. *Judging from the well-kept hull and fine lines she*
might have been a yacht rather than a working craft.

by Captain S. Lozier. The *Entire* was built in 1847 at an undisclosed New
Jersey shipyard. She was 78 feet long and 107 tons. The *A.R. Wetmore* was built
in Belleville in 1850; 229 tons, she was based in Hackensack.

It should be noted that these ships were not by any means the only ones
afloat at the time. Lloyds was attempting to rate these ships for insurance purposes. Those ships that did not meet their standards were not listed on their
register. The reader should also remember that these records are for those

HISTORIC NEWARK

Announcement of the opening of the steam passenger and freight service between Newark and New York. Established in 1849 by Thomas V. Johnson & Co.

Collection of Stephen Marshall

Launched in 1849, the steam powered Edward Payson could travel between Newark's Commercial Dock and New York City in about two and a half hours.

ships examined in 1867. Further research may reveal a more complete picture of the activities of these craft on New Jersey rivers.

Steamboats and Trains

The decision to divide this chapter into two parts between sailing and steam ships is completely arbitrary. The two types of vessels often worked side-by-side, serving the same ports, carrying many of the same cargoes, and in some cases, being commanded by the same men. The decision to include steam powered railways with steamboats is also subjective since both steamboat and sailing vessels competed against the railroad.

A brief description of the early steamboats on the Passaic River is given in Chapter 7. Because of the presence of copper (for boilers and cylinders), machine shops, and skilled workmen in the Passaic River area, Belleville became America's first center for steamboat building.

The first steamboat to travel on the Hackensack River was the *Thomas Swan*, owned by Schmults & Dunges. The available records do not indicate if her part owner was the same Schmults that would later enter into the brick business. She was unsuccessful because of her deep draft, and her later career is something of a mystery. The June 1, 1861 *New York Times* reported the *Thomas Swan* sailing for Fort Pickens, Florida with provisions, cannons, and gun carriages. *A History of American Steam Navigation* mentions a *Thomas Swan* as being chartered by the Quartermaster Bureau for $300 per day in 1861 and $200 per day in 1864. There is no hard evidence that this is the same ship, because no less than four *Thomas Swans* sailed in that period.

A steamboat with a documented Civil War career was the *Hackensack*, built in 1863 by a Belleville shipyard for Judge Huyler, John H.T. Banta, and John S. Lozier. She was a screw steamer, 175 tons, 110 ft. long, and 23 feet wide, commanded by Captain Henry Lozier.

Although intended for the coal and lumber trade between Philadelphia, Albany, and Hackensack, she was chartered to carry sutler's supplies for the Union Army. She carried supplies to City Point, Virginia which was the huge Union supply base during the siege of Petersburg. Throughout the fall and winter of 1864-65, Lee's Army of Northern Virginia was dug in and holding out against Grant's forces. As the siege was drawing to a close, the sound of distant artillery caused a nervous Union commander at City Point to order the *Hackensack* to remain in port, standing by, in case she was need to tow off a fleet of Union schooners and sloops should the Confederates break through Union lines. Far from this being the case, Lee's army was soon in retreat towards Richmond and ultimately from there to Appomattox Courthouse.

The *Hackensack* was lost in 1870, but Henry Lozier lived to an old age. He spent his last years running a canoe rental on the Hackensack. His granddaughter once told the author that she still remembered going with him for Sunday canoe rides as a special treat. (Henry Lozier seems to have been overlooked by biographers. His exact dates of birth and death have not been discovered. Judging by his career he was probably born in the 1830s or early 1840s and died between 1910-1930.)

Although large steamboats were used on the local rivers, the powerful and maneuverable tugboats were more common. Like modern tugboats,

THE CATSKILLS FROM THE HUDSON

Courtesy Project Guttenberg

A typical small coastal and river schooner of the mid-1800s. In many instances these vessels were towed up and down river channels instead of attempting to work under sail. This photograph was taken on the Hudson River but the scene was repeated on the Passaic and Hackensack. From The Hudson Three Centuries of History, Romance and Invention *by Wallace Bruce.*

these early vessels moved barges, but they also towed schooners through the river channels. Most of the early tugboats were tall stacked coal burners with wooden hulls. The boatman had a dangerous job, especially in the winter when decks were icy. Another source of danger was ice deposited on hawsers, cables, and winch barrels. It was not uncommon for men to lose fingertips by getting them caught between winch barrels and cables.

Numerous steam tugs were mentioned in newspaper advertisements, such as an item appearing on August 21, 1858, when a Mr. Van Saun chartered a "good steamboat" and a two decked pleasure barge *Irene* for an excursion down the Hackensack to Staten Island and back the same day.

According to the journalist and historian Eugene Bird, during the latter half of the 1800s the most famous steam-powered vessel on the Hackensack River was the tugboat *Wesley Stoney*. She was built in Belleville and owned jointly by her captain, D. Anderson Zabriskie, and her engineer, Henry Lozier. The tug towed hundreds of scows and sailing vessels up and down the river. After being sold, she was burned, but later rebuilt as the *Elisie K.* She

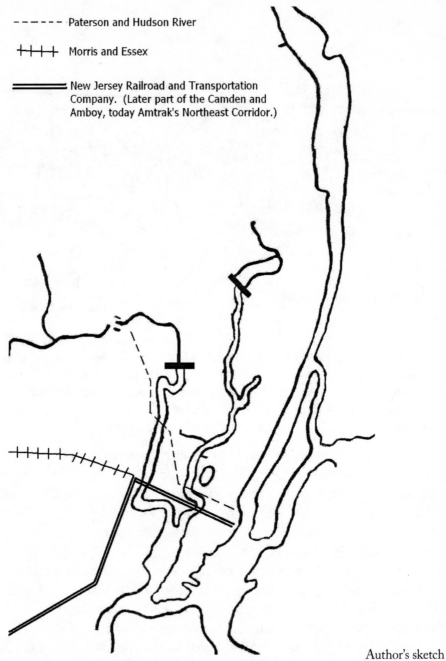

- - - - - Paterson and Hudson River

+ + + + Morris and Essex

New Jersey Railroad and Transportation Company. (Later part of the Camden and Amboy, today Amtrak's Northeast Corridor.)

Author's sketch

There several important early railroads crossing the Hackensack and Passaic rivers. Because the main line of the Camden and Amboy terminated at the port of Amboy on the Raritan River, it is not shown on this map. The Camden and Amboy eventually acquired the New Jersey Railroad and Transportation Company (double black line). All of these lines are still in use either by New Jersey Transit or Amtrak.

continued in service until 1915 when she sunk and her captain, whose name was not found in the available records, drowned.

There were four important early railroads operating in the watersheds of the Passaic River, Hackensack River, and Newark Bay. Reaching westward from Newark was the Morris and Essex. Chartered in January 1835, it offered service as far as Morristown three years later. Running between Newark, Elizabethtown, Rahway, and New Brunswick, the New Jersey Railroad and Transportation Company was chartered in 1832. Although originally intended to reach the Delaware River and points beyond (New Orleans was even mentioned), opposition by the established and politically powerful trans-state Camden and Amboy was strong. The line was eventually confined to the eastern side of the state where it served first as the Camden and Amboy's link to Newark, and later to Jersey City. (The Camden and Amboy was the first railroad to link the Raritan Bay and the Delaware River and its highly strategic route was guarded by monopoly privileges granted by the State Legislature.) The earliest line of the four, the Paterson and Hudson River Railroad, was chartered in 1831. Building eastwards from Paterson it reached Acquackanonck (Passaic) in 1832.

Between the time that the railroads reached the Passaic River and when they were completed to the Hudson, both passengers and freight had to transfer to boats at Acquackanonck. The railroad's agents sold passenger tickets and arranged for freight transfers. The railroad that ran through Acquackanonck passed down the center of what is today Main Avenue in Passaic. When it reached the river, the railroad swung inland and ran behind the Dutch Reformed Church on a route that is approximately that of present-day route 20. A small side road connected the railroad line to the site of the landing. (At that time the landing was also referred to as Paterson Landing, perhaps as a nod to the new railroad.) The railroad proceeded southward along the west bank of the Passaic before turning eastward and crossing the river a few miles south of Acquackanonck.

The railroad advertised connections to two schooners owned by John Hedden, the *Invincible* and the *Energy*. They departed the landing for New York on Wednesdays and Saturdays. Connections were also advertised with the "new, splendid, and commodious" steamboat *Proprietor*. Like the schooners, this boat did not run a daily service but only departed for New York on Mondays, Wednesdays, and Fridays. (These boats are discussed in Chapter 7.)

In 1834 the railroad line reached Bergen Hill. Temporary tracks carried the line over the hill until 1838, when the New Jersey Railroad and Transportation Company also reached the hill and the two lines collaborated on a deep cut through to Jersey City.

In addition to Bergen Hill, the route of the Paterson and Hudson River Railroad posed other significant engineering challenges. The Hackensack Meadowlands causeway required many pilings, followed by fill. The whole affair had to sit for a year before the engineers judged it stable enough to support track. This causeway led up to the Hackensack River drawbridge near Berry's Creek. Dating from 1832-33, it the first railroad drawbridge built in the United States and regrettably the site of one of the earliest drawbridge accidents. On December 17, 1833, a horse drawn car was traveling from Bergen Ridge to Paterson, when gale winds caused the draw platform to shift and upset it. Luckily, a passenger's bruised cheek was the only injury sustained. Twenty years later, on October 20, 1851, a sloop struck the same drawbridge and carried off a section of the span. Passengers were forced to stop and change cars until repairs were completed.

While crossing the Meadowlands, Paterson and Hudson River trains were reported to have stopped so that the passengers could get off and hunt for turtles. Although this seems extremely unlikely and obviously dangerous, it is true. In a 1901 interview, Paterson and Hudson River Railroad conductor John M. Garrison asserted that a stop to hunt turtles was customary. Garrison began his career on the Paterson and Hudson River in 1846. He described the early trains on the line:

> each train had two passenger coaches and several freight cars, except on holidays, when one or more coaches would be added to accommodate the "rush."

The first mention made of direct competition between the Paterson and Hudson River Railroad and the local steamboats was in the winter of 1843. Petitions from Bergen and Passaic counties had finally prodded the New Jersey State Legislature to force the widening of the railroad's Passaic River drawbridge. Cornelius C. Zabriskie and other steamboat operators had been pushing for such action since 1832. Once the work was finished the boat operators immediately went to work. They cut fares to half those of the railroad. In turn the Paterson and Hudson River cut its fares from 62 and one-half cents to 25 cents. But as soon as the river froze in November the railroad resumed its old fares. Thanks to the indignant 1843 editorials that appeared in the *Paterson Intelligencer*, we know the details of this early rate war.

Railroads did not reach into the Hackensack River Valley until the 1850s and 60s. The first was the Northern Railroad of New Jersey which built on the east side of the Hackensack. It began in the mid-1850s with construction westward from Bergen Hill. The line skirted the eastern edge of the

Courtesy Library of Congress

In this 1895 artist's drawing of the Passaic River north of Newark. A tugboat brings a barge northwards while an Erie train runs northward to Paterson. A schooner is moored on the east bank.

Meadowlands and then turned northward at Overpeck Creek. A New York lawyer named J. Wyman Jones bought up six farms in what would become Englewood and began selling building lots to fellow New Yorkers whom he considered "superior individuals." The line reached the New York border in the late 1870s and is today operated primarily as a freight route.

The first railroad on the west bank of the river was the Hackensack and New York Railroad, which, despite its name, linked Hackensack to the Paterson and Hudson River Railroad in Rutherford. It was charted in 1856, and the five miles from Rutherford to Essex Street in Hackensack were completed by 1861. Further construction was halted by the Civil War. In 1869 the Hackensack Extension Railroad was chartered to build the remaining 20 miles to the New York border to serve the towns of the Pascack Valley. This was completed in 1873 and the line became the New Jersey and New York Railway. Today the line is operated by New Jersey Transit as a commuter route.

As the New Jersey and New York Railroad was constructed on the Hackensack's western bank, it made river recreation accessible to passengers. The riverside towns were both homes to commuters and also the sites of hotels. Small resorts from New Bridge north to Oradell provided city dwellers with

Courtesy Library of Congress

The Erie Railroad crossed the Passaic River near Newark. This 1876 photograph shows the drawbridge and several schooners moored upstream.

nearby destinations devoted to boating, swimming, dancing, and strolling. (see Chapter 8).

Railroad drawbridges were vital to operating both through routes and local lines. Other spans soon followed the pioneering structures on the Paterson and Hudson River Railroad. An 1863 *New York Times* report of an accident on the Morris and Essex's Hackensack River Bridge casts some light on their operation. The morning passenger train from Newark to Hoboken left at 6:00 a.m. and usually arrived by 6:18. The Hackensack drawbridge was near the middle of this run. On the morning of the accident the train consisted of three cars - baggage, smoking, and passenger. (Because of the unsavory sanitary habits of 19th century tobacco users, they were relegated to their own car.) The drawbridge was usually left open all night and was supposed to be closed in time for the morning train. If a passing vessel prevented the bridge from being closed, a signal lamp was lit to warn approaching trains.

Surviving passengers reported that the whistle was blowing and brakes were screeching when the engine flew off the open end of the bridge. Although the tide was low, the engine had sufficient momentum to hurl itself into the deepest part of the channel, carrying engineer Jacob A. Woodruff to his death. The first two cars also followed over the edge and the passenger car was suspended with one end hanging over the water. The fireman jumped clear of the engine but was injured when hitting the water. William Havers, the conductor, was also hurt after being thrown out of the smoking car where he had been riding.

Because the engineer was killed, it can never be known if the correct signal was being displayed. The bridge tender was seen running from his house nearby wearing nothing but a shirt and pants. Witnesses suspected that he had been asleep. He pointed to the lit signal lantern but many believed that the bridge tender quickly hoisted it during the confusion immediately following the wreck.

Ultimately the railroads, and not the ships, transformed the landscape (see Chapter 8), but the memory of the river craft, their crews and captains lived on. Some of the more colorful characters were recalled by Bergen County historian and journalist Eugene Bird in his 1916 monograph *Wind Jammers of the Hackensack*. Among them was Captain David Bogart, who ran a schooner along the coast and Long Island Sound. A fastidious shipper, whenever passing another vessel, he would call for frock coat and stovepipe hat. Suitably attired, he would salute the passing vessel. But he also had a "cool and masterful" demeanor during heavy winds and was remembered for carrying all the canvas his masts could stand.

Captain Andrew Bogart, brother of David Bogart, was the master of the 300 ton schooner *Judge Baker*. On a November morning in 1855, he left Sandy Hook in tow with another schooner. He had hoped to make Philadelphia by Sunday morning as he was a devout man and wanted to arrive in time for church services. A storm rose from the south and the *Judge Baker* lost her tow. She went ashore at Long Branch losing a cargo of dyestuffs. On Sunday morning the bodies of Captain Bogart and his wife were found washed ashore. No crew members survived and their bodies were never recovered.

The Lozier family's origins in Bergen County go back to the late 1600s in New Milford. By the 1800s, several members of the family became either ship owners or masters. Captain Henry Lozier has already been mentioned as captain of the *Hackensack* and then as engineer and part owner of the tug *Wesley Stoney*. Lozier spent his entire working life at sea. As a young man he was said to have traveled to many foreign ports. Once he earned his master's certificate, he settled down to work the coasting trade between Jamestown, Virginia and New York. In 1870 he inherited a Spring Valley, New Jersey homestead. Lozier married Rachel Ann Voorhees and their son Arthur was born at his parent's home in 1874.

Arthur Lozier did not follow the sea, yet his career might be said to have had a profound influence on the trade patterns in the Hackensack River valley. He became one of the pioneers in truck farming, a type of agriculture that was new to the region, transforming his 90 acres into a specialized farm for fruits and vegetables. Once he and some other farmers proved it was possible, the local farms began moving away from the mix of grain, gardens, wood lots, and meadows that filled the holds of Hackensack River schooners.

A master mariner whose later career literally transformed the Hackensack River was Captain Richard R. Hawkey, who was born sometime around 1820. He commanded the schooner *Stewart* and was regarded as the most fearless man on the river for his daring feats of navigation. Hawkey was also keenly involved in politics and at various times served as county jailer and member of the Board of Chosen Freeholders from New Barbados Township. He was at times a real estate agent and held an interest in the Bergen Turnpike Company. In 1870, he was one of the original incorporators of the Hackensack Water Company, whose dams would someday restrict stream flow so completely that navigation on the upper river would become impossible for all craft but canoes.

The ship captains were all local men, respected in the community and still remembered today. There are remarkably few references, however, to the crewmen of these vessels or even to their officers. Eugene Bird in his *Wind Jammers of the Hackensack* claimed that there were many "wild and boisterous" incidents involving the rough sailors who manned the ships. Yet, curiously, he only related this one tale.

There was once a few sailors and chairmakers from North Hackensack who were enjoying the local apple jack. Deciding to attend church, they dropped in on the Sunday service of "Mart" Vreeland, a local preacher.

Preaching on the text from Proverbs "Look not thou upon the wine when it is red," Vreeland was busy denouncing sin in general and the habits of some church members in particular. As he was reminding the particularly unregenerate exactly where they were going, one of the sailors jumped up and shouted, "That's a damn lie!" Vreeland replied with a rebuke and cautionary admonition, but when the remark was again loudly repeated, the whole party of rabblerousers was ejected from the church.

The only other tale of sailors' doings recorded for posterity involved the commercial fishermen who worked out of Hackensack. Hackensack had a thriving fish market in the 1800s and the river was noted for both its commercial and recreational fishing. P. Christie Terhune, a Bergen County native whose reminiscences were recorded, stated that he remembered seeing fishermen empty their fish buckets and then drink river water. Terhune wryly remarked that "one drink today would finish them, but they all lived to a ripe old age." Sadly, he did not say why the fishermen did this, whether out of some custom or superstition, to prove the catch was fresh, or simply to quench their thirst.

The schooner's efficiency and ease of handling meant that coasting vessels could get by with relatively small crews. "Captain, cook and a man for each mast" was a general rule commonly quoted in the 1800s. Bird states that the local schooners commonly sailed with six man crews, and as the local schooners appear to be mostly two-masted, this rule appears to have been generally followed. But where did the men come from?

There are a number of possibilities. They could of course have been professional seamen who were recruited while the ships were in the large ports such as New York, Philadelphia, or Norfolk. Like the officers, some may have been relatives of the owners of the ships. Another possibly is suggested by research done on Hudson River sloops, where it was found that local tradesmen and farm workers would ship out for a few months or weeks during slow periods. It appears that these semi-professionals frequently switched between employment on land and on the river. It is not clear however if this was also the practice on northern New Jersey's rivers.

Chapter 7

The Ports

It is hard to overstate the importance of the landings in the communities that they served. Far more than just busy commercial centers built around a trans-shipment point, they were the socioeconomic link between the hinterland and outside world. In the early 1980s, the Rutgers University Center for Public Archaeology decided to excavate a section of the Raritan Landing. The landing was located on River Road in present-day Piscataway. The port was active for roughly 150 years between the early 1700s and the mid-1800s, and although it finally disappeared, there are several surviving structures from this period. The Metlar-Bodine House is now a museum. Other buildings from the period are preserved at the nearby open-air museum of East Jersey Olde Town.

Courtesy New Jersey Department of Transportation

In 1978 the Rutgers Archaeological Survey Office excavated a portion of Raritan Landing. The remains of a storehouse burned during the American Revolution are shown here.

After the excavations were complete, the archaeologists mapped the density of more than 30 artifact types including ceramics, bone, glass, and building debris. Study of these maps revealed how the patterns of land use changed over time. They also helped track specific artifact distributions from the different periods of destruction and rebuilding.

Two important concepts emerged from the Rutgers project. The first was that the landing was a very dynamic place that underwent frequent change. Raritan Landing was repeatedly flooded, burned by the British during the Revolution, and rebuilt several times as patterns of commerce shifted. The second major finding was that although the region was predominantly "Jersey Dutch" in culture, the people's material goods (as revealed by what was found in the excavations) were largely English.

As the predominant ethnic group in the Raritan valley, the Jersey Dutch had their own language, worshiped in the Dutch Reformed Church, and kept alive many Dutch customs. This would not be particularly remarkable if the Jersey Dutch were directly from Holland, but these were descendants of the original Dutch colonists in New Amsterdam and Long Island who came to New Jersey beginning in the 1650s. With the surrender of New Amsterdam to the English, more Dutch-speaking colonists moved into the region. In time, an ethnic enclave developed in the Raritan, Passaic, Hackensack, and Hudson River valleys which persisted well into the first half of the 1800s. Queen's College, later Rutgers University, at the southern end of the enclave and across the river from Raritan Landing, was originally established to train clergymen for the Reformed Church. But despite this persistent ethnic identity, the artifacts recovered at the landing were principally English. This is both a reflection of British mercantile policy and the realities of trade during that period.

Raritan Landing is the only one of New Jersey's small ports that has ever been archaeologically excavated. New Bridge Landing is the only one to have been preserved. Except for these two examples, we must turn to literature to glimpse the life of the ports that were the gateways to the outside world.

Acquackanonck

The founding of Acquackanonck was described in Chapter two. Aside from being at the head of navigation for the Passaic River, the site was well endowed with water power, was the location of important bridges, and was conveniently positioned to capture the freight traffic for much of the Passaic River

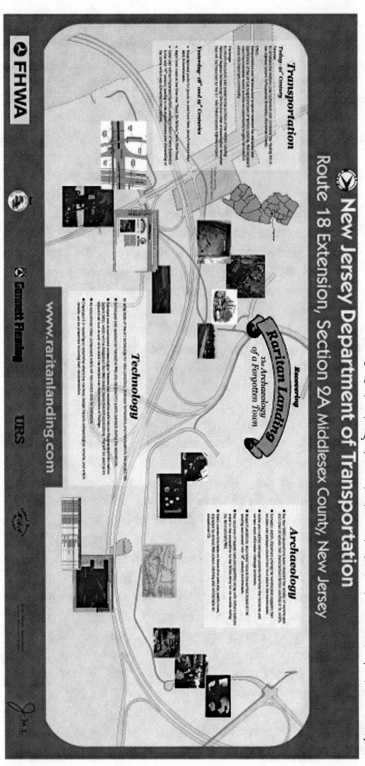

This poster was created by the archaeologists who worked at Raritan Landing for the 80th Annual Meeting of the Transportation Research Board held in Washington, D.C. It was displayed as part of a session titled: "Cultural Resources and Transportation: Outreach, Preservation, and Alternatives to Destruction."

Courtesy New Jersey Department of Transportation

77

watershed, which included the industrial cities of Paterson and Passaic. (Note: Because the name "Acquackanonck" was eventually replaced by "Passaic," the area will be referred to as "Acquackanonck" when describing events taking place prior to the 1860s and "Passaic" thereafter.)

Although preceded by the trading post operated by Michielson, the most important phase in the history of Acquackanonck landing began with a store operated by a one Major Robert Drummond, of whom little is known. The next owner was Abraham Ackerman (1752 - 1829), one of the richest men in Passaic County. In time, Ackerman took John Ryerson into partnership and was eventually bought out by Ryerson. Ryerson, in his turn, formed a partnership with Aaron Van Houton. Meanwhile, Ackerman built some docks and began running his own line of boats to New York City.

According to some recorded stories, local farmers brought their crops to Acquackanonck on Saturdays. Once the ships were loaded, the younger people stayed behind for dances on the summer evenings.

Eventually Ryerson and Van Houton were bought out by Peter Jackson in the early 1800s, who would be remembered as the most ambitious entrepreneur at the landing. Immediately after purchasing the property, Jackson erected a row of frame buildings and located his store at the end nearest the bridge. He bought large farms, expanded into the lumber and wood trade, and eventually built a hotel. The hotel was located on Main Avenue, across the street from the store, and was known as Ryerson's Hotel. (Did Peter Jackson put up the money while a Ryerson ran the hotel? The record is silent.) Jackson also had a "country" store as well as iron mines at Pompton. Prior to 1814, mail was only delivered as far as Newark. Jackson and Ackerman fought over who would become the postmaster for Acquackanonck, and Jackson prevailed.

Jackson was reported to have lived in fine style in a beautiful home that had elegant lawns and gardens. Mrs. Jackson was active in the Dutch Reformed Church. Although ambitious, Jackson was not noted for his thrift, and he lost everything in a financial panic. He was then forced to sell to Andrew Parsons, in 1830, but he did retain his postmaster's position for another eight years. Parsons ran the business until 1840. Finally, Jackson moved to Newark, where he died in poverty. His son John was born at the landing and learned business in his father's store. John eventually rose to prominence in a new form of transportation when he become president of United Railways of New Jersey (the United Railways later became part of the Pennsylvania Railroad.)

Surviving newspaper advertisements show that J.K. Flood & Co. was another emporium operating at Acquackanonck during the same period as

Courtesy Bergen County Historical Society

During the height of the family's prosperity at Acquackanonck Landing, Peter Jackson constructed this two-story house

the Jacksons. They used the towboats Maria and Independence to supply their store with fresh flour to be sold at "New York prices."

Newspaper advertisements of August 1853 mention the steamboat *Lodi* running as a freight boat between Acquackanonck and Barclay Street in New York City. Her captain was listed as John W. Speer. The *Lodi* made only one trip each day. She would leave Acquackanonck on a Monday and return on Wednesday. She would again depart for New York on Thursday but not return until Saturday. It would seem that the boat spent every Tuesday and Friday being unloaded and loaded in New York.

The steamboat *Proprietor* maintained a similar schedule, leaving Acquackanonck on Monday, Wednesday, and Friday and departing New York on Tuesday, Thursday, and Saturday. The *Proprietor* carried both freight and passengers. Her captain was listed as G.P. Andrews.

It is not clear why the *Lodi's* and *Proprietor's* schedules required two or more days for a round trip. The schedules were similar to those of the schooners *Invincible* and *Energy* which in 1833 were advertised as departing for New York on Wednesdays and Saturdays.

79

Acquackanonck Landing became noted for the lumber, timber, and building supplies businesses which grew up there. As late as the 1930s lumber continued to be brought from Albany to Passaic by barges operated by W.S. Anderson & Company. During the same period, two steamboats, the *Cora Mandel* and *Alfred Speer*, were making daily trips between Passaic and Newark. Within a few years, the Passaic to Newark commuter boats would be put out of business, the passengers being mortified by the stench of sewage and other wastes in the river.

Bergen County Historical Society

The Anderson Lumber Company across the river from Passaic had been an important destination for much river traffic for about 100 years when this 1922 photograph was made. A barge in visible on the river just beyond the unloading equipment.

The *Alfred Speer* was named for a Passaic newspaper publisher and civic leader. Born in Belleville, Speer was the son of a shoemaker. He was raised by his grandfather on a farm along the Passaic River. Although a man of little schooling, he rose to prominence as a publisher. Speer lobbied the government to improve river navigation, built the first public hall in the city, led a subscription campaign that raised money for streetlights and other improvements, and he was instrumental in getting the village's name changed from Acquackanonck to Passaic.

Water power was just as important a part Acquackanonck's history as navigation. The first dam was built just above the head of navigation in 1828. John S. Van Winkle and Brant Van Blarcom obtained a charter from the state legislature to erect an eight foot high dam across the river. It was later said to have been an "inefficient" structure which languished and was eventuality abandoned. The Dundee Manufacturing Company was originally established in 1832. The Company wanted to build a new dam but was unable to do so until it was reorganized as the Dundee Power and Land Company in 1870. This company built the present Dundee Dam and the Dundee Canal which ran through the southeast corner of Passaic. The dam is an immense structure, stretching 450 feet across the river. It is 40 feet wide at its base and 6 feet wide at the top. The canal was never seriously intended for navigation. The promises of the promoters guaranteed barge loads of raw materials delivered to factory docks and a passage way for steamboats carrying commuters from the upriver towns to Newark. On the day the canal was officially opened, a single boat carrying a party of VIP's locked into the canal and made a brief one-and-one-half mile trip along the waterway. This was the only time that any boat made the trip. The Dundee Canal did become immensely successful as a source of water for the factories lining its banks, which was exactly what the promoters had intended all along.

Today the name Acquackanonck appears no where except in history books. Even in the 1800s the port was often referred to as Passaic Landing. Until the latter half of the 1800s, the area that became the town of Clifton was also known as Acquackanonck. According to the short version of that story, as the area grew in size and prosperity, so did dissatisfaction with its name. The local citizens wanted something more progressive and easier to pronounce (easier to spell too, historians have counted more than 80 different spellings of Acquackanonck). Looking west to Garrett Mountain, a committee of civic leaders saw the sheer cliffs rising up from the valley and settled on "Clifton."

The actual story is somewhat more complicated. Originally part of Essex County, Acquackanonck Township was one of the original six townships included in Passaic County when the county was formed in 1846. By that time, parts of the original township had already been broken off. The earliest formed the original city of Paterson in 1791. The rest of present-day Paterson broke off in 1831 and another portion became Passaic in 1866. Finally, the remainder of Acquackanonck Township was absorbed by the city of Passaic. The name Clifton first appeared around 1867, but only in reference to the area around Main and Clifton Avenues. The present city of Clifton was not incorporated until 1917.

Today the cliffs that gave the city its name are all gone. Quarrying operations gradually reduced them until a by the 1980s only a thin wall of rock remained near the junction of Valley Road and Route 46. There was a brief effort to conserve these last remains, but they were too unstable to be left standing, and thus were demolished.

The site of Acquackanonck Landing proper, the area where Passaic's Gregory Avenue meets River Road, has been placed on the state register of historic places. Perhaps some day archaeologists will uncover the unwritten history of this important port.

Author's photograph

The east bank of the Passaic opposite Acquackanonk Landing is in the city of Wallington. The bridge in the background connects Gregory Avenue and Main Avenue. The site of Anderson Lumber has recently been made into the Liberty Crossing Municipal Park. A brightly painted bollard recalls the era of commercial navigation.

Belleville

Belleville has been a manufacturing center ever since entrepreneurs began expanding northwards from Newark in search of water power and land. Today, Belleville is remembered as an important center for the building of steamboats. The story of how that came to pass goes back to the 1600s.

In the 1680s Arent Schyler began mining copper in a hillside that rose near the west bank of the Hackensack River in what is today Moonachie. A native of Albany, Schyler had been an explorer, diplomat to Indian tribes, fur trader, and land speculator. His copper mine represented his last major enterprise in what had been a very full life. Schyler's mine continued to operate into the 1700s when removing water from the mine could no longer be done by simple drainage tunnels and crude pumps.

In the 1760s, a British built steam pumping engine was imported to the mine complete with an English mechanic, Josiah Hornblower, to set up the engine, run and maintain it. After the Revolution, however, Hornblower left the mine and formed a partnership with Nicolas Roosevelt. Roosevelt had operated a nearby copper foundry. Hornblower contributed his knowledge of engines, and Roosevelt his knowledge of copper working. Soon the two partners established the Soho Works in Belleville. To assemble steam engines and boilers, they hired skilled workers who were veterans of the firm of Boultan and Watt of Birmingham, England. In addition to the machine shops, the Soho Works possessed a copper smelter and rolling mill. This allowed the firm to supply the copper sheathing for America's early naval vessels.

A third member joined the team in the person of Colonel John Stevens, the pioneer industrialist who later would be instrumental in the construction of early railroads and steamships. A few years earlier Stevens had tried to build his own steamboat and had failed miserably. Now aware of his limitations, Stevens provided the funding for Hornblower and Roosevelt to build a new boat.

In 1798 the Soho Works of Belleville produced its first steamboat. On October 21 of that year the sixty foot *Polacca* made her trial run up the Passaic River from Belleville. The ship had been fitted with a twenty inch cylinder operating on a two foot stroke. On the upstream trip the engine's vibrations opened the seams between the hull planks and the *Polacca* was forced back to the dock for repair. Top speed on that voyage was three and one half miles an hour.

From then on Belleville became a regional center for the construction of steamboats. Several hulls from the Belleville yards found their way north to the Hackensack and Passaic rivers.

Bound Creek

Located west of Newark, the area known as Camptown was the site of Bound Creek. Although local tradition holds that the area was named for a Continental Army camp, there is no extant record of the army making use of the area. The name is believed to have come from the Camp family. Periaugers were built at the grandly named "Camptown Navy Yard" located in the Vinegar Hill section of Irvington between Irvington's town center and South Orange. The exact location of the yard is recored as being on the site of present day West Clinton Avenue between Ellery Avenue and Franklin Terrace. Completed boats were hauled four miles overland by oxen and launched into Bound Creek. The subsequent launching of boats at Bound Creek was reported to have been a day-long event with the Baldwins providing plenty of applejack and cider for the festive occasion.

The land was originally owned by a Moses Baldwin who transferred title for 37 acres to Jabez B. Baldwin in 1786. Jabez began building periaugers and other boats, many of which were built for Caleb Camp. The periauger *Sally and Betsey* was discussed in Chapter 3, but the Baldwins also constructed the schooner *Enterprise* for Camp. The sloop *Fair American*, owned by John Craig, Samuel Morse and David Shotwell, is also believed to have been constructed in Camptown. Two other ships, the sloops, *Maria* and *Minerva* are specifically mentioned by name in an account book kept by Samuel Roberts, a local cooper, in 1810.

The schooner *Enterprise* began her career as a cargo vessel. She is recorded as transporting shad and salt along the Jersey coast. Camp's records refer to the "Sale of Shad out of the Scuner interprise April 21, 1813" of $301.95. Another voyage made on the 30th of April netted a profit of $10.07. With the outbreak of war she also was employed in smuggling between Canada and Maine.

The area that is today the western edge of Weequahic Park was a transshipment point for farm products and other goods arriving from as far away as Morristown. Periaugers carried them down Bound Brook out to the Passaic River.

Weequahic Park was the site of New Jersey's state agricultural fairs between 1866 and 1889. It was later the site of horse and then automobile racing. For four days in the spring of 1916 it was the site of a pageant celebrating the 250th anniversary of Newark's founding. Boats on the lake reenacted the landing of the Puritans, which was then followed by costumed actors and actresses reenacting other sketches from Newark's history.

Bound Brook was diverted to feed the 80-acre Weequahic Lake, the largest in Essex County, and the centerpiece of Newark's 311-acre Weequahic Park. Over the years the lake has become shallow from silt, and its murky water contains high amounts of algae. The lake was closed for a two year dredging and shoreline stabilization project conducted in 1998 by the Environmental Protection Agency.

Elizabeth

The town of Elizabeth is located at the southern end of Newark Bay close to the Arthur Kill and Kill Van Kull. There is a great difference of opinion as to what the seaport associated with this city should be called, although officially the correct names of the marine complexes on the southwest side of Newark Bay are "Elizabeth Port Authority Marine Terminal," and "Elizabeth Marine Terminal." The Port Authority of New York and New Jersey deliberately chose not to give it name of "Port Elizabeth," in order to avoid confusion with a seaport town of that name in South Africa. "Port Elizabeth" is also the official name for a municipality and former colonial seaport on Maurice River, in Cumberland County.

"Elizabeth Port" and "Port Elizabeth" are in common use among journalists, historians, and the general public. "Elizabethport" is name of section of City of Elizabeth located just south of the present day Elizabeth Marine Terminal. It was originally a small settlement formed at the same time as Elizabethtown which was located about a half mile further inland. It served as the landing for Elizabethtown during colonial and post-colonial times. It is now separated from the remainder of the City of Elizabeth by the New Jersey Turnpike.

The town of Elizabeth had long been one of the sites where travelers transferred from boats to stagecoaches on voyages from New York to Philadelphia. With the construction of expanded docks after 1816 the town became a center for steamboat travel. On this development one traveler wrote that, "I noticed with pleasure that they are building a wharf to facilitate the getting on and off of the steamboats. Last year one had to go through water up to the knees for a distance of about 150 feet before getting to the boat." Of course there were existing wharves and dock facilities in Elizabeth serving sailing vessels, but it would appear from this account that steamboats either could not, or were not permitted, to make use of them.

By 1821 Elizabeth was the starting point for excursions aboard the steamboat *Atalanta* to Perth and South Amboy, where both ladies and gentlemen could bathe at the numerous facilities in that area. The fare was 33 cents, with children and servants paying half price. The *Atalanta* also took parties to the nearby fishing banks, with the excursion rate being one dollar, which included a cold cut. In July of 1847, there were evening excursions to "Princes Bay" off Staten Island by way of Amboy. The parties departed from Elizabeth at 7 p.m. on the steamboat *Water-Witch*, traveled through Staten Island Sound and returned by way of Amboy at about 10:00 pm. Passengers could travel to the docks via horse cars leaving Elizabeth Town 20 minutes before the 7:00 p.m. sailing. Cost of the excursions was set at 25 cents. On July 25, 1860, members of the Red Jacket Engine Company No. 4, of Elizabeth had a grand picnic and excursion to Fort Lee aboard the steamer *Red Jacket*. Baldwin's Band was hired to provide music. There were refreshments on board, and at Fort Lee there a dance hall was trimmed with awnings and provided with seating.

When the Elizabeth & Somerville Railroad (predecessor of the Jersey Central) was constructed in the 1830s and 1840s, it ran eastward from the Elizabeth Central Business District to Elizabethport to a connection with the ferries. This area was also an important freight terminal because the railroad served the iron mining region of western Morris County and the anthracite mining regions of Pennsylvania. For this reason Elizabethport became the site of major rail to water bulk-materials transfer facilities.

However, Elizabethport ceased to be the Central Railroad of New Jersey's primary coal handling terminal after the railroad completed a bridge over Newark Bay in 1864. This allowed coal trains to reach the Hudson River southeast of Jersey City. In an 1868 account the coal piers on the Hudson were described as "long black causeways" that "jut into the water like monstrous black arms seeking to embrace the trade of the metropolis." Today the site of the Central Railroad of New Jersey's terminal is part of Liberty State Park. The passenger station and ferry docks have been preserved as the park's visitor center, but the freight handling facilities have all disappeared.

The railroad's facilities at Elizabeth were also hampered by the constant silting of the navigation channels. In 1872 it was reported that only ships with a shallow draft could reach the docks. In the same year over 150 vessels ran aground near Port Elizabeth, but some $3,000,000 worth of coal and $175,000 worth of other cargoes were unloaded. Despite these difficulties, an estimated 10,800,000 tons of cargo passed through the port and thousands of vessels, ranging from 25 to 800 tons, called annually at the port.

The situation was caused by the confluence of currents from Newark Bay, the Kill Van Kull, and the Arthur Kill just off Port Elizabeth. As a result this became the site of heavy sediment deposition. The bar off Port Elizabeth was found to have moved 14 feet downstream in the years just prior to 1873.

Channel depths were less than 16 feet at low water. In addition to restricting the trade of Port Elizabeth, the sediments blocked access to the Arthur Kill and as a consequence the west shore of Staten Island.

The legislatures of both New York and New Jersey petitioned Congress to come up with remedial actions. Colonel John Newton of the Engineer Corps offered some preliminary ideas in 1873. He concluded that a proposed system of parallel dikes to direct the flows of the Kill Van Kull and Arthur Kills directly into one another would create a pool of quiet water and a new site for sediment deposition. A program of regular dredging was also called until a more permanent solution could be developed.

This permanent solution took the form of dikes that would channelize the Arthur Kill and create an increased water current that would scour the channel clean. The main drawback of this plan was that a gap would have to be left in the dikes so that ships could pass through to Newark Bay. Captain J.C. Gibbs of Elizabeth proposed that there should be separate channels dredged for access to Port Elizabeth and the rest of Newark Bay. This was to avoid the sediment accumulation which was occurring at the junction of the existing channels. Although the engineering studies and the cost analyses were submitted to Secretary of War William W. Belknap, the dikes were never built. The Corps of Engineers did perform regular dredging of the area, however.

Elizabethport was developed as a specialized container port in the 1950s and 1960s. By 1973 the port could handle 12,000,000 tons annually.

Hackensack

Hackensack has always been an important government and commercial center for Bergen County. For most of its history, even by the standards of a less populous world, Hackensack has never been considered a very large town. For this reason and because so many readers will only be familiar with the modern city, it is worth reviewing the town's growth since its official founding in 1693.

On December 23, 1776, the British 26th Regiment of Foot occupied Hackensack, and they found that it consisted of about thirty houses clustered around a village green. The First Dutch Reformed Church that stood on the green had been there since the 1690s, and the county buildings - a small courthouse and jail - dated to the early 1700s. There were, of course, many more dwellings in the surrounding countryside.

In 1834, there were 150 dwellings and 1,000 inhabitants in the town. There were three churches, two academies (in addition to a one female boarding school), ten shops, three taverns, and two paint factories. There was also a turnpike road leading eastward to Hoboken and westward to Paterson.

Hackensack did not become a true suburb until the 1860s. Direct rail connections were established to the outside world in 1861 and more lines were built in the 1870s and 80s, followed by a trolley line to Hoboken in 1889. The population in 1870 was 8,039, but by 1920, one year before Hackensack was officially incorporated as a city, it had grown to 17,667.

Courtesy Library of Congress

Hackensack in 1896.

As Hackensack grew, the river commerce reflected its growth, with the high point being the years before the railroads reached the city. Schooners, barges, and steamboats brought a wide variety of cargoes to the city including such diverse loads as chemicals, coal, lumber, and manufactured goods.

In the early years of the 1900s many of the mill workers at the Bogota Paper Mill lived across the river in Hackensack. Every day, even in the winter months, over 150 persons used an improvised ferry service of rowboats as a quick route over the river. Because there was no bridge near the mill a walk of three miles would have otherwise been required. Plans had been rejected to build a bridge when it became known that the projected cost was $158,000.

Over the years a number of mill workers were drowned when the rowboats overturned. Oddly, it is only through their obituaries that we know of the existence of this ferry.

In 1987, the Census Bureau estimated that the modern city of Hackensack had a population of 35,954. Today it is an important commercial center as well as the seat of Bergen County government (which employs some 4,000 persons serving a total county population of 830,467). It is the home of the county administration, courthouse, jail, child welfare department, and the Hackensack Medical Center.

Kearny

The town of Kearny is bordered by the Passaic River on the west and the Hackensack River on the east. Numerous marine facilities lined the banks on both rivers. Kearny's principle marine facility on the Hackensack, Federal Shipyards, is discussed elsewhere in this book.

The Newark Towboat Company was located in the Arlington section of the township. A 1928 issue of Donnelley's Industrial Directory listed the company as a boatbuilding yard located at 160 Wilson Avenue.

Little Ferry and Ridgefield Park

The site of an early ferry crossing this town on the west bank of the Hackensack was originally part of Lodi. A rope-drawn ferry (some period paintings show a periauger type vessel) ran from 1659 to 1826 when it was replaced by a toll bridge. The site of the original bridge and ferry is south of the modern Route 46 highway bridge. Little Ferry was the site of a number of important brickyards including facilities owned by the firms of Depeyster and Stagg, Cole and Showers, and the Mehrhof brothers. In 1904 the town had eight brickyards in operation, but the business declined after World War I, and by 1923 there were only four yards left. The last yard burned down in 1956.

Across the river from Little Ferry, Ridgefield Park is located on the site where Overpeck Creek enters the Hackensack. The New York Susquehanna & Western Railroad has a major freight yard and engine terminal along the river at this spot. The 1876 *Atlas of Bergen County* shows a hotel on the northern bank of Overpeck Creek. A bridge over the creek connected Little Ferry with Ridgefield. At the southern end of the bridge John V. Banta's establishment is shown as having several coal sheds along Bellman's Creek, a winding channel through the marshes south of town.

PAY — ROAD
TOLL HERE

Courtesy Bergen County Historical Society

*Multiple transportation technologies of 1910 converge at the Hackensack River Bridge
at Little Ferry. An open automobile, horse drawn wagon, and handcart wait to cross the
bridge. The trolley car tracks would turn northwards and continue to Hackensack. On the
left side of the picture, there are large brick drying sheds along the Hackensack River. Many
of the bricks will be loaded onto barges or schooners for shipment to market. The broken gate
at the entrance to the bridge is believed to have been damaged by an automobile.*

Newark

In the late 1820s Stephen, Condit, and Tomkins of Newark Bridge Dock ran
an advertisement that gives us a clue as to what the industrial city of Newark
was exporting:

> The Subscribers have A good substantial vessel running between
> Newark and Philadelphia, makes her passages about once a fort-
> night and will take freight at the following low rates. - viz: cot-
> ton yard, cotton goods, duck, and dry goods at $.20 per hundred
> pounds; heavy goods, such as iron castings, machinery etc., at
> $2 per ton and all other goods in proportion.

Other newspaper advertisements of the period identify similar vessels. Jonathan Cory placed an ad on February 27th, 1827 stating that his three sloops had re-commenced running to New York. They left from the Commercial Dock at the foot of Market Street and ran to White Hall in New York City. The three sloops were identified as the *Gov. Ogden* (Captain R. Earl), *Farmer* (Captain M. Baldwin), and the *Zephyrus* (Captain D. Baldwin). They were advertised as being "first class" with "judicious and experienced commanders." To handle his cargoes, Corey also advertised warehouses where freight might be stored free of expense as well as stables to accommodate teams of horses.

Regular sailings to more distant destinations were provided by other boats. In the 1790s, the sloop *Patty* made trips to Charlestown, South Carolina and in the early 1800s the schooner *Louisa* conducted a regular trade with Savannah, Georgia. It is likely that the major cargoes in these voyages were leather goods, of which Newark was a major production center, and apple brandy (also know as Jersey Lightning) a beverage that was widely famous and quite popular in the southern states.

In 1835 the Port Collector for Newark, Archer Gifford, reported that 82 ships used Newark as their home port. Only 9 of these ships were engaged in some sort of foreign trade. Twelve years later, 65 ships called Newark home. These 65 ships averaged 100 tons. The ships had undoubtedly increased in size in those twelve years but without Gifford's original reports it is impossible to say by how much.

As the city's commerce grew in volume it became apparent that Newark Bay needed a lighthouse. The project was taken up by Michael Nerny, a captain of a whaling ship in the South America trade, who was also a New Jersey pilot who guided ships into Newark. He long argued for lighthouses for Newark Bay and Bergen Point and in 1847 Congress finally appropriated $18,000 for two lights. They also appointed Nerney the first lighthouse keeper. Period photographs show the Newark Bay lighthouse as a two story clapboard structure with four gables. The light apparently rose from the main part of the house, where the keeper and family lived. The house was surrounded by a low picket fence and the entire establishment sat on a substantial base of hewn-stone. There was also a small dock and a few outbuildings. One of these was certainly an oil house, where the highly flammable lighting oil was stored.

The lighthouse was situated on the mud flats on the western side of Newark Bay. It was supposed to keep ships from running aground on the flats but as the silting in the bay worsened the channel was pushed out nearly half a mile from its 1847 location. Now instead of keeping ships away from the flats, the lighthouse was guiding them onto the flats. In 1914 the lighthouse was replaced by a series of four lighted channel markers.

David F. Brown operated a shipyard in Newark at Lister Avenue. Brown was the son of a prominent New York shipwright whose yard on the East River produced several important Navy vessels and privateers during the War of 1812. After the family's shipbuilding enterprise was moved to Newark, they were noted for their construction of cargo ships and schooner yachts for the area business owners. The yard constructed the tugboat *Newark* for the Stephens and Condit Transportation Company. She was 84-feet long, 18-feet in beam, and 8-feet deep. The Browns rebuilt two vessels for the Lister Brothers agricultural chemical company and repaired or overhauled some 76 vessels of various types. The yard's facilities could accomodate vessels 90-feet long with a 26-foot beam. The yachts built and repaired by the Brown's shipyard included the Boston-built schooner *Wivers*. The *Wivers* was 58-feet long, 13-feet in beam, and 7-feet deep. The yard also repaired steam yachts such as the *Duplex*, owned by Captain Lysander Wright.

THE J. F. SHANLEY CO., FT. MADISON STREET.

Courtesy Passaic County Historical Society

The J.F. Shanley Company was a major construction firm in the early years of the 1900s. Among their many projects were the Pennsylvania Railroad's line from Harrison to Newark and paving Main Street in East Orange. The company's supply depot was located on the Passaic River at the foot of Madison Street in Newark. Here a three-masted schooner is seen unloading materials circa 1912.

Newark is also unique in that the city's fire department operates the only municipal fireboats in New Jersey. Since 1918, the city of Newark's fire department has maintained a series of fireboats which engage in fighting fires that ignite on the shore side industries, ships in the harbor, and barges loaded with gasoline or other flammable liquids. Their boats are also engaged in search and rescue.

The earliest fireboat was the *Newarker* (sometimes referred to as the *Newark*.) She was mentioned in the newspaper accounts of the 1920s and 1930s. The *William J. Brennan* was the next boat and active in the 1950s.

Newark's most well-known is the *John F. Kennedy*, launched in 1964. She was built by the Hearn Shipbuilding Company of Somerset, Massachusetts. The *Kennedy* cost the city $96,000 but over the years has proved to be an invaluable addition to the fire department. The 47-foot long *Kennedy* had a top speed of 18 knots, could pump 5,280 gallons of water per minute, and only drew three feet.

The *John F. Kennedy* and the previous boats are valuable because so much of the city's industry is located along the river and inaccessible from the land. In 1975 alone, the Kennedy responded to 65 fires and was called out for 195 alarms.

The city's current boat, *Fireboat Number 1*, was purchased with funds from the Department of Homeland Security. She is a $1.1 million, 50-foot, multi-purpose boat equipped to handle emergencies both on Newark's waterways and at Port Newark. (It is not clear why the city ignored the previous boats when numbering this one.)

The story of Newark as a port is tied to the efforts to dredge Newark Bay and maintain a navigable channel. Congress first appropriated money for port maintenance in the 1840s. In May 1844, Archer Gifford, collector of customs, wrote about a congressional bill authorizing the dredging of Newark Bay and the nearby rivers. The work was supposed to be carried out by "apparatus of Mr. Griswold's dredging machine."

George Griswold was a director of the Morris Canal & Banking Company, and was also part owner of an unidentified shipping line. N.L. Griswold, George's brother and business partner, proposed a dredge for cleaning the bottom of the canal and deepening it to 5 feet.

The River and Harbor Act of 1852 marked the start of long term federal spending on the dredging of Newark Bay, the Passaic and Hackensack Rivers. Federal spending on port maintenance continued with the River and Harbor Act of 1922, and subsequent modifications in 1943, 1954, 1964, and 1975. The Act provided for the main channel in Newark Bay and Port Elizabeth, 37 feet deep in rock, 35 feet deep in soft material, and the 700 foot wide channel into Port Newark proper. Other channels through the bay and in or out of the port

areas were 800 to 900 feet wide. A more detailed description of port maintenance is provided in Chapter 10.

In August of 1864, the Central Railroad of New Jersey began running
trains over the newly opened bridge spanning Newark Bay. The bridge ran
from Elizabeth over the lower end of the bay so that all shipping was now
required to pass through the draw. The resulting inconvenience prompted
shippers, especially in Newark, to consider alternatives to the existing arrangement. For the next sixty or so years, plans were periodically brought
forward to create a ship canal across Bergen Neck, north of Jersey City. In the
marshland south of Newark there would be a network of canals and wharf
facilities. New railroad lines would be laid to the water's edges.

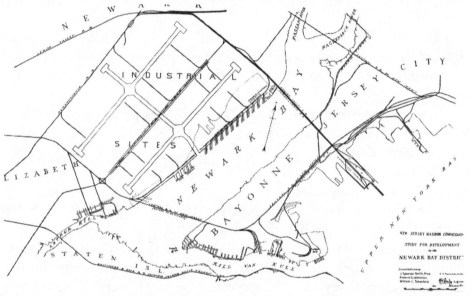

Collection of Stephen Marshall

Plans for the development of Port Newark in the late 1930s called for a network of 400-
foot wide canals extending from the western shore of the bay. The Pennsylvania Railroad,
Lehigh Valley Railroad, and Central Railroad of New Jersey would all have had access to
the new industrial parks lining the canals. Newark Airport now occupies most of the site
that was proposed for the canal network.

These plans divided Newark's leaders. The older Newark establishment
was generally opposed to them, while more recent immigrant groups, who
depended on the city's industries for their employment, were in favor of the
port expansion plan. It is not entirely clear if this division was the reason why
Newark languished even as New York's port traffic increased to the breaking
point.

Collection of Stephen Marshall

The plans for a ship canal across Bergen Neck and the Meadowlands near Newark were strongly opposed by many parties. This 1913 cartoon appeared in the Newark Evening News.

It could also be that there was simply not enough money to create a new port in an area where the water was shallow and the surrounding ground was marshy. As time went on, dredging made this part of Newark Bay deeper and the spoils were heaped onto the low-lying land to raise its elevation. Only then did the area become suitable for larger vessels and the cargo handling

95

facilities that they require.

The grandiose plans for the port were scaled back so that Ports' Newark and Elizabeth only had one channel each. The area that would have become the network of ship canals and wharves was instead turned into Newark Airport. A brief discussion of the building of Port Newark is found in Chapter 10.

Courtesy New Jersey Chamber of Commerce

The creation of Newark Airport (the "X" shaped landing strip) east of Port Newark forever halted plans to expand the port inland. The modern port occupies the same area as the one in this 1928 photograph.

By the year 2000 ocean going container ships had reached lengths of 1,100 or more feet with capacities of 6,600 containers. The 35 and 37 foot deep channels were too shallow for these ships, which require channel depths of at least 50 feet. Most east coast harbors are shallower and require extensive dredging. In 2003, 95% of imported goods reach the United States by water and Port Newark was the third largest container port in the country. The combined ports of New York and New Jersey are the country's largest automobile and petroleum ports. Each year some 5000 vessels move cargo into or out of the harbor.

Maintenance dredging of Newark Bay is necessitated by the sediments brought into the bay from the Passaic River, Hackensack River, Kill Van Kull, and Arthur Kill. In recent years scientists have discovered that there can be any number of sediment sources depending on the direction of the winds and currents. The implications of this discovery will be discussed later.

In previous years the sediments dredged from the channels were loaded onto barges and dumped at sea. A point about five miles offshore of Sandy

Hook became known as Mount Spike after years of continuous dumping created an artificial mountain under 80 feet of water. The mound became so tall that ships occasionally ran aground on it.

The sediments from Newark Bay were polluted with PCB's, dioxins, heavy metals, and a host of organic chemicals, all left over from decades of unregulated industrial activities. In the 1990s, environmental groups such as Clean Ocean Action began putting pressure on the Army Corps of Engineers to find alternatives to ocean dumping. In 1992, new analytical chemistry procedures revealed that the dredged materials were unsuitable for ocean disposal. By 1996 the practice was halted.

In 1997 the federal government opened up a new ocean disposal site, the Historic Area Remediation Site (HARS). This 54 square kilometer site encompasses the original 7.6 square kilometer site as well as some other earlier disposal areas. This new area is restricted to only the cleanest material and it is hoped that the earlier, more polluted sediments will be permanently trapped under it.

In order to contain the materials that cannot be disposed of at HARS, a large underwater pit was excavated in Newark Bay by the Army Corps of Engineers in 1996. This pit can hold approximately 1.2 million cubic meters of material deemed unsuited for ocean disposal.

The overall costs of dredge spoil removal has risen steadily. The average cost to dispose a cubic meter of material, which was $4 in 1992, rose to $40 by 2000. This has reduced the amount of dredging performed, and the total volume of material removed fell to 600,000 cubic meters in 1996.

Yet the need for deeper channels persisted. By 2003 a fleet of over 80 dredges, tugboats, and barges were working in the bay, part of a 3.2 billion dollar project slated to remove some 53 million cubic yards of material and scheduled to be completed in 2013.

Even though the materials were not destined for ocean disposal, the project was still controversial. A number of environmental organizations, including the Baykeeper program, insisted that dredging would release pollution back into the water column, damage local fisheries, and possibly deplete the water's oxygen supply. The Corps of Engineers did acknowledge these risks, but concluded that any damage to environment would be temporary, and that wildlife would soon move back into the disturbed areas.

The biggest problem with the sediment contamination is that removing the materials one time will not permanently clean up the bay. Scientists have discovered that when the winds blow from the either the east or the west, the water level in the bay will rise or fall. Water flows out of the bay and carries the polluted sediments into the other parts of New York Harbor. Under other conditions, sediments from the Hackensack River, Kill Van Kull, Arthur Kill, and the Passaic River are brought into the bay. The Passaic River sediments are the most worrisome since many of these materials are very badly contaminated.

Industrial wastes from Newark, Harrison, Kearny, Passaic, and other riverside towns have contaminated the sediments on the bottom of the Passaic River. Further upstream, erosion occurring on contaminated sites causes additional polluted sediments to wash into the river. Storm water runoff and combined sewer overflows also contribute to the total sediment contamination. Unless all of the adjoining waters are cleaned up, the sediments of Newark Bay will always present a serious disposal problem. Efforts to clean up the Passaic River sediments are described in Chapter 11.

The current estimates are that about 340,000 cubic yards of sediment reaches Newark Bay annually. While this might seem a very large volume, some of it leaves the bay, and what remains is distributed over a large area. The sources of these sediments, in cubic yards, are

- Passaic River - 12,400 to 79,100 (depending on how the river's sediment load is calculated)
- Hackensack River - 6,460
- Sewer and water treatment - 10,500
- Atmospheric Deposition - 285
- Kill Van Kull - 205,000 to 260,000 (depending on the method used to calculate sediment load)
- Arthur Kill - 41,900 to 53,200 (depending on the method used to calculate sediment load)

The Army Corps of Engineers, the EPA, and private engineering firms have created a number of creative alternatives to ocean dumping dredged sediments. Most are mixed with cement right on the barges just before unloading. The amount of cement used is kept low so that the sediment particles are bound together in small lumps that can still flow freely. This ensures that the sediment particles will not re-enter the environment.

These lumps are being transported to the meadowlands where they are used to cap old landfills. Current plans call for using the landfills for golf courses and limited amounts of housing. The work around the landfills requires far more than simply capping them. Trenches are dug around them and barriers are installed to prevent the migration of leachate into the marshes. Pumps can remove the leachate and send it to treatment plants. The author was privileged to visit the site of one of these projects and was astonished to see that the water inside the leachate barrier was bright orange but the marsh waters outside the barrier appeared clean.

The work of capping the landfills is being conducted by Encap Golf Holdings which has successfully completed a number of similar projects in the past. There is wide agreement that the capping would simply be too expensive as a public works project, although there is little agreement about how much Encap is entitled to be paid for the work.

New Bridge

Today New Bridge Landing is part of the town of River Edge. The house standing on the site is preserved as a state historic site called the Steuben House. It was given this name because the Prussian born Baron Von Steuben, Inspector General of the Continental Army, briefly owned the property. But this is only one reason why this site is so significant.

The recorded history of the site stretches back to 1682 when Cornelius Matheus purchased 420 acres on the west bank of the Hackensack River. In 1710 a gristmill was erected on the site by David Ackerman of Hackensack. The earliest part of the house that stands on the site today is believed to date from about 1713 when Ackerman's son Johannes, a shoemaker, inherited the portion of the property that bordered the river.

The area is best known for its association with the Zabriskie family who operated the store, gristmill, ships, and wharves on the site. Jan Zabriskie bought the house from Nicholas Ackerman, the son of Johannes, in 1745. The "new" bridge over the Hackensack was then a year old. The site almost immediately became an important trading point. The combination of a mill, road connection, and store attracted local farmers. Soon sloops were carrying flour and iron (from the Highlands region) to New York City and bringing back manufactured goods. In 1752, Jan Zabriskie doubled the size of the house and covered it with a gambrel roof. When work was completed, there were a total of twelve rooms and seven fireplaces.

The business prospered and grew. The family's interests eventually extended as far south as Puerto Rico. Other members of the Zabriskie shipped goods from points on the Hudson River. Among them were Christian and his son Cornelius, who operated a store in Paramus. The available records, however, do not reveal how closely this operation was tied to the one at New Bridge. Goods for sale at New Bridge included sugar, salt, candles, tea, coffee, rice, flour, tobacco, nails, gunpowder, shot, hats, cloth, umbrellas, tools, handkerchiefs, shoes, skates, spectacles, iron, quill pens (and pen knives), writing

Photograph by Dr. Michael Passow

New Bridge Landing as seen from a kayak at high tide. The Zabriski house on the river is museum building.

paper, and Bibles. Alcoholic beverages included brandy, gin, rum, and metheglin, a local wine made from fermented honey. Another locally produced item shipped from New Bridge were hoop poles, which were saplings cut and trimmed for use as barrel hoops.

In 1777, Jan Zabriskie was arrested by American soldiers and charged with passing intelligence to the British. Jan fled to New York in 1780 and in 1781 the Court of Common Pleas, then meeting in Pompton, determined that he had enlisted in the British army and ordered his property to be confiscated by the State of New Jersey. After the war, the property was offered to Baron Von Steuben in recognition of his services to the Continental Army. Steuben declined the offer but took the money from the rent and subsequent sale, and the house passed back into the Zabriskie family when Jan's son purchased the property in 1788. He died a few years later. When his widow, Catherine Hoagland Zabriskie, remarried, the house was sold out of the family.

Finally, in 1815, the house was purchased by a distant cousin, Andrew Zabriskie. He and wife Elizabeth Anderson raised 13 children, 11 of their own and 2 adopted infant girls. The store was located in the frame wing of their sandstone house. Andrew died in 1837 and his son, David Anderson Zabriskie, took over the operation. Captain David commanded the schooner *Farmer*. The *Farmer* was eventually wrecked off Bergen Point with a cargo of potatoes aboard. Captain David survived the wreck and lived until 1887.

His son and namesake, David Anderson Zabriskie, inherited the homestead. Like his father, he commanded schooners on the Hackensack River, and in later years commanded the tugboat *Wesley Stoney*.

Except when interrupted by the Revolution, the store and landing on the property were in continuous operation. The property had even been owned for a time by a miller, Luke Van Boskirk, and a tidal mill stood near the mouth of Cole's Brook, just south of the wharf of the east bank of the Hackensack. Andrew Zabriskie made bricks on the site. But by the time that the second Captain David worked on the river, the commercial importance of New Bridge Landing had waned. Finally, the wooden store wing was demolished and both house and land were rented to a tenant farmer.

After David Zabriskie's death in 1907, his unmarried daughter Magdelena inherited the house, only to sell it in 1909. The house passed through another series of owners and was even used as the location of a silent movie version of *The Mill On The Floss*.

In 1926, the State Legislature appropriated money to purchase the Steuben House as a shrine of historic significance. The State of New Jersey acquired the house and one surrounding acre on June 27, 1928. Since its restoration in 1939, the Steuben House has displayed the museum collections of the Bergen County Historical Society. It is owned and operated by the Division of Parks and Forestry, New Jersey Department of Environmental Protection.

The museum collection features many of the objects acquired by the Bergen County Historical Society. These are mostly locally produced pieces, including a magnificent 1775 cherry wood kas (a type of cabinet that is still used in Holland to store linens and clothes). Other locally made period furniture on display include a Hackensack Valley cupboard made by Jasper Westervelt, chairs displaying distinctive urn finials, a rare child's high chair, and a 1750 era oak settle which was made as a wedding present for Cornelius Livingston Hyatt. Local pottery is represented by a collection of slip-decorated redware pie dishes made in River Edge by George Wolfkiel (1805-1867). The textile collection contains garments, local quilts and woven spreads, including numerous examples of the pictorial coverlets produced by local weavers using the Jacquard loom.

Aside from the stone house which houses the museum, visitors can see the 1888 iron truss swing-bridge, the remains of the wharf. It was manufactured in Philadelphia and erected on site. A turntable in the center of the river allowed the bridge to open but this no longer operates. Just downstream from the bridge is the wharf and below that the outlet of Coles Brook and the site of the tidal mill. The State Park contains three relocated buildings. The Campbell-Christie was originally owned by Jacob Campbell. Jacob was a mason who built the house at about the time of his marriage in 1774. It was moved from its original location on Henley Avenue and River Road in New Milford in 1977. The Westervelt-Thomas Barn was built in 1889 by Peter J. Westervelt for use on his farm, and was donated to the Bergen County Historical Society in 1954. The Demarest House was reconstructed on the site in 1956 after having been removed from its original location near River Road in New Milford. All three buildings are only open for special events.

Near New Bridge in what is today River Edge, Westervelt mentions another general store in his *History of Bergen County, New Jersey, 1630-1923*. This one was operated by a Captain Stephan Lozier. The available records do not indicate what his relationship to Henry Lozier was. River Edge was also the site of Bloomer's shipyard which was active in the construction of sloops and schooners. Cedar shingles were split in a nearby factory from the logs brought north from the Meadowlands.

Christian Cole's schooner, the *Henry Brown* sailed New Bridge. She made voyages to Albany and in the coasting trade. The *Henry Brown* was reported to be a fast ship that and could (it was said) outrace steam powered freight boats on the Hudson River.

On the east bank of the Hackensack, an inn and tavern have operated at New Bridge since 1745. The original building is believed to have stood on land owned by Lawrence P. Van Buskirk. It was a stone building and so the tavern became known as the "old Stone Tavern." There was also a two-story frame house on the site for the innkeeper and his family which stood until the 1820s when it was torn down and the stones moved by scow to Hackensack for reuse.

The next inn was a frame building that, after a series of owners, eventually became Ackerman's Hotel in 1854. The Ackerman's sold the hotel in 1865 to C.G. Frederick Heine. As Heine's Hotel, it served as a community gathering place for many years. It had nine rooms, a ballroom, parlor, dining room, hall, and garrets. The hotel was sold in 1894 and the new owners advertised the hotel as a place for "sailing, fishing, hunting or pleasure parties." There were accommodations for twenty guests and "good German cooking" was guaranteed.

The hostelry at New Bridge served as the terminal for the stagecoaches that traveled between the landing and Paulus Hook from the 1760s to the 1850s.

Early on a Saturday morning in May of 1964, the nineteenth century

hotel building caught fire. Despite the efforts of firefighters from several surrounding towns, it was too badly damaged to be saved. A modern building
was raised to house the restaurant that continues to operate on the site.

Old Bridge

Old Bridge was also known as Demarest Landing after the first family to
settle in the region.

The author has discovered 1828 newspaper references to one Jasper
Demarest (1766-1844. He married Rachel Van Vorhees on 12 April, 1789)
who advertised cargoes such as 5,000 boards and planks, shingles, and similar
items at his store by Old Bridge. He promised a steady inventory and offered
reasonable terms.

Tomkins Terminal

Tomkins Terminal is a good example of a small facility offering trans-shipment services to local industries. Situated on the east bank of the Passaic opposite Newark in the town of Kearny, the 32-acre site offered river, railroad,
and road connections. The Plank Road formed the southern border of the
site.

The terminal was established in the late 1800s by the Newark Plaster
Company whose mill only occupied a small portion of the southern end of
the site. By 1912 private railroad sidings connected to the factory sites on the
terminal with the Pennsylvania Railroad. The Passaic River Channel had
recently been deepened to twenty feet at high water, and a stone bulkhead
600 feet long provided wharf space for customers. One factory building was
completed with several other plots leased.

The terminal expanded over the years with the Tomkins brothers opening
a second facility on the west bank of the river. By the mid 1960s the original
terminal had eleven buildings leased to various manufacturing and warehousing tenants, with twelve sidings connected to the Pennsylvania Railroad.
There were 425 feet bulkheads along the river, which had a depth varying
from 14 to 18 feet. In 1965 a sand and gravel company leased space along the
river front but it is not clear how often material was delivered by water.

Today the facility does not use water transportation, although its location
near highway and railroad networks makes it a valuable site for transportation
and warehousing companies.

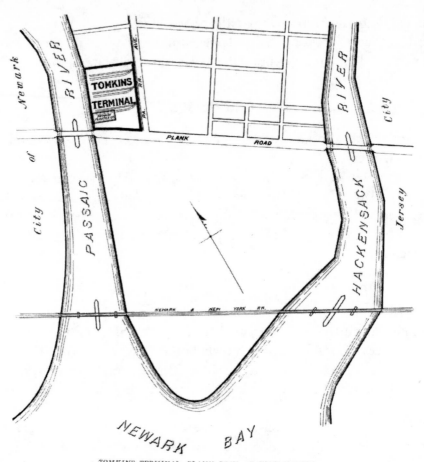

TOMKINS TERMINAL, PLANK ROAD, AT PASSAIC RIVER.

Courtesy Passaic County Historical Society

This 1912 map shows the locations and the railroad connections for the Tomkins Terminal. The ability to move freight between road, river, or railroad was the impetus for developing the site. The capability to move materials between railroads and roads is still an important asset for the site.

Van Buskirk's Landing

At the head of navigation on the Hackensack River, the channel splits in two and flows around two sides of a 13.3 acre island that is shaped like an isosceles triangle. This was the location of Van Buskirks' Landing. According to the research completed by the Waterworks Conservancy (see Chapter 11), this island is man-made. After the construction of a dam in 1802, water backed up into previously dry areas. At various times the landing was known as the Old Dock, Upper Landing, and Old Landing.

The earliest known structure at the site was the John Demarest Mill, which existed between 1681 and 1695. The earliest mention of the next mill on the site, owned by Jacob and Henry Van Buskirk, is in a letter from 1795. Jacob and Henry turned the southern tip of the islands into one of the most important store, gristmill, and wharf complexes in the Hackensack Valley. Their mill also produced animal feeds.

By 1829, a deed to a John Nightengale described the tract as containing Richard Cooper's Saw Mill, the saw-mill house, a bark mill and a dock. In 1873, the four-story (but short lived) Deed's Mill replaced the old Cooper mill. Finally in 1881, the Hackensack Water Company bought the land and developed it as a water pumping and filtration plant.

Chapter 8

Natural Resources

There are many stories of individuals and companies that took to the water and harvested the bounty of the rivers, marshes and nearby ocean. These endeavors ranged from a 1834 commercial whaling operation based in Newark, to a childhood afternoon picking huckleberries in the Hackensack Meadowlands. (A brief account of Newark's whaling ships is given in appendix B.)

In 1857, a carpenter from Paterson, Jacob Quackenbush, was dredging freshwater mussels from the Notch Brook. Notch Brook was a little known, minor tributary of the Passaic River located in Little Falls. But after Quackenbush discovered a large pink pearl and was said to have sold it to Tiffany's for $1500, the rush was on.

Just a few years earlier, many people had gone to the California gold fields and a few lucky individuals had come back rich. Now the chance to acquire wealth without leaving home offered itself. Thousands flocked to the rivers in northern New Jersey to search for pearls. There were hundreds of small brooks in the Hackensack and Passaic River watersheds and over $15,000 worth of pearls was reported to have been harvested in what local historians have humorously dubbed "The New Jersey Oyster Rush." Across the New York border, the area around Muddy Brook, a minor tributary of the Hackensack River, later became known as Pearl River. In this case, the name did not become official until years later when the railroad was searching for a station name that would attract commuters to the new suburbs. Although some historians scoff at the idea that the town of Pearl River was named for pearls found in the brook, the fact remains that in the 1960s a long-time resident donated a bag of freshwater pearls to the local library with the claim that they had come from Muddy Brook.

Although the Great Oyster Rush was a spectacular moment, fishing has always been an important part of life on the rivers. Several historians mention that Hackensack had a popular fish market near the docks downtown. The origins of this market are still obscure, but it was a well-established local institution by the 1860s, and appears to have survived into the early 1900s. There was also an extensive shell fishery which thrived in the shallow areas of Newark Bay, especially prior to the years before extensive dredging was carried out in order to deepen the waterway.

Data extracted from the New Jersey Fisheries Commission, the *Hackensack Republican*, and the *Evening Record* was studied by William Zeisel, who presented the material at the 1989 Hackensack River Symposium. Between 1860 and 1910 the fisheries primarily used nets. Different species were taken at different times of the year depending on their migratory patterns. From December to March, the Atlantic Tomcod was common. Between February and October, the European carp was taken. These were not native fish and therefore had to be stocked in the river. Carp were popular with Eastern European immigrants and rainbow smelt were also hatched in captivity and released. These were caught between February and April. Also common at this time of year, and popular for Lent, was the sucker. Bullheads (catfish) made up a smaller part of the fishery and were common from March to May. April and May were the months for shad and herring. Shad could be found as far north as New Milford. Sturgeon could also be taken during this season but became rare after 1870. The largest on record was 8½ feet long and weighed in at 271 pounds.

Good data is available from both the smelt and shad fisheries between the 1870s and 1914. The State of New Jersey maintained a hatchery on the Hackensack and used it for stocking that stream with smelt.

Until the hatching program began in earnest, smelt fishing was poor ("poor" being only about 60 pounds per net per night) in the 1870s. But thanks to the state program, 1881 was the best year ever, and up to 700 pounds could be taken in a single net. In 1884, there were 70 active nets that took a total of 8,964 pounds of smelt. Despite one crew's spectacular 1,200 pound catch between April 1 and 7, the 1885 season was short, intense, and disappointing. Nine years later, the 1894 season was only described as "fair." Six operators, Jacob Neighmond, the Bloomer Brothers, Charles Billings, Irving Brower, W & C Dawson, and Harvey McDonald took a total of 18,722 pounds. An estimated 6,000 pounds taken by non-commercial netters brought the total smelt catch up to about 25,000 pounds. Earnings for the individual operators ranged from Billing's $84.10 to Brower's $558.00. The remaining four earned two to three hundred dollars apiece.

For the first few years of the new century the catches were "good" but exact data is unavailable. The year 1902 was described as a particularly good one but again data is lacking. The fishery peaked briefly in 1904, when the best recorded single night catch per net was 350 pounds. The years between 1905 and 1914 were all described as "poor." The only high note was the smelt was in 1906, when they were of a particularly high quality, but quantity was still lacking. The best single-night catch was in the 15-20 pounds range.

Railroad connections to the Hackensack Valley spurred the growth of shad fishing once trains could quickly haul the catch to New York. Shad were caught by stretching nets across the river during their annual upstream migration. The net was held in place by hardwood poles that had been shaved absolutely smooth with a draw knife so that the net would not be torn. Once the shad swam into the net, two men went out in a boat to haul it in. The first, sitting in the bow, rowed against the current to keep the net tight. The second hauled the net into the boat over the gunwale.

The shad fishery was described as being "poor" in the 1870s but quickly revived itself in the early 1880s when annual catches could be as many as 50,000 to 100,000 fish (200,000 to 400,000 pounds.) In 1885 the catch was "disappointing" although individual fish were of a large size. Things improved in 1890, which was noted as one of the best years in memory. In 1894, when a stocking program began, the catch was only 17,406 fish (about 80,000 pounds). Nine operators took between 200 (Charles Billings) and 6,000 pounds (the Bloomer brothers) that year. Most of the fishermen netted about 1,100 pounds of shad and earned around $300. The list of shad fishermen included all of the names mentioned in the smelt fishery with the addition of Henry and Francis Terhune.

Shad harvests continued to fluctuate between 1900 and 1904. The earlier years were good, while 1903 was poor. Yields were up in 1904 and some nets took up to 2,000 pounds per night, with fish up to 11 pounds being recorded. Shad declined the next year. The single best haul in 1905 was only 200 pounds. There was a small improvement in 1908 but this year marked the last recorded shad run in the Hackensack estuary. By 1914, the shad fishery was totally depleted.

William Zeisel found that commercial fishing on the Hackensack River slowly died out between 1900 and 1920. He listed the key causes of this decline as overused cesspools and sanitary sewers that discharged directly into the river.

Ziesel's research also found that recreational fishing was an important part of life in Hackensack. He cited the newspaper account of a respected local journalist who, expecting guests for dinner, went to catch his main course before work. Slipping and falling into the muck below the high-tide line, the man's suit was ruined and he was forced to buy fish for the dinner. In consequence, his pride as an angler suffered greatly. Ziesel interprets this account to imply that fishing was common even among the leading citizens and that the recreational fishery was healthy enough for a man to trust it with important dinner plans.

The introduction of non-native species into the estuary is always a risk near any seaport, and Newark Bay was no exception. Frederick Voight of Central Avenue, Jersey City, was crabbing on the Hackensack River in August of 1903 when he hauled up an alligator in his net. According to the press reports, the alligator was about three feet long and greatly resented being pulled into a boat. Voight hit the alligator with his oars until the animal was quiet. He then took the alligator home and placed it in a specially constructed tank where it was reported to be content.

The 1860 to 1910 data from the recreational fisheries show pronounced seasonal patterns. Eels and white perch were common for most of the year. The striped bass, shad, tomcod, suckers (called roaches locally), and trout all had one or two month seasons. The greatest variety of species were taken in the spring and summer months. These included yellow perch, white perch, bullhead, sunfish, black bass, and blue crab. Fish taken by one boat in 1902 consisted of eleven perch, eight eels, and one bullhead, an example of the assortment of species available.

Naturally, the relative abundance of any species varied widely. While blue crabs were common and popular for most of this period, there was only one recorded run of Lafayettes (a type of drumfish, also referred to as "spots" by some authors) in 1908. Both the striped bass and white perch were off limits to netters. The white perch is still common while the former had declined dramatically by 1914. Trout had been fished out by the mid 1800s.

The New Jersey Department of Environmental Protections' Division of Fish, Game and Wildlife has recently discovered that there are brook trout directly descended from the trout that swam in the rivers of New Jersey 10,000 years ago, from the time of the Lenape/European contact. DNA analysis has revealed the presence of what the scientists called "heritage brook trout" populations in eleven streams in Passaic-Hackensack and the Raritan watersheds.

Surviving prints and paintings from the second half of the nineteenth century typically show small, one or two-man open boats being used for commercial fishing. None would appear to be more than 10 to 15 feet long. Some are depicted as being scow-shaped and built to be rowed. The sailing boats had more rounded hulls and generally carried two masts with lug, or gaff rigged sails and no headsails.

One of the working boats used in the Hackensack Meadowlands is preserved in the collections of the Hackensack Meadowlands Environmental

Center. It is a small boat typical of the hunting and fishing skiffs of the marshes. The boat has pointed ends to help it slip through the tall grasses. It also has great rocker, i.e., its bottom is curved, reducing waterline length and thus the turning radius. Overall, it is about 12 feet long and two feet wide with a single thwart in the center. Other sport boats found in the area exhibit similar characteristics.

During the last decades of the 1800s and the first decades of the 1900s, many hunters traveled to the Meadowlands to shoot railbirds. Railbirds, or simply rail, are related to the woodcock, and were common in the Meadowlands during the month of September. They were described as being "tame as kittens" or "wild as hawks" depending on the time of year and the location. Rail shooting was also described as being "ridiculously easy" but downed birds were often difficult to locate in the tall grasses of the Meadowlands. According to a 1912 article in the *New York Times*:

> The rail hunter typically took a train or trolley to Secaucus, Leonia, or any of the other villages near the Meadowlands. A local guide was known as a "pusher" because taking a boat to the shooting often required pushing it with a long pole through the marsh grasses and wild rice. The pole was also used to beat the bushes to flush the birds. Sportsmen were advised to set out with the start of the flood tide. The rail liked to feed at low tide and as the tide rose they would shelter in the long grasses from which is was often hard to dislodge them.

The large stands of cedar trees in the Meadowlands had mostly disappeared by the late 1600s, but in the 1800s there still enough buried cedar logs to make "shingle mining" worthwhile. Cedar is especially resistant to rot and this makes it very useful for shingles. Archaeologistss working in the Meadowlands have reported cedar stumps still persisting in the drier areas. The shingle miners first located the logs by probing with long iron rods. The logs were then dug up and split into shingles. Healthy trees that were knocked down by lightning or storms were still in good condition and brought better prices. Trees that begin to rot before they fell were less valuable but still worth the time to dig them out.

We have seen in Chapter Two how the earliest attempts to dig drainage canals in the Meadowlands were part of an effort to introduce English grass species which did not thrive in the brackish conditions. During the 1800s, the Meadowlands were the subject of far more determined efforts to dike, drain, and reclaim them.

Collection of Stephen Marshall

Harper's Magazine published this illustration showing railbird shooting in the Meadowlands. Note the "pusher" who used a long pole to propel the boat through the thick marsh vegetation.

In 1813 Samuel Swartwout began acquiring large tracts of marshland. His holdings eventually included much of the meadows on the east side of the Hackensack as far north as Overpeck Creek. Between 1813 and 1820, Samuel and his brother reclaimed approximately 1,300 acres of marsh by digging 120 miles of drainage ditches and erecting several miles of embankments. Their ambitious program became bogged down during the 1820s by legal troubles and the failure of the drainage systems themselves.

Some of the areas reclaimed by earthen dikes were successfully planted with gardens and at least one ornamental tree farm. However the land was abandoned shortly afterwards as a result of burrowing rodents that completely destroyed the dikes. The next attempt was the "Great Iron Diking Enterprise" undertaken in 1868. In this plan the burrowing animals were to be thwarted by iron plates inside the earthen dikes.

This project was commenced in 1867 with Spencer Driggs and Samuel N. Pike's New Jersey Land Reclamation Company. They acquired some of the former Swartwout lands south of Sawmill Creek with the hope of producing crops for the ever expanding population of New York and the surrounding areas.

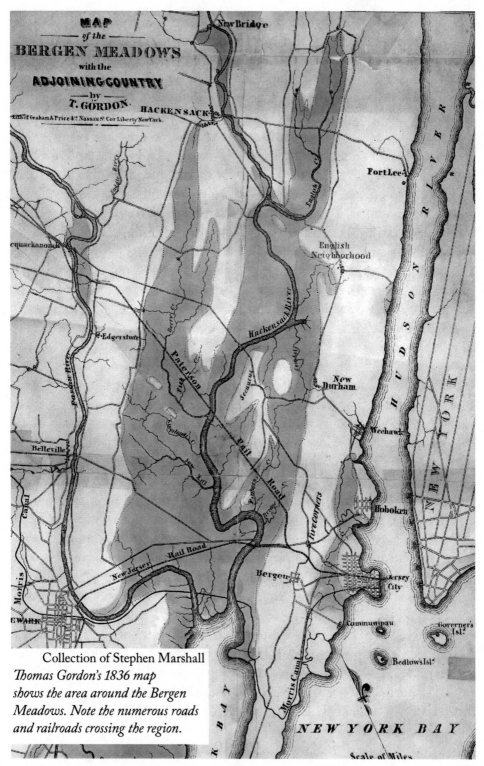

Collection of Stephen Marshall
*Thomas Gordon's 1836 map
shows the area around the Bergen
Meadows. Note the numerous roads
and railroads crossing the region.*

Soil conditions in the reclaimed land were reported to be poor and legend has long maintained that despite rapid growth, the tall cornstalks produced no ears. Another principal reason for the project's ultimate failure was that the reclaimed land was largely peat, which has a tendency to shrink and subside as it dries out. The drainage canals that were intended to use gravity soon required pumps and without any breach of the dikes the areas soon became flooded. The project was abandoned and the iron plates were said to have sunk into the muck and disappeared forever. However, only in legend had the iron dikes "sunk into the marsh and disappeared". The fact is that they held for almost eighty years and had a profound effect on the land forms within their confines. Those areas which had been successfully reclaimed and sold at a profit were later used for railroads and other industrial uses. Some of the dikes were re-used for mosquito control

Samuel N. Pike's death occurred in 1872, and this not only halted the project but initiated years of litigation. Pike's estate held certain of the lands in trust but Pike's former partners and business associates sought to have them sold to raise immediate cash. Pike's family resisted this idea, and the case dragged on for several years.

Michael McGowan and Mark Zdepski, consulting geologists with JMZ Geology of Flemington, New Jersey, investigated the remains of the dikes in the 1990s. In a brief archaeological project, they exposed the tops of the dikes and found that the basic structure was intact in many places, especially along the west bank of the Hackensack River. They discovered that the iron plates were driven to a depth of about 3½ feet. The original project prospectus called for slotted iron posts to form the junction of the sheets, but they were actually laid with a slight overlap and the posts were dispensed with. The iron plates were slightly narrower than the 15 foot square specifications; they were three feet wide and an estimated five feet deep. The excavations did not reach to the bottom of the dike and so their true depth still remains unknown. The dikes were only designed to be taller than the Hackensack's tidal range. Behind the dikes, a ditch was dug for water drainage, and the structure was completed by shoveling the dirt from the ditch to top of the dikes. Gates along their lower edge allowed water to flow out from behind the dike at low tide.

Except where preserved by subsequent filling, the land behind the dikes continued to drain and shrink so that the surface actually dropped several feet. In 1950, a hurricane breached them, and once the land flooded, the water was too deep to for the native plants to reestablish themselves, and today the area looks like a deep lake.

Except for some truck farming near Rutherford, only two agricultural activities, pig farming and floriculture, were successful on a commercial scale in the Meadowlands. Both were centered in the area around Secaucus, where the pig farmers had access to the growing refuse dumps, and flower growers presumably had ready access to pig manure. Secaucus was also known for vegetable growing. In 1875, 90% of the town's population consisted German immigrant farmers. Large scale hog farming was only possible in the twentieth century when improved roads allowed restaurant scraps and other food scraps to be brought from New York City and used for pig fodder. Hog production peaked in the years prior to and during the Second World War. The town was regarded as a major source of food for the war effort. It acquired a reputation for its strong odors and it has even been reported that high school sports teams refused to compete against the Secaucus students. [one has to wonder what their mascot was!!!] Only after the decline of pig farming after the Second World War was the town able to outlive its odiferous reputation. Secaucus has tried, with some success, to promote the memory of its other agricultural product, flowers, as a source of municipal pride.

After the unsuccessful attempts to promote agriculture in the Meadowlands in the 1800s, the next drainage efforts were for mosquito control. When announcing the Iron Diking Enterprise in 1868, Scientific American reported that the meadows were, "not only unproductive of anything which can subserve any important purpose, but they are productive of numerous evils." The article made a point of mentioning that meadows were home to "mischievous and annoying insects."

By the end of the 1800s, the mosquito had been confirmed as the vector of diseases such as malaria and yellow fever. John Smith, the New Jersey State Entomologist, identified the Meadowlands as an area where the mosquito problems were especially serious. Beginning in 1912 the mosquito control commissions were established in each of New Jersey's counties, with the Bergen County Mosquito Commission being created in 1914.

A joint survey to locate breeding sites in the Meadowlands was undertaken by the counties of Bergen, Essex, Hudson, and Union in 1914. The commission reported that large areas had been reclaimed by truck farming along Berry's Creek, north of the Erie Railroad in Rutherford. But they also noted factory wastes, refuse, and raw sewage scattered throughout the region. The Hackensack River was especially noted as being badly polluted with industrial effluent.

After dividing the Meadowlands into 27 districts, the diking began with the purpose of draining the breeding grounds. Where feasible the earlier ditches and dikes were reused.

Courtesy Bergen County Historical Society

One of the diking and drainage projects of the Bergen County Mosquito Control Commission under construction in this early 1900s photograph.

In April of 1916, the Commission began digging thousands of feet of ditches near the site of the Schuyler Copper Mine, near Moonachie Creek and the Carlstadt Meadow. The rate of mosquito born illnesses, especially around Newark, dropped immediately, but the drainage canals quickly reduced the salinity of the marshlands. This allowed cattails and phragmite reeds to dominate the vegetation. In time the ditching and diking was replaced by the spraying of chemical insecticides.

Almost all of the canals dug in the Meadowlands were for agricultural reclamation or mosquito control, and not navigation. The one exception to this was the Berry's Creek Canal (actually an expansion of the existing waterway) which left the Hackensack River near the present-day interchange between State Highway 3 and the New Jersey Turnpike. It ran eastward, parallel to Highway 3, and south of the Meadowlands Stadium and arena. The creek then turned northward to cross the Erie Railroad and the Paterson Plank Road.

Berry's Creek Canal was constructed between 1902 and 1908. It was prepared by dredging the existing creek and heaping the spoils onto the northeastern bank. In 1909, a 181 acre parcel bounded by the creek was sold to the Erie Land and Improvement Company. When the Erie Railroad was relaid

The Bergen County Mosquito Control Commission used this converted tractor to cut weeds during the early 1900s. Note the wide wheels that kept the machine from sinking into the moist ground.

through the Meadowlands, a portion of this parcel was used. The railroad divided the canal so that a moveable bridge would not have to be constructed over the waterway. It would appear that any plans for extensive industrial development went unrealized.

It is not clear how many boats used the Berry's Creek Canal. There were some industries located north of the Paterson Plank Road, which it crossed. In 1914, a newspaper reported that the barge *Crane* became stuck in the mud while passing through the Paterson Plank Road drawbridge. The *Crane* was carrying 500 barrels of tar, although the reports did not mention where she was bound. At that time, there was a trolley line on the Paterson Plank Road so that both automobiles and trolleys were temporarily halted by the accident.

The most effective scheme to fill, as opposed to reclaim, the meadows was started in the twentieth century. Land was filled for industrial use with ash, building rubble, cinders, and slag. Power plants were considered ideal since they produced a lot of ash, and they would soon be needed because once new land was created, another industry would be moved onto it. Then the cycle would begin again. Unfortunately these fill materials contained many toxic metals. Today those companies that located in these areas are coping with the consequences of the landfill process.

In 1908, Thomas Townsend of Hackensack wanted to show his children the rewards of constantly striving to live a virtuous life. To this end he wrote a delightful novel, *The Home Afloat or Boy Trappers of the Hackensack*. Townsend described the life of a wounded Civil War veteran, Jim Hull and his family. As the story begins, Jim is worried about the corrupting influences that his family encounters while living in New York City. Deciding to escape the moral decay and unhealthy environment, he journeys across Bergen Neck and finds a small house on the river. After their move, the family is befriended by Old Harry, a man described by Townsend as "colored." Harry was a man with much local knowledge of the river and marsh. Soon the boys are learning how to bob for eels, trap muskrat on Moonachie Creek, and catch turtles. They are very successful and soon catch a turtle so large that $60 was offered for it, and members of the Hoboken Turtle Club even came out for a look.

The Hull family built a sturdy scow that their young daughter christened *The Meadow Lark*. The scow was pressed immediately into service harvesting salt hay. Townsend's description of the process deserves attention as it was an important occupation for the area's actual residents. According to Old Harry, the scow should be sailed into a creek with deep water and perpendicular banks, so as to facilitate launching a heavily loaded vessel. Once the scow was secured, the worker would then take a sickle and cut a swath at right angles to the creek. He would then turn around and move back towards the boat throwing the second swath on top of the first. Once loaded, the scow would be towed down river and the tides would help move it back home. In this way Old Harry helped the boys cut hay that was "fit for a race horse."

After the death of their parents, the Hull children converted the scow into a houseboat and had numerous adventures with fires, thieves, and winter storms. The book ends with the construction of an iceboat and the winning of the annual regatta. *The Flying Harry* carried the crew to a happy ending in which goodness triumphs. No other references to iceboat racing on the marshes have been found, but the sport is not unlikely. Many residents recall skating on the marshes near Moonachie. (*A True Story of Boy Trappers of the Hackensack* can be found in Appendix C.)

Photograph by Gene O'Neill

Three eras of the Hackensack Meadowlands are depicted in this photograph. The cedar log in the foreground is at least several hundred years old. The wood's resistance to rot made these logs an important resource during the 1700s and 1800s. In the middle distance a twentieth century landfill rises above the marsh while in the far distance luxury condominiums rise on the east bank of the Hackensack. The trails and the footbridge are part of the visitor center and hiking facilities at the Meadowlands Commission headquarters.

Chapter 9

Suburbia Ascendant

Throughout the 1800s, the growth of the region's cities, population, and industries fueled much of the commercial river navigation. Well before 1900, the working vessels were joined by several new types of craft - pleasure launches, rowing shells, and canoes.

Courtesy Bergen County Historical Society

A boating party on the Hackensack River in the early 1900s. Note the youngster in the sailor suit on the bank. There are no life jackets visible anywhere in this photograph.

Recreational rowboat racing on the Passaic River was extremely popular in the years between the Civil War and at the turn of the century. There had been unofficial rowing matches on the Passaic stretching back to the 1850s. The noted English sports writer Henry William Herbert, whose pen name was Frank Forester, raced local hotel proprietor Frank Harrison, with the loser having to buy a wild-game dinner for the crowd. According to the accounts, Herbert was ahead but then lost both the lead and the race, when he paused to rest with a bottle of liquor.

A boat named *Lonely* was the first rowing craft on the Passaic that was specifically built for racing. She was placed on the river around 1860 by four young Newarkers. The *Lonely* is believed to have received that name because at the time there were no other racing boats on the river. This soon changed. The Passaic Boat Club began racing in 1865. Belleville's Nereid Boat Club launched their first six-oared boat a year later. By 1869, no fewer that ten rowing clubs participated in the first large regatta to be held on the river. After 1872, the annual Memorial Day boat races were the highlight of spring sports season. Other boat clubs founded afterwards were the Eureka (1873), Passaic River Amateur Rowing Association (1875), Essex Boat Club (1876), Institute Boat Club (1878), Atlantics Boat Club (1890), Riverside Athletic Club (1890), and the Newark Rowing Club (1894).

Controversies frequently arose when it was claimed that some boats contained too many mechanics and laborers. Although they continued to race, it was considered unfair that such brawny individuals competed against the largely white-collar rowers. The four-man crew of the Newark Institute had an undefeated season in 1895. Their international reputation led to an invitation to England for the famous Henley regatta on the Thames. There, the organizers ruled that three of the four crew members from the Newark Institutes were ineligible to compete in England because they were "mechanics." The fourth, who was a schoolteacher, was allowed to compete. Institute Club Commodore Michael A. Mullin protested, but the ban stood.

Women were not allowed at the Triton club's functions. It took a prominent sculler, Theodore F. Keer, who had just returned from his honeymoon, to break the taboo by bringing his bride to the forty-eighth anniversary of the club's founding.

Nationally, the decline in the popularity of rowing was caused by a number of factors. Among these were the rising popularity of the bicycle and the proliferation of other sports. On the Passaic River though, the principle reason was the growing amount of sewage and industrial pollution.

By the 1970s, the Belleville, Nutley, and Kearny High Schools were only three crews on the Passaic River. These crews rowed 13 to 15 miles a day, six days a week. The only two other high school crews in New Jersey were both based in Atlantic City, so teams needed to travel either to Philadelphia or Poughkeepsie to attend competitions. All three schools shared the same boat house and rowed the same stretch of river, yet the activity drew plenty of students. In the 1973 season, Belleville had 80 candidates for their three varsity boats, a "lightweight" boat (135-pound competitors), and two freshman boats. In 1973, Belleville added women to the team for the first time. One of the original four women served as club statistician (responsible for recording practice times) and the others competed as the coxswains who steered the boats. Belleville coach Sam Giuffrida commented "We get kids who can discipline themselves. It's that kind of sport, and I've never heard a kid moan or complain. I think crew brings out the best in them because each has to pull his own weight or the other seven kids in the boat will know it."

Courtesy Library of Congress

An artist's conception of rowing races on the Passaic River in 1874.

At the time of this writing, there are two clubs active on the Passaic River, the Neriad Club and the Passaic River Rowing Association. The Neriad Club is the last surviving club from the 1800s, and shares facilities with the high school crews. The Passaic River Rowing Association was founded in 1998 with a specific goal of becoming a community based club. They have a new boat storage building on the grounds of the Bergen County Riverside Park South. In 2007, the Association has more than 200 members and the vast majority are youth members. The Association sponsors competitive teams for all ages and a "Learn to Row" program.

Photograph by Paul Lerin

Modern four-man rowing shells and their coach's boat move down the Passaic River north of Newark.

There were other rowing clubs competing on the Hackensack River. The Ridgefield New Jersey Rowing club competed near Little Ferry. Their September 1873 regatta featured a one-mile course from the Little Ferry Bridge downstream to a stake boat and back again to the bridge. The United States Revenue Schooner *Dana* was moored near the bridge for the accommodation of the judges and invited guests, and the small brass signal gun on the bow of the *Dana* was used to start the races. Races began with a single scull event for the Ridgefield club championship. The next race was open to four-man boats from all clubs. The prize was a silk pennant, which was won by the Atlantic Club of Hoboken with a time of 15 minutes and 15 seconds. The final events were races for single sculls open to all clubs and a junior sculling event for the Ridgefield club. After the races, the club members and their guests returned to the clubhouse for clam chowder and the awards ceremony.

If pollution was driving recreation from the Lower Passaic River, there was still plenty of room for recreation in other parts of the Passaic and Hackensack watersheds. As much as 50% of the more than 200 square mile watershed remained open space as late as the 1970s. A rising middle class, trolley lines, more railroads, and better roads meant new opportunities for suburban developers like Gustave Pete, of New York. In 1890, he purchased a tract of farmland near Oradell. Modestly naming the area Peetzburg, he urged his fellow New Yorkers to stop paying rent and escape city life by purchasing a home from him. Advertisements for the community touted good boating, fishing, hunting, and bathing in the Hackensack River. And at the turn of the century, many Bergen County residents were doing all of those things with great enthusiasm.

A newspaper article of September 8, 1905, listed the competitions at the Bogota Boat Club Regatta; competitors came from the Oritani, Rosedale, and Overpeck Clubs for the Labor Day event. Diving, double canoe races, lady's double races, men's swimming, single gig, single scull, mixed double canoe races, and boy's swimming events were featured. Winning the launch race was the *Mary*, owned by Joseph White of the Bogota Boat Club, who beat the *Genevieve A.*, owned by W.D. Adams of the West View Boat Club, by one minute, 33 seconds. These were probably steam powered crafts as the "Auto Boat" race was won by the *Nina*. Other contests included horse races (on barrels) and a tilting tournament.

Among the most famous sports enthusiasts of the era was Kittie Miller of Hackensack. Daughter of Captain Chris Miller she was known as an adventurous traveler, crack rifle shot, expert rower, swimmer, all around athlete, and the first woman to ride a bicycle in Hackensack. Her best remembered exploit on the river was the commotion she caused during a sailboat race. After rounding a turn the judges saw her boat disappear from among the racers. Then out of nowhere, a new boat suddenly appeared in the fleet. Both were really Kittie's boat. She had painted it black on one side, and gold on the other.

Several canoe clubs appeared on the Hackensack in the early 20th century. The Hackensack Yacht Club was founded in 1903 and encompassed both yachting and canoeing interests. The club still exists today and operates a clubhouse, docks, and a marine railway.

Another canoe club was headquartered at New Bridge in the frame building directly across from the Steuben House. The WaWa Canoe Club is still active and maintains a club house and public dock south of Hackensack

Courtesy Waterworks Conservancy

This late 1800s photograph shows the clubhouse of an unidentified canoe club near Oradell. Such organizations were popular during this period when both local people and summer visitors paddled, fished, and swam in the upper Hackensack.

in Bogota. This club specializes in the training of Olympic Style canoe racers. Emily Krieger, daughter of a Bogota boathouse owner, recalled many years later, the fun times with the old canoe clubs:

> In the fall, the clubs organized canoe carnivals. Men would spend days decorating their shells and canoes with Japanese lanterns and paper decorations, and you would see 50 or more boats on the river. There were tilting contests, and music and dancing.

Another woman reminisced about the now extinct Kinderkamack Canoe Club. It was situated in the area later flooded for the Oradell Reservoir.

> "Our object was to have good times together and enjoy paddling. We had steak and fish dinners at the club once a month."

Most members lived on the water's edge and only had to launch from their backyards and paddle the seven miles to the club house.

A much longer canoe trip could be made by following the Hackensack

126

northwards into Rockland County and ascending to the uppermost portions of the eastern tributaries. From there it was a short portage to another brook that led down to the Hudson. Then the paddlers descended to Newark Bay and back upriver to their starting point. Although this was a very popular canoe route, no one has been able to use it since the construction of the Hackensack Water Company's reservoirs. Tracing the route is also made difficult today because of a lack of documentary evidence. Historian Arthur Adams speculates that the easiest route would have been north on the main branch of the Hackensack to the junction of the Dwarkill. Then up the Dwarkill to the site of Piermont road. At that point there would be a four-fifths mile portage across level, solid ground to the headwaters of the Sparkill, in present day Rockleigh, New Jersey. The Sparkill could then be paddled through the Sparkill Gap to the Hudson River at Piermont.

Courtesy Bergen County Historical Society
Boathouses and rental liveries were found on the Passaic River upstream of the Great Falls in Totowa and Little Falls. This 1907 postcard shows a facility at Spruce Street in Paterson.

Recreational use was also made of the upper portions of the Passaic River. In the early decades of the twentieth century, the reaches west of Paterson, immediately upstream of the Great Falls, were popular for rowing and strolling in the riverside parks. Summer bungalow communities grew in the area around Wayne Township, especially along the Pompton River. About five miles long, the Pompton is formed by the confluence of the Ramapo, Wanaque, and Pequannock Rivers in the town of Pompton Lakes. It flows south along the border of Wayne and Pequannock townships and finally enters the Passaic

127

near Two Bridges. With its many summer-home communities and opportunities for boating, fishing, and swimming, the area was advertised during the 1920s as the "Venice of America."

Wayne Township perhaps did not appreciate the title. With the summer vacationers came noisy parties, loud music, and dancing in the streets. The town council eventually passed a law that prohibited the wearing of bathing suits on the streets after 10 p.m.

Newark Yacht Club, Passaic River.

Author's collection

The Newark Yacht Club on the Passaic River is shown in this 1907 postcard. Note the large number of rowing boats in the foreground. There is a scow-hull shanty boat hauled up in the yard and several steam launches moored at the pier.

The pollution of the lower rivers did not discourage children from swimming. Writing at the turn of the century, a Newarker recalled some of the places in and around the city where as a young boy, during the Civil War, he and his friends often swam. There was a small creek near a zinc works, which had a sand bar that the boys called Coney Island. Ripley's sawmill had a pond which was also popular, although there were some tough kids from the 12th Ward who would rent a rowboat and come over to steal pennies, marbles, and knives from the pockets of the clothes left on shore. Another popular spot was the tar dock where a lampblack factory would later be established. Behind this site was a shallow pond in the meadows, where despite the many leeches, younger children learned to swim. What is surprising to the modern reader is just how many fish, eels, crabs, and shrimp were thriving in these waterways during the 1860s.

A very popular recreational crab fishery developed on the Hackensack River, Meadowlands, and Newark Bay. From several docks in the riverside towns, one could rent a boat and keep all the crabs you could catch. One such boat livery, Meyerholtz & Bressigs, was located in Newark at the Central Railroad Bridge. According to their 1893 advertisements, they could provide scoops, drops, nets, and hooks used in crabbing. A steam launch provisioned with the best wines and liquors was also available.

The Erie Lackawanna Railroad had a large lift bridge near Secaucus and the author was fortunate enough to speak to a former member of one of the bridge tending crews. This former railroader said that crabbing was a favorite pastime for the crew members. Having a steam engine that raised and lowered the bridge, they cleverly bled some hot steam to cook the catch.

Courtesy New Jersey Chamber of Commerce

1920s-era pleasure boats are moored on the Hackensack River near Jersey City. The sloop in the foreground appears to be a type with a deep keel that would require a well-dredged channel.

In the years before and immediately after the Second World War, the American Power Boat Association sanctioned races on the Hackensack River at Carlstadt. Open only to association members and registered boats, the races followed a five-mile course. Most competitions were for outboard powered hydroplanes. The "midget" class of hydroplanes raced a three mile course.

Excursion vessels provided a day on the water without the cost and trouble of owning a boat. Although there were a number of passenger and freight boats operating on the Passaic, excursion boats made their appearance in the late 1830s, when the *Olive Branch*, *Wadsworth* and *Experiment* were making regular weekend runs between Newark and Passaic.

The first excursions out to Coney Island and Rockaway were scheduled in the 1840s. A July 20, 1845 excursion aboard the Wave between Newark and Coney Island was canceled after protests that the Sunday trip would profane the Sabbath. But before the Civil War the boats were carrying as many as 3,500 passengers annually to the oceanside resort. The Stephens and Condit Transportation Company even built several boats dedicated to this purpose, including the *Thomas P. Way*, *Chicopee*, and *Jamaica*. These boats were later joined by the *Maryland*, *Jonas C. Hurst*, *Maria*, and *Magenta*.

In 1845, a grand excursion around Staten Island was scheduled for July 12 at 8:00 a.m. on the large and elegant steamboat *R. L. Stevens*, which was to leave Newark at the foot of Center Street. Passengers would have a view of the island, the fortifications, and other government works. They would also have an excellent opportunity for inhaling the sea breeze. On the return trip there was to be a stopover at Coney Island of about two hours of sea bathing. If time permitted, a stop was to be made at Fort Hamilton. The Newark Brass Band was to play during the trip and dinner and refreshments were available on board. The fare was 75 cents for adults and for children under 12 years, one-half fare.

An 1868 newspaper account describes a trip on the *Thomas P. Way* from the Hudson River at Barclay Street in New York City to Newark. The boat made two trips daily, departing at 10:30 a.m. and 4:30 p.m. It took about half an hour to reach Staten Island where the boat turned west. She then docked at the Latourette House hotel at Bergen Point, which was popular with guests from the city. Each time the steamboat arrived the wharf was crowded with those inspecting the new arrivals. The trip up Newark Bay was noted for the greenery along the shores and the views of villas that overlooked the water. The newspaper reporter observed that railroad passengers saw very little of the city as they passed through Newark but from the water a person could appreciate the full extent of the city, which although already immense, would have a future "its founders never dreamed of." The trip on the *Thomas P. Way* cost 20 cents, and according to the newspaper, the boat might carry as many as 1,500 passengers on a busy Sunday. It was "a pleasant and a cheap trip for those who cannot conveniently leave the city for a term of weeks in the summer time."

A brief inspection of the Newark newspapers for the summer of 1893 revealed a number of steamboat excursions. One could take the People's Line every Sunday, Tuesday, or Thursday morning to Far Rockaway. The $.50 round trip included music, food, and drink. A.W. McCabe on Broad Street had a 60 passenger steam yacht, *Howard*, for charter. The Epworth League Methodist Church sponsored an excursion to Long Branch, Asbury Park, and Ocean Grove. The trip was 6 hours by sea. And finally, if one was not a Methodist or serious sportsman, the *Schuyler* sailing from Franklin Street offered fishing and a $1 coupon for drinks.

The Landscape Changes

Any developments that changed the face of the land would naturally have a profound affect on the rivers. This was especially true in the upper Hackensack River valley. For example in 1908, another real estate agency began selling "Brookchester" homes in New Milford. Eventually commuters from the area formed the River Edge Manor Improvement Association and succeeded in getting improvements to roads and schools, and the installation of gas pipes. By forming a Republican Club in 1915 and electing a member to the Township Committee, they began to set the pattern of change towards suburban development.

Courtesy Waterworks Conservancy

A proud boatbuilder displays a newly constructed rowboat somewhere near Oradell.

131

Courtesy Bergen County Historical Society

Peetzburg, near Oradell, was an early planned suburban development meant to attract city dwellers. The Hackensack River with its fishing, swimming, and boating was an important asset for the new community. This 1907 postcard shows one of the homes built in the community and a gazebo on the Hackensack.

Bergen County Historical Society

A pleasure boat somewhere near Oradell around the time of the First World War. Well-dressed passengers lounge on the cabin roof. Note the folding deck chair set up on the stern.

This did more than just change the scenery. As woodland and pasturage were leveled for housing construction, erosion followed, and stormwater runoff began carrying huge amounts of silt into the river channels. This process was gradual at first, but was greatly accelerated in the twentieth century and still continues today. After the Second World War portions of both the lower Passaic and Hackensack rivers were channelized. Stone rip-rap or concrete channeling was added to the banks to prevent further erosion and control flooding.

Collection of Stephen Marshall

This 1946 aerial photograph of the Hackensack River shows how much open space was still present in the Meadowlands. Snake Hill (14) and Secaucus (7) are the only developed areas. The New Jersey Turnpike would not be built for another five years.

The choking effect of the silting on the Hackensack River was exacerbated by the reduction in stream flow by the dams of the Hackensack Water Company. Not only was there less water to flush the silt away, but tidal currents carried brackish water farther upstream than ever before. In 1874, before the construction of any major reservoirs, the water company was pumping water out of the Hackensack River at Cherry Hill, just north of the city of Hackensack. Although the river was brackish, historian Adrian Leiby pointed out that there was apparently enough fresh water in the channel to serve the needs of the company's customers. Either there were two distinct layers of water, lighter fresh water flowing along the river's surface over a layer of heavier brackish water, or the fresh water was only available during low tide. Either way, the water was reported to be of good quality, and the residents boasted that it was superior to New York City's Croton Reservoir water.

The Hackensack Water Company was reorganized in 1880 and shortly afterwards soon obtained a ten year contract to supply Hoboken's 30,000 citizens with water for $75,000 annually. A new source of water was needed somewhere farther upstream than the existing inlet at Cherry Hill. There were some reservations on the part of Hoboken's leaders about relying on a small river for all of their city's water. During a drought in 1881 all doubts vanished when they saw a large schooner sailing the Hackensack several miles north of the existing pumping house.

Construction on what would someday become the Oradell Reservoir and the New Milford Waterworks began in 1881, with the purchase of J & H Van Buskirk's mill with its 11 acres for $50,000. (See Chapter 7) The original New Milford pumping station was completed in 1882 and in November of that year its first water reached the city of Hoboken. The station expanded in 1902 in conjunction with construction of the first of several Oradell Reservoirs. The reservoir was needed so that sediments would have a chance to settle out of the water before it entered the filtration plant. The new filtration plant was completed in 1904 and it was expanded again in 1911 when 25,000,000 gallons a day was being pumped from it.

In 1902, the Oradell Reservoir was only one-half of a mile long, 150 to 200 feet wide, and had a capacity of 250,000,000 gallons. Plans to build Woodcliff Lake Reservoir (on Pascack Creek) were announced in 1903. This facility had been planned for some time when a two month drought made the need immediate. In October 1900, the Hackensack Water Company bought out the Spring Valley Water Works and Supply Company in Rockland County. It was not a large concern, having only one employee. But the move was a far-sighted one as it embraced the idea that a watershed and its management could not be restricted by state borders. In the 1950s, the purchase would give the company the necessary rights to build the DeForest Lake Reservoir.

Starting in 1911, the Oradell Reservoir was expanded again. The company built what was until then the largest vessel ever used on the upper river, the dredge barge *Reliance*. Named for the America's Cup defender of that year, she had 12 inch suction pumps. A second dredge was added shortly thereafter. Late one night, a water company executive boarded one of the dredges and found the vessel's floodlights all shining, the pump engines chugging at full speed, and the entire 12 man crew asleep. (The line was sucking up only river

Courtesy Waterworks Conservancy

The exterior of the Hackensack Water Company's pumping station on Van Buskirk's Island is shown in this period photograph. The large building in the foreground was where the pumping equipment was housed.

water.) The crew was fired on the spot.

Dredging continued until 1916. Sediments found their way into the water system and there were also reports of muddy water downstream ruining the river for bathing and recreation. Some silting occurred in the channel south of New Milford. The Oradell Reservoir was dredged and expanded again in the early 1920s. The 1921 enlargement program extended the reservoir as far north as Harrington Park and Closter and increased its capacity to 1,600,000,000 gallons.

Aside from the silting problems, the reduction of freshwater flow increased the salinity of the Hackensack River. The loss of riverfront land to reservoir construction also meant the loss of recreational opportunities such as the famous Thirty-foot Hole (at the junction of the Dwarskill in Harrington Park) which was a favorite swimming hole. Canoeing was forbidden in the reservoirs and was also restricted wherever the water company fenced off riverfront land, to prevent contamination. On the other hand, modern-day Bergen County and parts of Hudson County were made possible by the Hackensack Water Company. The water company also preserved large tracts of open space in what would become one of the most densely populated places in the United States.

Except for the resentment of certain Rockland County leaders over the

Courtesy Bergen County Historical Society

Around the time of the First World War, in order to achieve maximum storage capacity, the Oradell Reservoir was deepened using several large suction dredges. These were too large to be moved up river and had to be constructed on the site. It is not recorded what became of them after the reservoir was completed.

loss of land for the construction of a reservoir that served out of state interests, the damming of the Hackensack River has generally been a politically quiet process. Passaic River water, on the other hand, has been hotly contested since the early 1800s. Paterson's industries depended on the water power in the Passaic River where it passes over the Great Falls. By the time the river reaches the Falls, it contains the combined flows of four rivers - the Passaic, Pequannock, Wanaque, and Ramapo. Beginning in the 1830s, the eastern end of the Morris Canal was kept full by diverting the flows of the Pequannock, Wanaque, and Ramapo into the Pompton Feeder canal, which joined the main canal in what is today the Mountain View section of Wayne Township. Some Patersonians resented the Morris Canal because it provided neither water power or transportation for their city. It was built too high up on the side of Garret Mountain for easy access and did nothing to power Paterson's factories. For their part, the canal builders were zealous in defense of their rights to use the water. By the end of the canal era, the Wanaque and Pequannock Rivers were part of municipal water systems and there was little reason for further dispute. What arguments persisted over the use of canal

Courtesy Walter Nickelsberg

The Passaic River has long been known for its flooding. Some indication of the volume of water can be obtained in these photographs at Paterson's Great Falls.

137

waters had shifted westward to Lake Hopatcong.

Starting in the 1970s, Patersonians saw the Great Falls as the centerpiece of their city's urban renewal efforts. There was even serious talk of rebuilding the old hydroelectric power plant at the falls. Upstream communities were more interested in diverting the Passaic for flood control and drinking water. For a brief time, the old arguments were revived as Paterson resisted efforts that would detract from their urban showpiece.

New Cargoes

As the region continued to grow, the commercial traffic on the lower reaches of the rivers served the needs of the population with such cargoes as coal, fuel oil, asphalt, crushed stone, and concrete. These last few were especially important with the widespread acceptance of automobiles.

The first of these cargoes (and the best documented) was coal. In New Jersey, the Morris Canal and the Delaware and Raritan Canal, which linked Pennsylvania's coalfields with New York Harbor, was opened for traffic in the 1830s.

The outlet of the Delaware and Raritan Canal was New Brunswick, and the original outlet of the Morris Canal was the Passaic River at Newark. Later, the Morris Canal was extended across the Kearny Peninsula and around the base of Bergen Ridge into Jersey City, where it connected to the Hudson River at what is now Liberty State Park. The Morris Canal had a guard lock at Newark's Mulberry Street to allow boats into the Passaic River and then across the peninsula formed by the Passaic and Hackensack rivers. The Hackensack could be crossed at high tide, pulled by mules walking across a bridge. According to Simon Johnston (1886-1976), an old canal hand, "You had to know your job to do it."

George Mowder (1875-1968), a canal driver at 11 and eventually a captain, describes crossing the Hackensack. "This was a channel made through the meadows about one mile long, and this brought you to the Hackensack River, which is approximately 300 yards wide. The team went over the long bridge, which is also a drawbridge, and pulled the boat across the river going into a lock which passed you into the eight mile level on the way to Jersey City."

He recalled the time he and his father, while in their canal boat, were blown across the meadows and stranded for two days and nights by a storm. George was worried but his father comforted him by saying, "Now son, don't be afraid, our Heavenly Father will take care of us." In his many years ahead, George would remember his steadfast father at the tiller, and would draw

Courtesy Canal Society of New Jersey

After boats crossed the Passaic and Hackensack, they re-entered the Morris Canal on the west shore of Newark Bay. From there the boats traveled around the southern tip of the Bayonne Peninsula and entered Jersey City from the south. Note how only a narrow tow-path separated the canal from the bay.

upon the deep faith he learned on the boat's deck.

Many Canalers recall leaving their mules behind in Newark and taking tows from steamboats up the Passaic and Hackensack rivers. In a 1960 interview, Oliver Warman told James Lee about bringing 65 to 80 ton loads using this method from the canal to Hackensack and Englewood.

Canal boats on the New Jersey waterways were constructed in two sections. They were joined amidships and the two halves could be separated for easier passage through locks or on the inclined planes of the Morris Canal.

Some accounts mention the boats traveling up the Hackensack on the tide until New Bridge. There they could be separated and poled through the narrower channels all the way to the head of navigation at New Milford.

The connection between the Highland iron industry and the Hackensack River was broken by railroads in the 1800s, but for a while it was re-established by the Hudson Iron Company. In 1905 this company took over the Forest of Dean Mine, located four miles west of Fort Montgomery and seven miles south of West Point, New York. The mine shipped much of its production via the Hudson and Hackensack rivers to its furnace in Secaucus.

The ore began its journey 700 feet underground and traveled up a 1,700 foot long incline. Once through a crusher and storage bin, it was loaded onto a narrow gauge railway for a 3½ mile ride down to the Hudson. There it was loaded on an aerial tramway and taken down to a loading dock. The ore not destined for Secaucus usually went by rail to furnaces in eastern Pennsylvania.

The Public Service Company which provided gas and electricity was

139

an important user of river transportation. In the days before natural gas was widely available, gas for lighting purposes was manufactured by individual companies from coal. "Pipeline" or natural gas did not arrive in New Jersey until 1949.

In the earliest gas manufacturing process, coal was sealed into huge ovens called retorts and heated in the absence of air. Instead of burning, the coal began to decompose and form smaller, more volatile molecules. In the late 1800s the Water Gas process was introduced. A charge of coke was raised to white heat in a hot air blast. After the heat was turned off, steam was admitted into the retort. Carbon monoxide and hydrogen gas were produced but taken together they did not have much heating value (only about 320 to 350 BTU/ft3). These were then passed into a second vessel, the carburetor. The carburetor was an air-tight brick chamber that was heated to extremely high temperatures. When a kerosene type oil was sprayed onto the hot bricks, it was quickly vaporized and passed to a superheater, along with the carbon monoxide and hydrogen. At temperatures of up to 1,500 degrees, the oil "cracked," i.e., the molecules split apart, helped by the reactive carbon monoxide, and then combined with the hydrogen to form volatile molecules that could be burned for lighting and heating.

In both processes production was cyclical. Even when production alternated between two or more retorts, there was always a down time between batches. There were also periods when the gas producing apparatus was shut down for repairs or recharging. The gas had to stored in huge reservoirs and released into the delivery pipes at a constant rate.

Numerous valuable chemicals were produced by the gas manufacturing process. These included toluol, Bakelite, dyes, fertilizers, and ammonia (a by-product of the water gas purification step). Another derivative was a gooey brown tar that was considered unwanted waste.

This gooey brown tar often was often dumped into the nearest river. By the late 1800s, this practice was so widespread that it led to the nation's first laws against water pollution. These laws were less concerned with ecological damage than with hazards to commercial navigation. But all the same, today's legal protection for streams, rivers, and oceans can all be traced back to gasworks and gooey tars.

The coal used in the gasworks often arrived via water either in canal boats or in the larger barges that were used in the coasting trade. Late nineteenth century photographs of gasworks in Newark show Morris Canal boats being unloaded from the Passaic River docks. By the 1920s, the canals were closed but the larger coal barges were a major segment of river traffic. By then of course, coal was also needed for electrical generation.

The first two gasworks in New Jersey both began operations in 1847. The Paterson Gas Light Company had been chartered in 1825, but remained dormant for a score of years. In 1845, the Newark Gas Light Company was chartered. The latter company established their Broad Street Works on the Passaic River. The riverbanks would later be home to the Newark gasworks of the People's Light and Power Company. By the late 1890s, electrical generators were also installed on this site. After a disastrous fire in 1896, it was rebuilt as the River Station, and again rebuilt in 1902. After the 1903 consolidation of dozens of local electrical, gas, and trolley companies to form the Public Service Electric and Gas, it became Public Service's City Dock Station.

Courtesy NOAA

The Kearny Station of Public Service Electric and Gas can be seen across the Hackensack River from Jersey City.

Across the meadows from Newark, Public Service's electric railway division built the Marion Generating Station (later known as the Hudson Station) to power its street cars. The station was on the east bank of the Hackensack, below the hill upon which Jersey City is sited. Completed in 1906, the Marion station was one of the first in the Public Service system to use 6,000 kilowatt steam turbines, instead of reciprocating engines to turn the generators.

The Essex Station was built in 1915 on the Passaic River in Newark with a single 22,500 kilowatt turbine. Another was soon added, and came on line just in time to meet the power demands caused by the United States entering the First World War.

In 1926, the fires in the Harrison Gas Works on the Passaic River were started with coals taken from the Market Street Gas Works. In this ceremonial lighting the company made a point of perpetuating the flame that had first produced gas for in Newark in 1847. The Harrison Gas Works extracted an amazing 80% of heating value from the 230,000 lbs boiler fuel, 730,000 lbs generator fuel, and 80,000 lbs of oil that fed its water gas sets each day. By the end of the 1920s, the company's largest coke plant was in Newark. It could produce 11,000,000 cubic feet of gas each day using 9 water gas sets.

The Kearny station also came on line in 1926. It was built on marshland about half a mile north of the Plank Road, opposite Jersey City. Its 5 generators, 15 boilers, 12,000 tons of steel and 7,000,000 bricks sat atop 22,000 piles driven into the soft marshy ground. The Kearny Station was noted for its suitability for receiving coal loads by water.

Bergen Generating Station, which opened in 1959, was built in Ridgefield, near the New Jersey Turnpike. Between 1946 and 1965 Public Service added 2,410,000 kilowatts of generating capacity by adding the Essex generating station on the Passaic River and the Linden generating station near Newark Bay. In 1964 the 400,000 kilowatt Hudson Station came on line. It was located just north of the Marion Station, which it replaced. Today the Hudson Station still receives barge loads of fuel from the docks on the Hackensack River.

Although coal was the usual cargo unloaded on Public Service's docks, Darrow Sage, former generating station chief, tells this story from the era of Prohibition involving the Essex Station and some rumrunners:

> I always got into the station (Essex, that is) between eight and fifteen minutes past eight, driving down from Short Hills. One foggy morning I had just gotten to my office on the fifth floor when someone called me on the phone and said, "There are a bunch of gangsters down here on the dock and they have driven us off with loaded guns and we can't operate the coal car." I said, "What do you mean, gangsters?" They said, "Four or five men, they all have guns and they say no one must come on the (coal) barges and no one must come on that end of the dock." So I went down to the dock and a fellow came over and said, "Sorry, we are not going to let you on the dock or on the barges for

about an hour." This was during Prohibition. "One of our rum-runners has crashed into one of your coal barges and is sinking," he said, "and we've got it full of Scotch and we are putting it on the barge now and we are having another motor boat come to take it off in about an hour. We are going to take possession of the dock and if you don't like it we'll kill you."

So I figured I could stop coal handling for an hour. It wouldn't bother anybody. I thought, "This is pretty serious, I'd better call my boss, Jake Barron." And he said, "What do you want to tell me that for? I don't want to know anything like that. Now that you've told me I've got to do something about it." So in a few minutes the fire department arrived, the ambulances arrived, the reporters arrived, the Prohibitionists arrived, and a lot of other people. Seventy-five people were down there within a half hour and the chief of the fire department walks over and says, "Shut everything down." I said, "Chief, there isn't anything wrong, inside. I'm not going to shut anything down." He said, "When I give an order everything is going to be shut down, everything is going to be shut down." And I said, "As long as I've got a license and nothing is wrong, nothing is going to be shut down. Listen, chief, you didn't come down here to put out a fire. You came down to catch some firewater." And everyone giggled and that saved the day. Otherwise, they would have had me in jail.

Well, another motorboat came up. It was a very thick fog; that's why the first boat hit the barge. They transferred the booze and were all gone (with the gunmen) in less than an hour. They were all gone by the time the police got down there. We were all standing on the dock looking at one another when we heard the motorboat coming down, the rum-runner. And we all looked at each other and looked out. And God just gave us a hole in that fog and as the boat went by, the gunmen all thumbed their noses at us. They could travel faster than any boat on the river and they knew the river as no one else did.

The next morning when we came in, sitting on the stringpiece of the dock was a case of Scotch with a note saying, "Thanks for your cooperation." I took one bottle and gave the rest to the yard gang.

Bridges and Boats

In the late 1800s and into the early 1900s, as both the port of New York and the northern New Jersey suburbs spread out, the number of railroad lines crossing the Passaic and Hackensack rivers also increased. The number of trains using each line, especially during the morning and evening commutation hours, continued to rise. Under the existing laws of navigation, boats had the right of way and trains had to stop while the bridges opened.

The railroad companies backed by the commuting public demanded that the bridge openings be restricted to certain hours. The ship and tugboat operators naturally resisted this suggestion. Freeman Putney Junior published a poem On February 8th, 1907, in the New York Times about the debate.

Rights of Navigation

A schooner emerged from the morning fog.
With a load of bricks and a yellow dog.
And the Captain, the same who was likewise crew,
stood by her wheel, as the old sails drew,
her slowly up the Hackensack.

"I hear," said the captain, with stiffened back,
"The railroads are asking the government powers,
to close the bridge in their busy hours."

"Shipping has rights, they must understand,
on this here river, if not on land.
And the railroad system can take its shock,
for I don't wait til 11 o'clock.
And the bridge, by the laws of navigation,
must open to me, if it stops creation!"
They opened the bridge, and a train stood still,
while the schooner crawled at her own sweet will;
Another train halted, then many more,
while passengers fidgeted, grumbled, or swore.
When the boat was through, and the draw swung back,
they were late for miles up the railroad track.

Five thousand commuters in such a fix,
held up by the voyage of a load of bricks!
The schooner went on at a leisurely jog,
the captain grinned at the yellow dog.
The captain winked and the dog winked back,
navigation was safe on the Hackensack!

The number of passengers delayed by the open drawbridges numbered in the thousands. In March 1901, the newly constructed Lackawanna Railroad Hackensack River drawbridge became stuck in the open position. It had been opened to allow the passage of a lumber schooner. As the bridge was closing, one of the steel rollers that allowed the bridge to pivot came loose and jammed with the bridge just five feet short of fully closed position. After an hour of frantic repair efforts the bridge was finally closed. River traffic had to be halted until the cause of the failure was investigated and remedial measures put in place.

In May of 1910, fourteen Erie mainline trains with an estimated 7,000 morning commuters were delayed between twenty minutes and an hour and a half when the two-masted brick schooner, *Mary Ann*, became stuck in the mud while passing through the Hackensack River drawbridge. The captain was witnessed making frantic efforts to keep the schooner in the channel, but her steering gear was broken. A train was halted at the open bridge and every ten minutes another train was forced to halt behind it until the line of halted trains stretched back a full mile. The railroad moved the stalled trains to sidings so that a large freight engine could be brought to the bridge. A cable was passed from the engine to the schooner, and inch by slow inch the locomotive pulled the stranded schooner free from the mud.

In the early 1900s it was estimated that 70% of Erie commuter train delays were caused by open bridges. The issue of limiting times that bridges could be opened was once again introduced in local political circles.

In addition to the problems created by delays, the narrow openings under the bridges were ideal places for boats to become stuck or collide with the piers. At least once, a delay was caused by merely having a boat at anchor. In 1891, schooner Captain Thomas Fitzpatrick of Little Ferry had moored his schooner to a Hackensack River bridge, presumably in such a way as to prevent it from closing. He was indicted in United States District Court for obstructing the mails. Although he had originally pled not guilty to the charge, he withdrew his plea and was fined $50 plus costs.

In March of 1881, the tugboat *Mary Ann* of South Amboy (not to be confused with the schooner of the same name) had a barge lashed to her side while trying to pass through the open Pennsylvania Railroad Hackensack drawbridge. The *Mary Ann* and the barge were too wide and became stuck. Unfortunately the morning commuter rush was in progress and for an hour and a half the trains all came to a halt, and an estimated 5,000 passengers were delayed. Some seized the opportunity and walked across an adjacent drawbridge where special trains were waiting to carry them for the remainder of their trip. Several other tugboats came to the *Mary Ann's* assistance and she was finally pulled free.

In February of 1946, a 6,643 gross ton coal-carrying ship *Jagger Seam* crashed into the Central Railroad of New Jersey's drawbridge between Jersey City and Kearny. The ship had unloaded her cargo in Kearny and was heading down the river and back to her home port of Boston. Two spans of the structure were thrown off their piers and into the river while a third was partly submerged.

The cause of the accident was human error. The *Jagger Seam* and a tugboat both arrived at the open drawbridge at the same time. Her pilot signaled to the tugboat that he would proceed through the bridge first and proceeded to increase speed. The tugboat's captain did not acknowledge the signal and the *Jagger Seam* sounded a distress call and attempted to stop by dropping her anchor.

The coal ship's bow was damaged and was taking in water but the ship was not in any imminent danger of sinking. Fortunately for the railroad, this bridge was not part of their main line, because it was estimated that three months would be required for repairs to be completed.

Just over a year later, in April of 1947, traffic was halted on the Pennsylvania Railroad's main line. At 4:46 a.m. the tugboat *Samson* was towing an oil barge through the Pennsylvania's Hackensack river bridge. The barge was swung against the side of the drawbridge by the strong current. The collision damaged the bridge's power cable, leaving it in the open position, halting trains for two hours while repairs were made.

The problem of bridge collisions has not entirely disappeared, despite the use of modern navigational aids. On December 1, 1994, the *Asphalt Trader* was being towed downriver by two tugboats after delivering her cargo the Bergen Asphalt Company. One of the tugs broke loose and the ship drifted into the fixed portion of a Hackensack River bridge. The bridge supported New Jersey Transit's Morris & Essex line over the river. The accident halted rail traffic on that line between 4 and 5 p.m. New Jersey Transit workers were called out to repair the damage, which was not serious. They were able to lower the span and lock it into place, and train service resumed, but ten trains were prevented from leaving the Hoboken Terminal while the repairs were being made.

The most serious type of bridge accident was caused by a train plunging through an open drawbridge. Most of these accidents were the result of signals being misinterpreted or ignored.

On Erie Railroad's Greenwood Lake branch, a passenger train consisting of the engine *Orange* and one passenger car left Montclair at 5:50 a.m. on November 4, 1879. Engineer Ira Dexter, a veteran of four years service on the Erie, was at the throttle. Making stops at Bloomfield, Woodside, and Arlington, the train approached the Hackensack River drawbridge at about 6:15.

The fifty-foot long swing type drawbridge was open at the time to allow a schooner to pass. On a frame constructed over the tracks on the east side, signal lanterns hung to warn engineers that the draw was open. As required, a red light was displayed but as it was broad daylight, it was not bright enough for engineer Dexter to see it. At that time of the morning, the train would have been traveling directly into the rising sun.

Bridge tender James Moore and his partner Michael Mannion were both standing near the track and saw the train rushing toward the bridge over the meadows. Seeing the train now nearing the bridge approaches, Mannion began to wave furiously. The next thing the bridge tenders saw was engineer Dexter jumping from the cab window. Meanwhile, the fireman, John Masker, was busy putting out the fire and did not have time to jump out of the cab.

The *Orange* careened out over the water, smashed into the trestle work on the east side of the bridge, and immediately sank in fifty feet of water. Fortunately, the passenger coach became uncoupled from the engine and the trucks fell off after the car went off the end. The coach also struck the eastern side of the bridge but floated downstream partially submerged.

Baggage Master J.D. Wood was riding in the front of the passenger car when he heard the engine slamming into reverse. He got up to move back when he saw fireman Masker climb back over the tender to the front platform of the coach, from where he jumped overboard. J.D. Wood also jumped off the coach and began swimming to shore, pausing in the river to hold a passenger's head out of the water until help arrived.

Some of the passengers were already crawling out of the car when Mannion rowed out in a skiff. James Davis was the first passenger to climb from the car onto the skiff. By this time Bridge Tender Moore brought an axe and it was used to smash a hole in the coach roof. The remaining passengers crawled through this opening and everyone was soon huddled in the bridge tenders' shanty, cold and wet.

Fireman Masker walked to the Bergen telegraph station to call for help. Superintendent C.W. Douglas brought an engine to the site. Attaching a rope to the car, rescuers used the engine to drag the car to the riverbank. There was a large hole in the side where it had struck the engine, and the seats were broken and scattered, but no bodies were found.

The body of Engineer Dexter was discovered where he had jumped, his neck broken. Dexter, who was forty years old, left a wife and two children. Some of the passengers and crewmen were injured. Conductor William H. Stark, who had suffered a head injury, was in shock, and remembered nothing of the accident until finding himself in the bridge tenders' shanty. Brakeman Jesse Williams had cuts and bruises on his head, sides, and arms. J.D. Wood suffered a back injury but it did not appear serious. F.B. Tuttle of Montclair suffered internal injuries and was taken to a Newark hospital. William Harrison of Belleville had a broken collar bone and internal injuries, but none of the remaining passengers were seriously injured.

Superintendent Douglas immediately declared that Engineer Dexter was at fault. The signals that the bridge was open were properly displayed and he should have seen that the bridge was open.

Although some railroad enthusiasts have suggested that the *Orange* might still be on the bottom of the Hackensack River, she certainly would have had to have been removed during construction of the current drawbridge, if not sooner.

The most serious type of accident occurred on the Central of New Jersey in September of 1958. A commuter train from Bay Head ran a red signal indicating that the Newark Bay drawbridge had been opened. The train ran off the end of the open bridge and plunged into Newark Bay. Fortunately the first car of the train had been locked and was not occupied. This reduced casualties but even so 47 persons were killed and another 48 injured.

Sabotage was the cause of a Jersey Central Railroad 17-car freight train running off the end of the Newark to Kearny Point drawbridge over the Passaic on October 6, 1970. The bridge was on a secondary line that served industrial customers in Kearny. An unidentified person broke into the cab of a switching locomotive parked in Newark's riverside freight yard and managed to throw switches, couple together a 17-car train, and attach four additional locomotives. The train was then run off the opening of the drawbridge.

The bridge was normally left open at night so that ships could pass. All five locomotives and 15 of the 17 freight cars plunged into the river. The perpetrator was never caught and it was believed that he may have drowned after the locomotive fell in the river. The only certainty was that whoever was

Author's photograph

The powerful gearing system under the swing bridge at Gregory Avenue - Main Avenue is still visible under the span.

responsible knew a great deal about railroading, such as how to loosen the freight car brakes and how to operate the locomotive.

Many of the major highway bridges were constructed with enough clearance so that they would not have to open frequently, but this was not always the case. In 1936, it was reported that the Lincoln Highway Bridge over the Passaic River was obliged to open 48 times per day!

Chapter 10
The Port Expands

In Chapter 9, we saw how suburban development affected both commercial and recreational uses of the Hackensack and Passaic rivers. The second great influence that would transform both the lower reaches of the rivers and Newark Bay was the incredible expansion of the Port of New York. Between 1898 and 1913, foreign commerce in New York increased by 131% but available wharf space only increased by 25%. On any given day in 1914, there were an estimated 3,000 barges, tugs, scows, and floating derricks in the harbor. In addition, there were also between 1,500 and 2,000 railroad car floats in operation. The port would soon expand up the local rivers and onto the marshy shores of Newark Bay.

The River and Harbor Act of 1907 and 1927 (modified 1911, 1912, and 1930) provided the Passaic River with a channel 30 feet deep and 300 feet wide from Newark Bay to a point 3,000 feet north of the Lincoln Highway Bridge. From there to Congoleum Industries (a major linoleum manufacturer) in Kearny, the channel would be 20 feet deep and 300 feet wide. The channel also began to narrow and become shallower as it moved upriver. It would be 16 feet deep and 200 feet deep to the railroad bridge at Nutley, and finally 10 feet deep and 100 feet wide to the Eighth Street Bridge in the city of Passaic.

The River and Harbor Act of 1912, (modified 1922-1927, 1954, and 1966) provided for 16.3 miles of dredged channels in the Hackensack River. These would be 34 feet deep in rock, 32 feet deep in soft material. The channel would start at 400 feet wide near Newark Bay and narrow to 300 feet when it reached the Erie Lackawanna Railroad Bridge. A 25 foot deep turning basin would be provided here. The channel became progressively narrower and shallower the farther it moved upstream, 15 feet deep and 200 feet wide to Little Ferry, and finally 15 feet deep and 150 feet wide to the Court Street Bridge in Hackensack.

The River and Harbor Act of 1922, (later modified by the Acts of 1943, 1954, 1964, and 1975) provided for the main channel in Newark Bay and Port Elizabeth, 37 feet deep in rock, 35 feet deep in other material, and a 700 foot wide channel into Port Newark proper. Other channels into and out of the port areas were 800 to 900 feet wide.

Courtesy New Jersey Chamber of Commerce

This compact workboat was engaged in laying telephone cables under the Hackensack River in the late 1920s. She is typical of the small working vessels of the period.

Canal boats, barges, and lighters were common types of freighting vessels but the term "lighter" deserves special explanation. Traditionally a "lighter" is a small harbor craft. When an ocean-going ship was too heavily loaded to maneuver in the shallow waters of a port, the "lighters" would come out and take off cargo, making the ship lighter, and thus more buoyant. Sometimes this was only done to reduce the draft sufficiently so that the ship could reach the dock. In some very shallow ports, lighters were used exclusively to unload big ships. Some form of lighterage is still used in many if the world's ports. Because New York Harbor is so expansive, lighters were also used as intra-port, short-haul cargo vessels. Most railroads operating in the port had a fleet of these vessels to handle cargoes between the railhead and points along the shoreline. In the resulting "lighterage" system, "lighters" could be covered barges (these had a barn-like wooden superstructure that protected the cargo), ordinary barges, barge-mounted cranes (which also had deck space for cargo), or small steamboats equipped with cranes for cargo handling.

During the Depression in the 1920s and 30s, lighters were used to move cargoes directly from the harbor to the factories in the Dundee section of Passaic, adjacent to the Passaic Street Bridge. As the lighters were pushed upstream by tugboats, the tug's whistling to request drawbridges to open announced their progress. This served as a signal for men and boys to gather around the gates of the factory. Soon a foreman would appear and arbitrarily select 10 to 20 members from the hopeful crowd. Using hand trucks, they would then unload the vessel for 50 cents an hour, and if they did not work fast enough, they would not be picked again. If the tide was high, the unloading was easier, since the lighter's deck was level with the shore, but as the tide went down, the gangplank became steeper and the work was more difficult.

Author's Photograph

Three young men in a canoe are exploring the Passaic River upstream of the Acquakanonk Bridge site. The heavily industrialized Dundee section of the Passaic is visible in the background. Note the use of concrete to stabilize the river banks. In the past, the river would have been crowded with barges and lighters bringing freight to these factories.

Lighters and other small cargo craft were useful, but their presence alone on the Passaic and Hackensack rivers could not entirely relieve port congestion. That could only be accomplished by massive capital improvement projects.

During the year 1935 an estimated $106,891,591 worth of cargoes passed up and down the Passaic River. Incoming cargoes included fuel oil, gypsum, coal tar pitch, crude coal tar, plaster, fabrics, wool, steel, molasses, sand, lime, turpentine, rosin, and lumber. Ten tankers each day were required to handle the fuel oil, including one that made a daily trip all the way to Wallington, a distance of approximately 14 miles. Outgoing cargoes included clay, petroleum products, paint, calcium compounds, tallow, and alcohols. With Japan fighting a war in Manchuria and Italy and another war in Ethiopia, scrap metal exports were also rising. Many of the 8,000 ships, boats, and barges were engaged in local traffic with cargoes bound for New York, where they would be loaded onto ocean-going ships for export. Only about 6,500 tons were shipped overseas directly from Newark and only eight foreign flag vessels called at the city annually.

Ground was broken for what would eventually become Port Newark near Peddle Creek in 1913. A 20 foot deep channel, bulkheads, and two miles of railroad track were completed by 1915. The first ship to unload its cargo there was the four masted schooner *AJ West* with a load of mahogany from Manila.

On September 14, 1917, as a result of World War One, the Submarine Boat Company received an 18 million dollar contract to build 50 freighters at Port Newark. Although Port Newark was completely undeveloped, construction began immediately. Shops, warehouses, trolley tracks, and shipways quickly rose alongside Newark Bay. The first keel was laid on December 20, 1917. The

Courtesy U.S. Naval Historical Center

The USS Piave was launched at Federal Shipyards in December 1918. She was assigned to the Naval Overseas Transportation Service for trans-Atlantic but was wrecked near Deal, England, in January 1919.

Agawam was eventually launched on Memorial Day 1918. The work quickly picked up. The yard launched three ships simultaneously on July 4, 1918, and by Memorial Day 1919, the company's fifty-second ship slid down the ways.

Until taken over by the Port Authority in 1948, the port had only 14 usable deep sea berths. With the capital funds provided by the agency, the area continued to grow as a maritime center. In 1997, over 2,800 ships used the Port Authorities Marine Terminals, which also include facilities in Brooklyn, Staten Island, and Bayonne. Today the Port Newark and Port Elizabeth Marine Terminals cover 2,100 acres and handle more than one million containers annually.

The year 1917 also saw the Federal Ship Building Company chartered at Trenton. The company was a subsidiary of United States Steel which hoped to create a market for the steel and a means to bring it to overseas markets. The yard was constructed in Kearny facing the Hackensack River and stretching back towards the Passaic River. During the First World War, the yard constructed some 30 steel freighters totaling 288,000 deadweight tons and in

Courtesy New Jersey Chamber of Commerce

What appears to merchant ship is under construction at Federal Shipyards in this 1920s era photograph. Federal Shipyards was also active in the conversion of steam powered ships to diesel engines during this period.

the process became the third New Jersey shipyard among the country's most productive ten.

A government contract in 1933 assigned the shipyard to begin building Navy vessels at the height of the Great Depression. Among their other projects were a series of freighters, tankers, and passenger liners. One of these, the *Steel-Seafarer*, of the Isthmian Line, which was another U.S.S. subsidiary, was sunk in the Red Sea, an early casualty of World War Two.

During the Second World War, Federal employed 32,000 people around the clock. On one day in May 1942, it simultaneously launched four destroyers and four more auxiliary vessels, and to complete the day workers at the yard laid four keels. By 1943, a new ship was launched every 4½ working days.

Courtesy National Archives

The 1630-ton Gleaves *class destroyer,* USS McCalla *is shown on her delivery voyage from the Federal Shipyard in May 1942. Note the Federal Shipbuilding & Dry Dock Co. flag flying just below her starboard yardarm.*

Completed warships were sent to the Brooklyn Navy Yard to receive their armament and final outfitting. Ships from the Federal yards served in all theaters of the war. The *USS Kearny* was torpedoed in the North Atlantic and the *USS Juneau* was sunk in the Pacific. The *Juneau* is still remembered as the ship aboard which the five seamen, the now famous Sullivan brothers, were killed. The loss of so many members of one family at a single blow ended the Navy's practice of allowing brothers to serve aboard the same ship.

Courtesy National Archives

The USS Juneau was a 6,000-ton Atlanta class light cruiser. Here she is shown ready for launching in October 1941. Fitted out at the Brooklyn Navy Yard and commissioned in February 1942, she was damaged in the Naval Battle of Guadalcanal in November of 1942 torpedoed by a Japanese submarine. She sank rapidly and there were only 10 survivors.

Less noticeable, but just as essential, were the troopships and transports built at Federal. The transport ships were named for stars such as the *Andromeda, Castor, Centaurus, Diphda,* and *Libra,* while the P2-type troopships were named for military leaders like the *General John Pope* and the *General W.A. Mann.* A troop transport was described in October of 1943 as being like "a small city on the move." Their exact size was classified at the time but the Navy did say that they were among the largest transport ships ever constructed in the New York area. The single-funnel ships had sleek, knife-nosed hulls which were designed to outrun enemy warships and submarines. After the war, it was revealed that the P-2 troopships carried 5,142 men, measured 623 feet long, 76 feet wide, and had a top speed of 20.6 knots. Nicknamed "invasion specialists," their sole purpose was to get as many soldiers safely and quickly overseas as possible.

Courtesy US Navy History Center.

The USS General John Pope *was a P-2 type troop transport launched by Federal Shipyards in 1943. During World War Two she served throughout the Pacific Theater and was laid up after making five "Magic Carpet" trips to bring veterans home from the western Pacific. She was returned to active service in the both the Korean and Vietnamese conflicts before being transferred to the Maritime Administration's Reserve Fleet in 1970. The* USS General John Pope *is the last surviving member of this class and as of 2006 was in storage at Suisun Bay, California. While the Navy is aware of her historic status, there are no definite plans to use this ship as a museum.*

The troop ship designs were based on ocean liners, but unlike their civilian counterparts there were no portholes. All fresh air was provided by mechanical ventilation. The galleys were fitted with a machine nicknamed "Mrs. Moo," which blended butter, condensed milk, and water to create a drink that was alleged to taste remarkably like fresh milk. There were complete medical facilities aboard, including battle dressing stations. The smaller lifeboats held 75 men while the larger ones could accommodate 135 persons each.

Some of the transport ships built at Federal were transferred to civilian owners after the Second World War, and several were later employed during the Korean Conflict.

The first of many women who would work at Federal was hired in October of 1942. By this time many of the male shipyard workers had abandoned their jobs to serve in the military. Although men were still showing up regularly for the morning hiring line-up, there was a real shortage of skilled labor. Company officials estimated that about 15% of the jobs in the shipyards could be performed by women.

As a result, many area women took up the challenge and enlisted for work at the yards. Miss Dorothy Darmanin was an experienced pump-press operator when she started work at the Port Newark site, where she was trained to operate a drill press. Mrs. Neil Dennithorne, the wife of a machine shop worker at the Kearny yard, was a former silk mill worker. Mrs. Sophie Zaborowski was the mother of two, who trained to become a pipe-threader. She had formerly worked in the fur trade. Miss Betty Rogers, who had worked assembling mounts for radio tubes, was trained to operate a power hacksaw. Four other women, whose names were not mentioned in the press reports, were hired for the machine shop. Federal called their former Supervisor of Women, Isabel Kelly Roth, out of retirement to help train the new hires. Mrs. Roth had held the same position in the First World War at the Kearny yard.

Federal's impressive production record was sometimes marred by labor unrest and charges of corruption. The first serious labor difficulty was an extended strike which took place in the summer of 1941. The National Defense Mediation Board ordered the management to subscribe to a maintenance of membership clause. Such a clause requires all employees who are union members to remain in the union as long as the contract is in effect, however employees not in the union can't be forced to join. The unions representing Federal Shipyard workers objected to this clause and so the Navy commandeered the shipyard, on August 21st. President Roosevelt later ordered the yard returned to private management, on January 6, 1942, even though the dispute still had not been resolved. The union approved the maintenance of membership concession in a contract finally signed in May of 1942.

Minor labor disputes continued to plague the shipyards but there were no severe labor problems until the night of Thursday, October 14, 1943, when 6,000 night shift workers walked off the job to protest the dismissal of five union leaders. The unrest could be traced to an incident dating to August of that year. John Dempsey, then the president of Local 16 of the Industrial Union of Marine and Shipbuilding Workers, was removed from his post following charges that he was cooperating with the management against the interest of the union. Dempsey was later reinstated as the chair of the grievance committee. On Tuesday night, a group of five union committeemen staged a protest against Dempsey's reinstatement. When the committeemen were dismissed, the night shift walked off in protest. When the day shift arrived on Friday morning, about 1,100 workers stayed off the job, and it appeared that the strike would extend to the day shift. Local 16s Administrator, Gavin MacPherson, deplored the walkout and stated that the union would not sanction it. He and the five committeemen called for the union members to return to work. The committeemen also called upon the then US Senator Harry Truman to investigate conditions at the yard.

During the Second World War, men employed in the shipyard were exempt from the draft, and highly skilled jobs were illegally sold to unqualified men. In one instance an Army Air Force private from Brooklyn testified that he paid $500 for job as a skilled machinist (he was in fact a professional photographer). When his draft board rated the man as 1-A, his money was returned. Prosecutors contended that as many as 54 men purchased similar positions with their corresponding draft deferments.

In 1948, Federal Shipyards was sold to the US Navy for $2,375,000. The Navy did not plan to use the yard for either construction or repair, but instead planned to lease the property for civilian industrial use on the condition that the 11 shipways and other equipment would be available to the military should an emergency arise. With about 5,000 people about to be laid off, the shipyard unions loudly complained that US Steel was putting "profits ahead of patriotism." They argued that Congress had recently appropriated $100,000,000 for new ship construction and that US Steel had rejected contracts to build a new and badly needed fleet of oil tankers. The union further charged that US Steel had buried the wartime profits from the yard in its consolidated earnings statements, and then claimed that the yard was losing money.

On a rainy December 31, 1948, Captain William E. Sullivan, USN, superintendent of shipbuilding for the Third Naval District, took possession of the property during a brief noontime ceremony. The yard officially became the Navy Industrial Reserve Shipyard, Kearny, New Jersey, and was to be operated as an annex of the Brooklyn Navy Yard. It was hoped that the development of the site for civilian industrial use would provide employment for any laid off workers. The Navy also left the possibility open that the yard would be used for ship construction and repair either by the Navy or another civilian shipbuilder.

The shipyard remained under government control until 1964. The yard's subsequent closing was a devastating blow to the South Kearny area, but today the city still remains proud of the shipyard. Volunteers from the city's Museum Commission assembled an exhibit of memorabilia for display at Liberty State Park, and it was shown in the park during the summer of 1997. When a newspaper article erroneously stated that the *USS Juneau* was built in

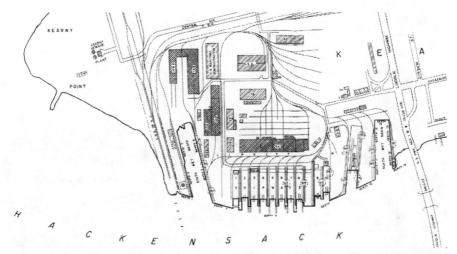

When this 1965 map was created, Federal Shipyards was owned by the Navy, but would soon be permanently closed.

Brooklyn, residents fired angry "letters to the editor" correcting the mistake. Several former employees helped to salvage records from the yard. Both the city library and Museum Commission have additional information in their collections and interested readers should contact them. Unfortunately, the Navy has been unable to provide the Kearny Public library with copies of the records from 1948 to 1964.

The Federal Shipyards area became an industrial park managed by the River Terminal Development Company. For a time, the slips and wharfs at Federal became the location for a ship breaking industry. The site still had five of the large traveling gantry cranes left over from the shipbuilding and servicing operations. These cranes had 92-foot booms and a combined lifting capacity of 100 tons. The shipyard also had their diesel-powered railroad cranes and crawler cranes. The railroad connections that once brought steel to the shipyard were now used to haul it out. The last use of water transportation at the site was during the 1970s when some of the scrap was loaded onto barges for removal.

After the ship breaking operations ceased in the 1980s the entire Federal Shipyard site was converted to other uses. Today it is used almost entirely by warehousing and distribution companies, none of which use water transportation.

During the 1920s and 30s, the coastwise sailing trade entered its last days. One of the final remaining four-masted schooners, the *Dustin C. Cressy*, came to Newark in 1928 with a cargo of lumber from Saint John's, Newfoundland.

Courtesy US Army Corps of Engineers

The mood of this 1978 photograph is suitably somber for the task of ship breaking at the former Federal Shipyards.

She also was carrying 6,000 cases and 500 kegs of illicit whiskey. The alcohol had been secretly transferred to the ship once she was out on the open sea. After an uneventful voyage south through Long Island Sound, the *Cressy* was towed into port, with neither the Coast Guard nor US Customs showing any interest in the ship. She docked at the Sears-Roebuck pier on Newark Bay where the lumber was unloaded. Under the cover of darkness, she was towed up the Passaic River to Harrison where the whiskey was briskly unloaded and transferred into waiting vans. The *Cressy* then returned to the Sears-Roebuck pier.

Everything to this point had proceeded flawlessly and the liquor was safely carried off. The captain, James Hanrahan, left the five-man crew alone on the ship, but the crew had not been paid and they grew restless and started to complain loudly. This created a disturbance on the waterfront, and the noise attracted the attention of Michael Sweeney, a customs agent, who became suspicious. When the captain returned he paid the crew off to quell the disturbance, but all six men were subsequently arrested and their vessel was seized.

The *Dustin C. Cressy* was later purchased by a group in Hackensack. Calling themselves the Junior Mariners, their intent was to convert her into a training ship. They did get her towed from Newark to Hackensack, but the vessel burned and sank in 1933. The charred remains are still visible behind the

Author's sketch

The Dustin C. Cressy was a fairly typical Maine-built schooner of the late 1800s. She would have looked something like this under sail.

Bergen Record building just south of the New York and the Susquehanna and Western Railroad bridge. With the sinking of the *Cressey*, the era of working sail on the river was over.

Yet another era was also drawing to a close. The pollution caused by all the development in region made boating, fishing, and swimming less attractive. Recreation suffered a decline well before the 1930s, first on the lower reaches of the rivers, and then farther north. Richard Hitt, an elderly yachtsman of the author's acquaintance, recalled the time before the Second World War when he and some friends set sail southward from Hackensack on a cruise. He vividly recalled sailing through filth and stench before reaching the open sea.

After the Second World War, there were more changes for the worse. In Chapter 8, we have seen how rapid land exploitation led to vastly accelerated erosion and silting and narrowing of the stream channel. In the process many toxic compounds and heavy metals became trapped in the sediment. The Meadowlands in particular became dumping grounds (this was nothing new, but the scale of it was) and the waterfront towns turned to the highways, ignoring and forgetting about the rivers.

Passage of the Clean Water Act in 1972 allowed the federal and state governments to control dumping and pollution. The cleansing action of time and tides began to clear the rivers. Species of birds and animals began returning to the Meadowlands. Cleaner rivers presented many challenges and opportunities. Land could now be set aside for recreation, or inappropriate development. Pollution could be monitored and controlled, or left totally unchecked. Individuals could once again explore and enjoy the river from boats, canoes, and walkways, or ignore the river.

The last chapter of this story is the tale of many individuals who rose to meet those challenges in a positive way.

Chapter 11
Benches Facing the River

In some of the waterfront parks lining the Passaic River, the benches have been turned around so they face away from the water. These serve as suitable symbols for the years of pollution and neglect of the waterway.

Commercial Navigation

At the time of this writing, commercial traffic on the Hackensack River is limited to the locale south of Hackensack. The Court Street Bridge in Hackensack is the official head of navigation. On the Passaic River, commercial traffic is limited to the vicinity around and immediately north of Newark, while on Newark Bay, Port Newark continues to serve container ships and tankers.

In 1960, the freight traffic between Newark Bay and the Hackensack River was estimated to be between 3 and 4 million tons annually. The Army Corps of Engineers calculated that in 1970, 5.6 million tons moved on the river, including one million tons of coal; 800,000 tons of sand, gravel, and stone; and 400,000 tons of heating oil and gasoline. There were smaller amounts of chemicals, crude tar oil, newsprint, scrap metals, and sewage sludge.

The navigable channel ran for 16.5 miles, varied between 100 and 400 feet wide, and was crossed by 17 railroad and highway bridges. Depths ranged from 36 feet in Newark Bay to 5 feet (at low tide) at Hackensack. Currents ranged from 4 to 6 knots. There were, according to William Cleary, President of the New York Towboat and Harbor Carriers Association, "some very tricky bends to it." The typical tugboats ranged from 85 to 100 feet in length and their barges were up to 312 feet long, 40 feet in beam, with a capacity of 5,000 tons.

The typical river towboat or barge of the second half of the twentieth century might be 65 to 75 feet in width, and its tow had to squeeze through

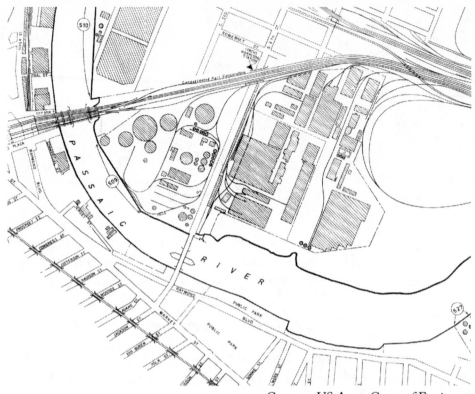

Courtesy US Army Corps of Engineers

The area of the Passaic River between Newark and Harrison, immediately upstream of the Harrison Reach, as it appeared in 1977. The multiple track railroad bridge over the Passaic is Amtrak's Northeast Corridor line between Boston, New York, Philadelphia, and Washington, DC. The Newark Fire Department's dock is located on the west bank just to the north of the area shown on this map.

510 Otis Elevator, fuel oil for plant consumption.
509 Public Service Harrison Gas Plant. This plant received fuel oil, kerosene, and naptha by barge. It shipped out tar by barge.
527 British Petroleum

bridge openings about 100 feet wide. The older bridges, where collisions were frequent, were especially worrisome. Captain Robert Markuske, who commanded a tug for McAllister Brothers Towing, explained in an interview conducted in 1972, that coming with the tide and advancing toward an open bridge was like "threading a needle with a runaway locomotive." He explained that currents tended to push the tow sideways so that passing the bridge was a "sort of wiggle through."

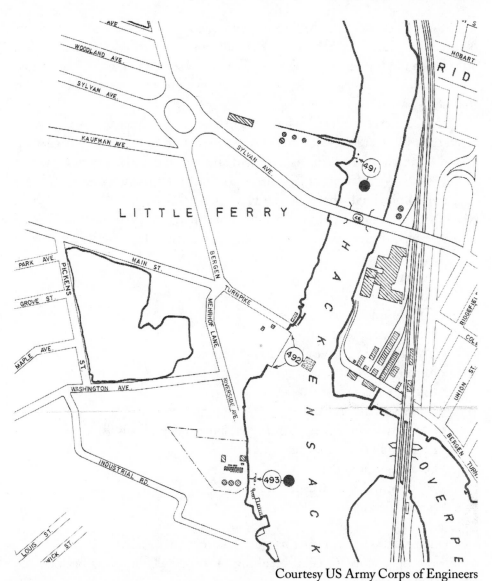

Courtesy US Army Corps of Engineers

Overpeck Creek in 1977 with the tracks and bridges of the New York Susquehanna and Western Railroad along the Hackensack's east bank.

491 Ameranda Hess, Little Ferry
492 Little Ferry Asphalt Corp.
493 R.K.D. Oil Corp.

Aside from the problems created by bridges, there were also recreational boatmen on the river ignorant of the rules of the road. William Sjovall, a 30 year veteran tug captain for Moran Towing, observed that when he signaled pleasure boats with his whistle, "they think you're blowing to say "Hello" and they start waving."

The 22 diesel powered Moran tugboats at the time averaged slightly more than 100 feet long with an average beam of 28 feet. They drew between 13 and 16 feet when fully loaded and had an average of 3100 horsepower.

The US Army Corps of Engineers port facilities inventory for 1978 listed 36 active commercial wharfs on the Hackensack River, and 37 on the Passaic River. These numbers did not include wharf space in Newark Bay. Broken down by type of cargo handled, the wharves on the Hackensack River were dedicated to

- Asphalt...1
- Bulk Cement...1
- Coal for plant consumption...2
- Coal Tar Products...1
- Construction Materials and Equipment...1
- Kerosene / Naptha...2
- Liquid Caustic Soda...2
- Liquids, Misc. Bulk...1
- Newsprint...1 (Bergen Record, dock never actually used)
- Packaged Food Products...1
- Petroleum products...19
- Sand Gravel and Crushed stone...6
- Scrap Metal...2

Wharves use for Mooring barges and other vessels...3

Mooring vessels for Ship breaking...4 (Federal Shipyards became the site of ship scrapping)

Note: Several of these wharves were used for more than one type of cargo. Thus the total number of cargo handling facilities is higher than the number of wharves.

On the Passaic River the wharf space broken down by types of cargo handled is as follows:

- Construction Materials and Equipment...1
- Fuel Oil for plant consumption...5
- Fuel Oil...4

- Kerosene / Naptha...3
- Loading Bunker Oil...2
- Liquids, Misc. Bulk...1
- Liquid sulfur...1
- Packaged Food Products...1...
- Petroleum products...12
- Petrochemicals...1
- Sand Gravel and Crushed stone...5
- Sludge...1
- Tallow...1
- Tar...1

Wharves use for Mooring barges and other vessels...4
Source: The Port of New York and New Jersey, Port Series No. 5, Revised 1978, US Army Corps of Engineers, United States Government Printing Office, 1978.

By 1999 the numbers of commercial users had declined on both rivers. On the Hackensack:
- Asphalt...1
- Coal for plant consumption...2
- Kerosene / Naptha...2
- Liquid Caustic Soda...2
- Petroleum products...4

Wharves use for Mooring barges and other vessels...1
Note: The wharves for handling coal, kerosene, and liquid caustic soda are all examples where one user has more than one wharf.

On the Passaic River:
- Cement...1
- Sulfuric acid...1
- Petroleum products...6
- Sludge...1
- Tallow...1

Wharves use for Mooring barges and other vessels...1
Source: The Port of New York and New Jersey, Port Series, Revised 1999, US Army Corps of Engineers, United States Government Printing Office, 1999

Courtesy US Army Corps of Engineers

The coal unloading dock at the Public Service Gas and Electric Company's Hudson Generating Station on the Hackensack River. This mid-1970s era photograph shows the unloading tower which could extend a 37-ton capacity bucket up to 42 feet from the shore.

One of the last of the northern Hackensack River barge customers was located immediately north of the Court Street Bridge. The Raia Industries cement plant accepted barge loads of sand and gravel until the late 1980s. Across the river, there is a dock behind the Bergen Record building. Although intended for barge loads of newsprint, it was never used, and it remains as a remnant of the past. Two other cement plants on the river also are served by barges. Several oil terminals dot the river's banks. Ameranda Hess has a fuel oil terminal in Secaucus and another in Bogota. The latter had formerly been the site of a yacht club and a Sea Scout base.

Coal and other fuels are still being brought to the electrical generating stations on the lower Hackensack River. The 1999 US Army Corps of Engineers Port Series listed the Hudson Generating Station as receiving coal by water, and it still does so today. The plant has an open air storage capacity of 300,000 tons. The channel is maintained at a depth of 30 to 35 feet off its 750-foot long wharf. At one time the plant was also receiving fuel oil by barge, but this dock was no longer in use in 1999. The Kearny Station also had rail and water connections for both coal and fuel oil. This

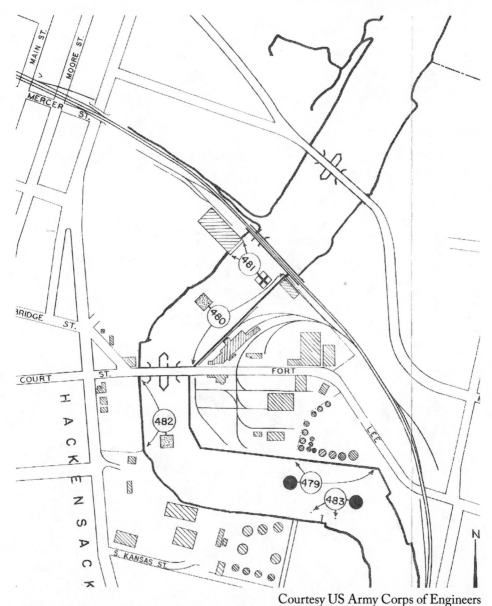

Courtesy US Army Corps of Engineers

Hackensack's commercial wharves as of 1977 included petroleum, stone, and newsprint for the Bergen Record. The newsprint dock was never used for this purpose however.

479, Ameranda Hess
480, Bergen Asphalt Company
481, Bergen Record Newsprint wharf
482, Tidewater Stone and Supply
483, Exxon USA

Courtesy US Army Corps of Engineers

The Marion Generating Station (also known as the Hudson Generating Station) and its water and rail connections for receiving coal (black square) and fuel oil (black circle) are shown on this 1965 map. The Public Service Gasworks site is to the south of the station. It was receiving coal deliveries by water at this time.

station was occasionally receiving barge loads of kerosene for plant consumption in 1999. A large pipeline connects the station to the Amarada Hess Newark Terminal. The Essex Generating Station on the Passaic River where Darrow Sage once encountered rum runners, was no longer receiving fuel by water in 1999.

At the Bergen County Utility Authority's sewage treatment plant there was a small set of pilings at the end of a large horizontal pipe. Here barges were loaded with treated sludge, which was then dumped into the Atlantic Ocean. New York and New Jersey were the last two states allowing this practice. Although a number of sewage plants recycled treated sludge as fertilizers, heavy metals from the region's many industrial plants are concentrated in the material and this prevented its use as compost or fertilizer. The utility ultimately found alternatives to its ocean dumping in the late 1980s, and the barge dumping ceased.

When one barge per week began running again, they carried sewage not to the open ocean but to the Passaic Valley Sewerage Commission's (PVSC) treatment plant on Newark Bay. This arrangement now allows Bergen County to use the Commission's excess treatment capacity. Moving sewage by barge

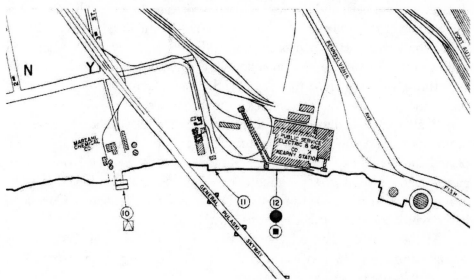

Courtesy US Army Corps of Engineers

The Kearny Generating Station of Public Service Electric and Gas is located on the Hackensack River upstream of the Pulaski Skyway Bridge. This 1965 map shows the plant receiving coal and fuel oil by water. The railroad not only delivers coal, the track leading into the station allows heavy equipment to be delivered directly to where it is needed.

avoids the need to connect the two plants by pipeline or convey stinking loads of raw sewage over the highways.

The original plant at the Newark site was built in 1924 and the last major addition to the current facility was a new Interim Sludge Dewatering Facility in 1991. The Passaic Valley Sewerage Commission plant can treat 330 million gallons per day to secondary standards (i.e. removal of all solids and destruction of pathogens but not the removal of nutrients.)

As an indication of the quantity of river traffic on the Hackensack, in 2005 the Lincoln Highway Bridge was opening between 20 and 30 times a month, according to Erin Phalon, a spokeswoman for the New Jersey Department of Transportation.

Governmental Cleanup and Pollution Control Initiatives

In 1932, a plan was proposed by the Passaic County Parks Commission to beautify the Passaic Riverfront in conjunction with road improvements being conducted in the area. Under this regional plan, part of the land between Newark and Paterson would be made "dry and usable" by means of flood gates, dams, new channels, and improvements to existing channels. Unfortunately the authors of this proposal did not specify how it might be funded. By the 1930s, the lower Passaic had been long suffering from severe pollution and had been the site of several serious floods. While not the first to realize that something had to be done for the river, the Parks Commission did develop one of the earliest serious regional clean-up proposals.

Real progress had to wait until the 1970s, when the state and federal governments created environmental protection agencies and specific laws were passed addressing clean water issues. At that time the Passaic River was regarded as the second-most polluted river in the country. The dubious distinction of the most polluted river is usually reserved for Cleveland's Cuyahoga River, which ignominiously caught fire in 1969.

At the time the Federal Clean Water Act was passed in 1972, it was estimated that the Hudson-Raritan estuary was receiving nearly two million cubic meters of raw sewage every day.

The New Jersey Department of Environmental Protection and Energy began maintaining a monitoring system for all of the state's waterways. They established a network of about 110 freshwater monitoring points statewide. The agency has been joined in this effort by a loose coalition of academic institutions, citizen groups, federal agencies, and community volunteers.

The large number of participants who began to study the region's waterways was to some extent the result of the proximity of several universities in the area. The area's population density also gave it the political clout necessary to support such sustained efforts. Many university researchers have become involved because they realized that many other urban areas had similar water pollution problems, and what could be learned on the Passaic and Hackensack rivers could be applied throughout the world.

One of the first discoveries made prior to 1982 was that high levels of PCB's and certain pesticides (primarily chlordane) were present in finfish taken from the region's tidal waters. Recreational fishermen were cautioned to limit their consumption of fish taken from the tidal areas of the Passaic, Hackensack, and Raritan rivers, as well as Newark Bay. Commercial fishing was totally banned in these waters. Because of high levels of dioxin, the state has prohibited consumption of all finfish and shellfish taken from the lower Passaic River. This ban has been extended to striped bass and blue crabs taken from the tidal Hackensack River, Newark Bay, Kill Van Kull, and Arthur Kill. In the early 1990s, a ban was also placed on the harvesting of Newark Bay's blue claw crabs (the favorite catch in those waters), due to high levels of dioxins and PCBs. The crabs were so badly contaminated that it was calculated that a person could safely eat only one crab every 20 years. When one scientist went to measure the dioxin concentration in crabs, he was shocked to find that it was higher than what his laboratory instruments were designed to measure!

Despite the warnings, people continued to eat fish from these waters. In response the New Jersey Department of Environmental Protection created the Toxic Crab Outreach Program in 2002. The program conducts an average of six public courses each year. Partner agencies and local organizations have also conducted public programs as part of the outreach, and this has allowed the department to reach many additional anglers.

Public education is also the goal of the Passaic Valley Sewerage Commissioners' Education and Outreach Program. Full time staffers teach grammar school children about the effects of pollution on the Passaic River. The program is available in the 47 municipalities served by the commission. A typical school visit includes an hour-long presentation on pollution prevention and floatables control. Commission staff members create all of the materials used in the programs, including videos, coloring books, games, and models.

The cartoon mascot of the program is "Messy Marvin," a young boy who takes on a journey on a polluted waterway and learns how his own actions impact the river. The program has been presented to over 25,000 students in more than 300 schools.

Messy Marvin and the educational outreach are part of a larger Passaic River restoration effort. In 1998, the commissioners initiated the Passaic River/Newark Bay Restoration Program. The program combines shoreline clean-ups, floatables removal, and clean-up efforts with the assistance of Sewage Commission employees. The restoration program seeks to promote the recreation and continued safe economic use of Newark Bay, the Passaic River, and its tributaries.

These restoration efforts work as partnerships between volunteer organizations and the Sewage Commission. In a stream clean up, a community organization will provide volunteer labor while the Commission will provide logistical support and removal of the trash. Since the program's inception there have been more than 250 shoreline clean-ups, which removed over 1,000 tons of litter and debris. Local municipalities may request an "in-house" clean-up with the help of the Commission's employees.

In 1999, floatables removal began with the purchase of a trash skimmer vessel. Financed with state grant monies and operated by the Commission, the *S.V. Newark Bay* patrols the Passaic River and Newark Bay scooping up trash and driftwood. The Newark Bay is a 50-foot long twin hull vessel with an 11-foot beam built by United Marine International. She only draws 17" when empty and 26" when loaded. Her capacity is 700 cubic feet of trash.

Photograph by Paul Lerin

Passaic Valley Sewerage Commission's dock on Newark Bay is home to the skimmer boats. The smaller S.V. Passaic River *is tied up at the wharf. The small motorboat is used by the Commission for environmental research and monitoring.*

A second, smaller vessel was added to the program in 2001. The *S.V. Passaic River* is 32 feet long, with an 8 foot beam. Her loaded draft is only 20 inches and her capacity is 120 cubic feet. The *S.V. Passaic River* is able to operate in shallower waters and more cramped environments than the *S.V. Newark Bay*. Both skimmer vessels operate from Newark Bay north to the head of navigation, but the river clean ups are organized in communities throughout the sewage district.

Vessels like the skimmer boats are required on the Passaic River because of the influx of storm water pollution. Every time there is rain or snowmelt, local rivers fill with litter and debris washed into them from storm sewers or streets. While floatables are unsightly and threatening to wildlife, there are many more invisible pollutants in storm runoff which threaten the entire ecological health of the rivers.

There are still a number of combined sewer overflows in the Passaic and Hackensack river basins. Combined sewer overflows (or CSO's) are antiquated waste water systems designed to handle both sewage wastes and stormwater. The pipes are constructed so that in periods of normal flow all waters are transported to a treatment plant, and during periods of heavy flows, excess water is drained out of the system and into nearby rivers. A CSO system can result in waterways being contaminated with high bacteria levels as well as runoff from streets and roads.

In areas like the Lower Passaic River basin, where industrial plants and other waste generators are hooked up to the sewers, CSO outfalls have been found to be contaminated with a range of chemicals including toxic metals, polycyclic aromatic hydrocarbons (polycyclic aromatic hydrocarbons or PAHs are among the carcinogenic compounds found in cigarette smoke), polychlorinated biphenyls (PCBs), pesticides, and other organic chemicals. CSO's allow these materials to be washed into the river where they are incorporated into the sediments.

The good news is that there has been considerable effort expended to separate sewage and runoff within utility systems and most CSO's are not expected to be in operation much longer.

Even without sewage mixed into it, stormwater overspill remains a serious threat to the Hackensack and Passaic Rivers. The problem is most acute on the Passaic, where there are more heavily industrialized sites, especially around Newark, and in densely populated areas downstream of Paterson. When a property near the river has any sort of pollutants in the soil, erosion washes them into the river and the contaminated sediments contribute to the already overburdened environment.

With several EPA Superfund sites along near its banks, the Passaic River is constantly being re-charged with contaminated sediments. An example of this process is the Bayonne Barrel and Drum site in Newark, New Jersey. This facility washed and reconditioned chemical storage drums from the 1940s to 1982. The Harbor Project of the New York Academy of Sciences calculated that soil being eroded from the site annually carried off between one and nine grams of dioxin. (This may not seem like a great amount but there is no known "safe dose" or "threshold" below which dioxin will not cause cancer.) The Academy of Sciences recommended that at any site where erosion of polluted soils is likely (what environmental scientists call remobilization), preventive measures like stormwater diversion structures, silt and sediment barriers, and settling basins should be used. The exposed areas may also be covered.

Urban stormwater runoff is often reported as the second most frequent cause of surface water pollution in the United States, and as a result the State of New Jersey enacted the Municipal Stormwater Regulation Program (MSRP) in 2004. This regulatory program grew out of the US EPA's stormwater rules of 1999. The New Jersey regulations affect 560 municipalities, 77 public complexes, and 33 highway agencies. In the entire Passaic River basin, there are three watershed management areas, five counties, and 118 regulated municipalities

Each "entity" affected by the rules (municipalities, large university campuses, golf courses, industrial sites, and others) is issued a permit by the New Jersey Department of Environmental Protection. The permittee is then required to prepare a stormwater program which includes a written Stormwater Pollution Prevention Plan, a Post-Construction Stormwater Management in New Development and Redevelopment Plan, as well as a public education component. Pollution prevention activities might include better controls on the improper disposal of waste, elimination of unlawful connections to storm sewers, mapping of outfalls, and control of floatables. The DEP hopes that this program will greatly alleviate the non-point source pollutants entering New Jersey's rivers.

Old landfills in the Hackensack Meadowlands are another source of pollution into the rivers. Water percolating through the layers of trash becomes contaminated and then leaches into the environment. Most of the modern landfills have engineering controls to prevent the loss of leachate but the older ones require remediation. A more complete description of this process is found in the section about Newark in Chapter 7.

The overall results of the Hackensack River research have been generally encouraging. A study by the Meadowlands Commission, Rutgers University, and the New Jersey Institute of Technology was completed in 2007. A comparison of results of metals analysis from research in 1987 and 2007 shows that the amounts of cadmium, lead, chromium, copper, lead, nickel, zinc, and arsenic are indeed decreasing. The only bad news is that at 2.9 parts per million, mercury levels remain high. The Meadowlands Commission attributes these mercury levels to leaching from the former Ventron/Velsicol chemical plant near Berry's Creek. Approximately 160 tons of waste was buried on that site between 1929 and 1974. Although the waste and contaminated soils were removed in 1990, further clean up efforts have been stalled by litigation.

On the Passaic River, the most prominent Federal efforts of recent years have been the Lower Passaic River Study Area, which was followed by the CARP program (Contaminant Assessment and Reduction Program.) The Lower Passaic River Study Area was defined as an area from one mile south of its junction with the Second River, which is located in northern Newark, extending six miles into Newark Bay to the abandoned Conrail Railroad Bridge. The study is primarily an EPA project, although the U.S. Army Corps of Engineers and the National Oceanographic and Atmospheric Administration [NOAA] are assisting the EPA. Volunteers from AmeriCorps, the federal government's domestic national service organization for young men and women, have worked on environmental sampling. On the state level, the New Jersey Department of Environmental Protection and Energy (NJDEP) is also involved.

In establishing the Lower Passaic River Study Area, the EPA had three goals. First, determine the location and concentrations of the hazardous substances in the sediments of the Passaic River Study Area. Secondly, to identify human and animal populations at risk. Thirdly, to determine where the contamination is moving within the study area.

The CARP program is an expanded sampling and assessment program. It is funded by the Port Authority of New York and New Jersey and performed by the states of New York and New Jersey, with cooperation from EPA Region II, the Hudson River Foundation, US Army Corps of Engineers, the New Jersey Harbor Dischargers Group (NJHDG), and the Passaic Valley Sewerage Commissioners, the lead agency for the NJHDG.

The Passaic Valley Sewerage Commissioners worked with the Great Lakes Environmental Center on sampling and measuring a wide range of contaminants in treated waste water, stormwater and combined sewer overflows. The Stevens Institute of Technology assisted the program by sampling and measuring contaminant concentrations in all New Jersey rivers that drain into the harbor.

Ultimately, the data collected by the CARP program will be employed by the EPA and the states of New York and New Jersey to evaluate the current water and sediment quality throughout the harbor and its major tributaries. It will also be used to develop predictive water and sediment quality computer models that can be used to make water and sediment management decisions.

The impetus behind these studies was the discovery of pesticides, dioxin, PCB's, heavy metals, and other hazardous substances in Passaic River sediments. Although many corporations which used, produced, and sometimes discharged these materials have been located in the study area for many years, one particular contaminant, dioxin, is especially worrisome. Dioxin can be formed as a byproduct to many industrial chemical processes including the manufacture of herbicides and pesticides. The Diamond Shamrock Chemicals Company's (now Occidental Chemical Corporation) Diamond Alkali plant on the Passaic River was the site of pesticide manufacturing in the 1950s and 1960s. According to the EPA, during that time, contaminated waters were piped from the plant directly into the Passaic River.

Courtesy NOAA

Federal scientists are shown conducting sediment sampling at the Diamond Alkali Site in Newark, New Jersey. The sediments in this portion of the Passaic River are regarded by many scientists as among the most highly contaminated anywhere in the United States.

The area where the Diamond Shamrock plant was located is known as Harrison Reach. This short stretch of the Passaic River, where it briefly flows in an east-west direction, is widely considered to be the most polluted section of one of the most polluted rivers in the United States. The writer and historian Stephen Marshall has identified a long list of pollution sources along both banks of the reach. The 1830s saw the construction of railroad tracks along the northern riverbank and the Morris Canal on the south side of the river. Most of the northern riverbank is characterized by transportation facilities, including the Port Authority Trans Hudson railroad system (PATH), New Jersey Transit's Meadowlands Maintenance Shops, and the New Jersey Turnpike.

Industrial pollution began in the 1850s when Alfred and Edwin Lister established a factory for grinding animal bones into fertilizer. The Army Corps of Engineers began dredging the lower Passaic River in the 1870s and this encouraged more industrial development (and pollution) along The Reach and upriver. As on the Hackensack River, construction of dams and reservoirs along the Pequannock River and other tributaries of the Upper Passaic diverted large amounts of fresh water and altered the salinity gradient of the Lower Passaic.

Wetlands bordering the southern riverbank were filled in by the Manufacturer's Branch of the Central Railroad of New Jersey during the 1890s for the specific purpose of creating new industrial sites. The industries on or near Lister Avenue included the Fiske Brothers oil refinery across the street from the Lister Agricultural Chemical Works. The A.J. & J.O Pilar Company purchased buildings for their textile and leather dye manufacturing at the corner of Lister Avenue and Chapel Street in 1927. These buildings were formerly occupied by a manufacturer of lead batteries.

During Prohibition, the buildings that had housed the Lister Agricultural Chemical Works were taken over by bootleggers who operated a large distillery. The facility included two 50,000-gallon stills, 14 fermentation vats capable of holding 25,000 gallons of molasses and mash, and six 40,000-gallon receiving vats for molasses. Prohibition agents raiding the plant in February of 1932 found 15,000 gallons of alcohol. Pipes led from the receiving vats to a dock on the Passaic River where barges of molasses were unloaded. The plant even had its own narrow gauge railroad for internal transportation. An alarm system of red and green lights was controlled by push buttons at the plant gate. This system was apparently working as no arrests were made during the raid.

Sometime in the mid to late 1930s, chemical engineer Leon Kolker selected 80 Lister Avenue as the site of his Kolker Chemical Works. During the 1940s it became one of the nation's largest producers of DDT. In 1951 the site was acquired by the Diamond Alkali Corporation and became the site of

Agent Orange manufacture during the Vietnam War.

All of this would be bad enough but as we have seen in Chapter 7, the movement of sediments spreads the contamination throughout the harbor system. Although the region's waterways are becoming increasingly cleaner today, scientists believe that certain areas with large amounts of polluted sediments are always re-introducing fresh contamination. Sediments traveling from the lower Passaic River are believed to be the source of 80% of the dioxin in Newark Bay.

The EPA's analytical laboratory and the environmental consulting firm Malcolm Pirnie participated in an extensive geochemical evaluation of the historical data relating to contamination in the Lower Passaic River. Both the vertical and horizontal extent of sediment contamination was mapped out and contamination sources were identified. This study also included an underwater 15.5-mile side-scan sonar survey conducted in 2005 and extensive studies of the historical navigational charts. Additional data was also provided by the government and academic institutions, including the Lamont-Doherty Earth Observatory of Columbia University and the Rensselaer Polytechnic Institute. Estimates of the total volume of contaminated sediments in the Passaic River range from 2.8 million cubic yards to 8 million cubic yards. Sediment cores have shown that many contaminants have no known "bottom," indicating additional contamination lies below the areas studied.

The evaluation led to a number of important conclusions regarding the Lower Passaic River. Among the more important was that there was little evidence of "hot spots" areas where remedial dredging and clean up efforts could be focused. Because of tidal mixing and sediment re-suspension, there are broad areas of contamination more than a mile in length and nearly the width of the river. This is a serious set back for those river clean up plans which were made under the assumption small areas could be cleaned up while leaving the uncontaminated portions of the riverbed alone.

At the 2004 Passaic River Symposium at Montclair State University, Lisa Baron of the New Jersey Department of Transportation, Office of Maritime Resources, presented a paper on the Lower Passaic River Restoration Feasibility Study. Among her most important announcements was that a demonstration dredging project in the Harrison Reach for the purpose of pollution remediation would commence in the summer of 2005. About 5,000 cubic yards of material would be removed from a one-half square mile area of the Harrison Reach.

The pilot dredging project would evaluate dredging technology performance, monitor sediment transport, and determine the effectiveness of decontamination technologies. Hopefully a full scale project would follow.

Preparations for the dredging lasted over two years and included detailed hydrographic surveys which resulted in a three-dimensional mathematical model of the river flows and tidal currents, the position and movement of the salt wedge, and its variation of salinity and temperature with depth.

Courtesy Lisa Baron, NJDOT

The Passaic River remediation project was closely monitored by a number of environmental agencies. The large white boat to the left of the dredging barge is the USEPA's research vessel.

The results of the dredging operation were reported in the December 2005 issue of the journal *World Dredging Mining & Construction*. The consortium of agencies that performed the dredging project included the New Jersey Department of Transportation, Office of Maritime Resources (local sponsor for the overall Feasibility Study), US Environmental Protection Agency (which provided analytical chemistry services and was the lead agency on the decontamination technologies), the US Fish and Wildlife Service (which provided a shuttle vessel and field staff), Rutgers University (conducted the water quality monitoring program), and the US Army Corps of Engineers (which provided vessels, field personnel, and dredging construction oversight).

Courtesy *World Dredging Magazine*

The Passaic River remediation dredging project was of great interest to the civil engineering community because of the large number of innovative technologies it employed. These included special position monitoring sensors on the dredge equipment, as well as sediment decontamination systems.

The private firms participating in the study were Earthtech, Inc. (NJDOT's prime consultant), Malcolm Pirnie, and AquaSurvey (which conducted many of the preparatory surveys and provided support vessels.) The Passaic Valley Sewage Commissioners made their docks available for vessel and equipment storage.

Critical to any future dredging projects would be evaluating the performance of the dredging equipment for productivity and its ability to precisely remove the material at predetermined depths and bottom locations. The equipment had to do this without allowing any material to fall back into the river to be re-suspended.

The dredge prism consisted of three cut lines approximately 300 ft long at elevations of 11 ft, 13 ft, and 15 ft below mean low water. The river depth at the project area was about 10 to 15 feet at low tide. The operation removed about 1,000 cubic yards in a 12 hour workday. The dredgers were equipped with a custom-manufactured 8.0 cubic yard mechanical clamshell bucket. For precision placement, the bucket was fitted with a depth sensors while other sensors measured its penetration into the river bottom which prevented overfilling. Closure sensors ensured that the bucket was fully closed prior to hoisting it up from the river bottom.

While the dredging took place, four smaller vessels were collecting water samples for comparison with the background or pre-dredging water quality. There were also six fixed monitoring stations. This ensured that the levels of pollution in the river were not being increased by the dredge activities. Post dredging monitoring measured how quickly the river returned to its normal conditions.

Removal of the sediments was only the first half of the project. They were loaded onto barges and transported to the Bayshore Recycling's facility on the Raritan River in Keasbey, New Jersey. Because the sediment could be dredged faster than it could be decontaminated, Bayshore brought a 730-foot Great Lakes bulk freighter, the *Valgocen*, to the site to use as a floating storage facility.

The *Valgocen* (officially christened the *Algocen*) was launched in 1968 for the Algoma Central Corporation at Sault Ste. Marie, Ontario. She is a traditional styled straight deck bulk carrier typical of the Great Lakes powered by 12-cylinder 2,000 b.h.p. diesel engines with a single screw. She was also equipped with an 800 h.p. bow thruster. The ship has 6 holds capable of holding just under 30,000 tons of bulk cargo. Her usual cargoes were grain and iron ore with occasional shipments of cement. She was laid up in Montreal in January of 2005. After being renamed and registered under the Panamanian flag, she was towed to New Jersey by the *Atlantic Oak*, and arrived in Keasbey on August 3, 2005.

It should be stressed that the treatment technologies used for decontaminating the Passaic River sediments from Harrison Reach were not applied to the Newark Bay dredge spoils. The two projects were completely separate and they used different approaches to treatment.

The Bio-Genesis plant used a patented sediment washing technology. Both metal and organic contaminants were stripped from the sediment particles using a combination of impact forces generated by high pressure water jets and a special biodegradable detergent. The end product was a manufactured soil that could be used in landscaping and other land-based applications.

The other approach to sediment decontamination was thermal destruction. A smaller portion of the sediments were incinerated by the Endesco Clean Harbors Corporation with their Cement- Lock thermal destruction technology. The kiln was erected at the International-Matex Tank Terminal in Bayonne. The Cement-Lock thermal destruction technology employs a rotary kiln operating at temperatures up to 2,600 F. Even at this high temperature, the sediments will not melt, so proprietary additives help lower the melting point and convert the sediments to liquid glass.

Any toxic gases released during the melting are fed to a combustion chamber where they are incinerated at high temperature. A scrubber system removes any particulates or acid gases from the exhaust stream.

The molten mixture is rapidly cooled which "locks in" the organic contaminants. The resulting material is a glassy, granular product called Ecomelt. The Ecomelt is ground and blended with Portland cement to produce construction grade blended cement. Once the cement hardens, the contaminants are tightly locked into the solids and will remain there even if the cement cracks or breaks apart.

Although there are a great many individuals who participated in the project, special mention should be made of Eric Stern of the United States EPA and Lisa Baron of the New Jersey DEP for their leadership in getting the project underway and encouraging and engaging the participation of the private sector.

Another approach to remediation is the use of plants and bacteria to remove toxic materials from the environment. The Gaia Institute, a non-profit research institute dedicated to sustainable development, has proposed developing a Green Port demonstration project for the Passaic River using bioremediation technologies.

Salt marsh plants can normally help remove a wide range of organic compounds and even heavy metals from the environment, but in the lower Passaic River these botanic environments have largely disappeared. Even if they could be restored, the roots would not reach far enough into the sediments to remove the deeply buried pollutants. The Gaia Institute project would begin by adding additional carbon to the sediments that will establish the anaerobic conditions that allow certain types of bacteria to break down the dioxins. The riverbank and tidal flats would next be replanted with grasses that will help remove the shallower contamination while at the same time providing wildlife habitat. Riverside industries can continue to have the transportation benefits, because the plans call for the cargo handling facilities to be moved onto floating platforms moored in the river.

But one big question remains. Who will pay for all of this?

Since the establishment of the current environmental laws, the goal has been that the "polluter pays." Yet in an environment as complex as the Passaic River where there were literally hundreds of industries, assigning responsibility is an extremely complex task. The single exception to this generalization is dioxin where there is wide agreement that the Diamond Shamrock site is the single most significant source on the river.

Occidental Chemical, the successor company on the site, has resisted demands that it pay for any dredging and remediation. The company did sign an agreement to conduct a study that would augment the "Passaic River Restoration Initiative" by expanding the analysis of how the dioxin contamination has spread through the river and into Newark Bay, as well as possible methods of remediation.

Opponents to the plan describe it as a taxpayer bailout and an excuse to delay substantial action. The New York / New Jersey Baykeeper Association leads the opposition to the proposal. In cooperation with other environmental groups the Baykeeper brought suit against Occidental which would force them to pay for an independent study followed by an actual cleanup of the sediments.

Speaking at the Second Passaic River Symposium at Montclair State University, Baykeeper Executive Director Andrew Willner said that if the federal government agrees to Occidental's plan for more studies, "They are putting the fox in charge of the hen house."

The EPA had already conducted its own study of the Passaic River from Newark Bay to Dundee Dam, when it was announced that a consortium of 73 corporations would be conducting another study whose purpose was to characterize the pollutants and develop clean up strategies. These companies had been identified as being responsible for pollution in the Lower Passaic and under the Federal Superfund Law, they are responsible for cleaning it up. The study would last for several years and any actual clean up is not expected to begin until 2012 at the earliest.

While it may be argued that the responsible parties have the right to conduct their own study, a number of environmental advocacy groups have seen this as little more than a delaying tactic. Ella Fillppone of the Passaic River Coalition flatly stated that "We need to start dredging this river." New Jersey Department of Environmental Protection Commissioner Lisa Jackson took pains to point out that her agency was not asked to help negotiate the agreement in which the EPA allowed the study. According to Jackson, the EPA should be focused on going after the companies responsible for the dioxin in the lower Passaic. She feared that the new study would provide polluters with "ammunition to use against us." The results of the study might be used to argue that the river was too polluted to clean or that the number of responsible parties was larger than the 73 companies already identified.

What characterizes the clean up and remediation efforts on the Passaic River during the 1990s and into the twenty-first century is the emphasis on comprehensive and coordinated solutions. Government agencies are not only coordinating their efforts. They have formed partnerships with the academic community and citizen groups. There has also been an emphasis to try to understand the New York Harbor estuarine system as a whole and the associated role that the Passaic River plays in it.

This regional approach to environmental action has been used in the Hackensack Meadowlands since 1969. The New Jersey legislature recognized the potential of the area as both an environmental asset to New Jersey and as prime real estate. They created the Hackensack Meadowlands Environmental Commission (HMDC.) Since its creation in 1969, the commission has tried to balance economic development with wetlands protection and preservation. They began by creating a master plan for the 32 square mile (20,480 acres) district and attempted to direct development. Originally intended to be islands of office spaces, residential towers, and recreational spaces linked by floating taxis, the somewhat utopian plans have been scaled back. In its first two decades, the commission had been able to attract over 1,800 companies to the district and has created more than 44,000 jobs. In large part the success has been attributable to good planning and strict land use controls. For example, someone building an office tower would be guaranteed that no one else could put a dump next door. In 2005, Rutgers University reported that there were 9,322 companies operating in the region employing more than 154,000 workers.

At the time that the commission was created in 1969, the area was receiving 11,000 tons of trash a day from New York City and northern New Jersey. The stench was unbearable, and during the dry summer months uncontrollable trash fires would sometimes burn for weeks on end.

Since the inception of the HMDC, the number of regulatory agencies with jurisdiction over wetlands has grown. (The HMDC is one year older than the United States Environmental Protection Agency or USEPA.) In 1988, the HMDC began revising its master plan. As a consequence, a great deal of work had to be devoted to reconciling the conflicts and inconsistencies between the existing master plan and the federal regulations passed since its inception. The result was that the HMDC entered into a cooperative effort with the Corps or Engineers, New Jersey Department of Environmental Protection and Energy (NJDEPE), and EPA to create a special district. The need for the district was more apparent in light of continued development pressures. Also, potential solutions were still not being found for the continued degradation of both the land and the water quality.

The U. S. Environmental Protection Agency has created a Meadowlands Special Area Management Plan (SAMP). It considers the area as a complete watershed in order to achieve "integrated environmental protection." As defined by the plan, the district contains approximately 8,500 acres of wetlands, and 11,000 acres of upland. This is about half of the historic wetland area and slightly smaller than the 32 square miles covered by the original HMDC plan. Even so, it still includes much of the Hackensack River's lower watershed. Of course, most of the upland areas have already been developed. The EPA immediately recognized that despite the landfills, agricultural and mosquito control drainage, and alteration of the water flows by tidal gates, the Meadowlands are still valuable to fish and wildlife, particularly migrating birds. More than 260 bird species are known to use the Meadowlands for at least some portion of their life history and at least 60 species nest there. It is also used as an over-wintering habitat for numerous water fowl and raptor species. In addition, the Meadowlands still supports reptile and fur trapping. And while the Hackensack River is still closed to fishing for human consumption, it does provide habitat for estuarine and freshwater fishes.

In order to better evaluate these wetlands as a whole and to provide guidance for decision making, the U. S. Environmental Protection Agency (EPA), the New York District Army Corps of Engineers (Corps), the HMDC, the U.S. Fish and Wildlife Service (FWS), the New Jersey Department of Environmental Protection (NJDEP), and the National Marine Fisheries Service (NMFS) undertook a joint study to develop an Advanced Identification

(AVID) of the Meadowlands. These agencies evaluated 92% of the District's wetlands. The found that approximately 88% are generally unsuitable for fill, 2-3 % are potentially suitable for fill, and approximately 9% of the wetlands in the district are of indeterminate value as landfill sites.

Six different land-use scenarios were evaluated to see which would best accommodate the projected human needs for additional land. Five scenarios examined how development and redevelopment could be confined: how the uplands could be redeveloped, or if new construction could be confined to specific growth centers, highway corridors, areas of dispersed development, and even out-of-district development. The sixth scenario was called "no-action," which was defined as a continuation of the existing master plan. Not surprisingly, none of these six alternatives met the needs of additional land use and protection of the wetlands. The solution was to encourage construction outside of the district and restrict it within the district to projects with the lowest impact.

The draft plan proposed 2,200 acres of land for development, including 842 acres of wetlands. A mitigation program would enhance more than 3,400 acres of existing wetlands so that there would be no net loss to wildlife habitat or water quality. Permanent preservation through zoning, deed restrictions, and conservation easements would protect the district's remaining acres of wetlands.

Over time the SAMP plan proved awkward because it was "trying to please too many masters," according to the commission. A new planning process had to be implemented, which would bring together the large number of interested parties, municipalities, environmentalists, the business community, and citizens. The resulting Meadowlands Master Plan was the product of public hearings at both the commission's offices and in two municipalities. The public was encouraged to participate, and final review of the draft plan was done with their comments in hand. The goal of the resulting Meadowlands Master Plan is to preserve wetlands and open space while allowing for the redevelopment of older properties.

As the region's needs have changed the role of the commission has evolved. Speaking in 2001, Alan J. Steinberg, Executive Director of the Meadowlands Commission, summed up the process,

> In the 1970s we brought order to the chaos of illegal dumping in the district and stopped the growth of additional landfills being built on wetlands. By the mid-1980s we brought an end to the disposal of solid waste coming to the Meadowlands from

nearly two-thirds of New Jersey's communities. Our concentration in the 1980s was planned development and infrastructure improvement, and when Governor Whitman took office, our focus turned to environmental improvement and wetlands and open space acquisition.

To reflect the shift from promoting new development to open space preservation and environmental stewardship, the HMDC was renamed the New Jersey Meadowlands Commission in August of 2001.

The headquarters of the commission is located at the Hackensack Meadowlands Environment Center. This center is located at DeKorte State Park in Lyndhurst and is open to visitors. Perched above Kingsland Marsh, the center offers visitors exhibits relating to the estuary's wildlife and ecology. They can observe birds and also view the Manhattan skyline from the glass enclosed deck.

Author's photograph

The pavilion built over the marsh is used for public programs and as a bird observatory at the Meadowlands Commission Headquarters.

191

The on-site laboratory is certified by the Department of Environmental Protection. It is operated as an ongoing monitoring facility for the marsh's surface water, biological health, and groundwater. The laboratory also monitors the large landfills to measure the impact of leachate decontamination. The facility provides opportunities for student interns and graduate research. Scholars are also invited to conduct their own investigations using the laboratory's facilities.

The scientific study of the Meadowlands is considered important because there are other urban wetlands throughout the world. Just as on the Passaic River, scientists hope to apply the lessons learned in New Jersey to other locations. The leader in this scientific effort is the Meadowlands Environmental Research Institute, which grew out of and expanded on the activities of the original commission laboratory. Projects have included air and water quality monitoring, wetland plants and ecology, the effects of contamination on bluefish, and the role of nutrients in wetlands.

In terms of habitat protection, open space, water quality, and recreation, it is widely agreed that the single largest challenge on the upper Hackensack River has always been the multiple-use management of watershed lands. The Hackensack Water Company has recognized the difficulties in protecting potable water supplies while making this land available for recreational use. The watershed land is not a trivial issue because it represents some of the largest area of remaining open space in Bergen County as 85 percent of the Hackensack River watershed is already developed.

United Water, formerly the Hackensack Water Company, is one of the largest investor-owned water utilities in the United States. It serves approximately 750,000 customers in the New York metropolitan area and its major source of supply is surface water contained in three reservoirs; Lake Tappan, Woodcliff Lake, and Oradell. Additional capacity is provided by Lake DeForest and its watershed in Rockland County, New York, and other sources, including the Saddle River.

The company currently owns 31 square miles or 3.6% percent of the watershed area, which is typical of water utilities nationwide. Because the land extends over multiple political and use boundaries there have always been controversies over its management. Today's basic management objective is to control specific pollutants without resorting to changes in treatment methods, while equitably sharing in the cost, and benefits of watershed protection.

Water quality is monitored at approximately 30 locations throughout the watershed at a frequency of 12 times each year, in addition to the routine raw water analysis at the Haworth Water Treatment Plant. Whenever a new land use is proposed near the watershed lands (in actual practice this generally means within 200 feet), the company has some statutory authority to review potential water quality impacts, including storm water runoffs. To further protect water quality, the company has supported municipalities applying for Green Acres open space preservation funding.

Until the early 1980s, over 650 acres of watershed land was at least partially open to the public as part of several golf courses in the towns of Emerson, Oradell, River Vale, Harrington Park, and Haworth. Proposed development on this land was fought by a coalition of environmental organizations who took United Water to court. In 1993, after more than a year of negotiation, the United Water signed an agreement with the Environmental Defense Fund, Save the Watershed Action Network, and the State Department of the Public Advocate, which represents rate payers. United Water agreed to transfer 290 acres of the golf courses to an affiliated company, Riverdale Reality. The transfer is accompanied by deed restrictions that guarantee the land will remain as open space and that future owners will follow best management practices. The company re-acquired some 355 acres that had been transferred to Riverdale Reality and set this land aside as a water quality buffer zone

Citizens Groups and Non-Profit Organizations.

One of the first clubs to take an active interest in cleaning up the Hackensack River, from the water level, was the Hackensack River Canoe Club. It was founded in the early 1980s and remained active for several years thereafter. The club ran several trips on the river as well as on other waterways in the state. One of its first organized activities was canoe races. During the inaugural race, several canoes overturned, including the one with the first aid squad members who had set out with the intention of protecting the other paddlers. The club held social events and participated in the annual Hackensack River Festival. Members also created a canoe trail through the marshes at DeKorte State Park, enabling fellow canoeists to enjoy the area without specialized knowledge of the myriad channels in the marsh.

In addition, the organization conducted regular river monitoring expeditions. Traveling with the tide and armed with pH paper, thermometers, and sample jars, the club members kept an eye out for unauthorized dumping, oil slicks, and other abuses. On one trip they discovered and tracked an oil slick to a storm drain in the town of Teaneck. They notified the Department of Environmental Protection and the fire department was called out, but unfortunately the slick had largely dispersed by the time help arrived with containment booms and cleanup equipment. On another trip on the Passaic River, the club discovered unlawful filling of the stream channel. As of this writing, the club is largely inactive. The American Littoral Society's Baykeeper program has taken over many of its functions and some of its former members participate in that program.

A group with a more narrowly defined objective is the Hackensack River Coalition, which was founded in 1985 with the purpose of lobbying on behalf of a clean river. Initial efforts have been to open the riverbanks for boaters and strollers. The coalition has also opposed the sale of unused watershed land for development, especially the land surrounding the Oradell Reservoir that was considered unnecessary for water quality protection. Members have rallied against overdevelopment of the Meadowlands and against the projected widening of the New Jersey Turnpike. A concern at the time that the group was founded was the cooling water discharge from the PSE & G Bergen generating station. The plant was discharging up to 634 million gallons of water at temperatures approaching 106 F every day. Water at such a high temperature robs the river of dissolved oxygen and can cause the death of fish and other aquatic life.

The award for the most dramatic, roll-up-the-sleeves-and-get-dirty effort has to go to students at New Jersey's colleges and universities who perform hands-on cleanups. One of the first was done by students at Fairleigh Dickinson University's Teaneck campus. A group waded into the river at the campus and wrestled out shopping carts and other debris. Most participants expressed a sense of responsibility for the river and a cleaner environment. The domestic-service program AmeriCorps has organized a series of cleanups using volunteers recruited from college campuses and riverside communities.

New Jersey Community Water Watch is a joint program between AmeriCorps and the New Jersey Public Interest Research Group's Law and Policy Center. The organization has three major program areas, river cleanups, stream monitoring, and environmental education. The organization has a small corps of full time coordinators, usually members of AmeriCorps, based at a college or university, who recruit and organize part time volunteers. Since the program's inception in 1994, Community Water Watch has organized 303 waterway cleanups removing almost 800 tons of trash from waterways throughout New Jersey. More then 81,000 students have participated in the group's educational programs. The Water Watch carries out monitoring programs in 50 waterways.

As of the late 1990s, the largest, most politically astute and active organization working for the rivers and bays is the Baykeeper program of the American Littoral Society. Although the littoral society is a nationwide coastal advocacy and educational organization, the Baykeeper program is a local organization for Hudson/Raritan Estuary, which for their purposes is roughly defined as a 15 mile radius around Statue of Liberty. It is involved with management plans for the Meadowlands, and works with the Hackensack Meadowlands Development Commission, the United States Environmental Protection Agency, the New Jersey Department of Environmental Protection, and Energy and the Army Corps of Engineers. Baykeeper members serve as members of these agencies as well as on the citizen advisory committees for dredging and filling permits.

The Baykeeper organization has also been involved in water quality monitoring since 1990. They have monitoring points on the Hackensack River, at Lincoln Park on the Passaic River, and west of Jersey City on Newark Bay. They have acted as advisors on habitat restoration and preservation, and have worked with AmeriCorps and other volunteer organizations. They also help out with the annual River Festival.

One participant in the Baykeeper program is the full-time Riverkeeper. Captain Bill Sheehan is a retired commercial fisherman who had worked Newark and Raritan Bays. His father was a barge captain and grandfather was a longshoreman and foreman in Hoboken. Today his outboard-powered pontoon boat *K/V Edward Abbey* (K/V – Keeper Vessel) with the fixed aluminum canopy is a regular feature on the Hackensack River.

Courtesy Hackensack Riverkeeper, Inc.

Aboard the Edward Abbey, *Captain Bill conducts a tour for the Red Hat Ladies the Sawmill Creek Marsh in Lyndhurst.*

One of his duties is to make the Hackensack River accessible to scientists by providing a boat with himself as guide. Rich Kane, of the Audubon Society, was aboard for a bird census in the Meadowlands, when he remarked to Captain Sheehan that "There's a market for what you do." This was the birth of ecotourism in the urban estuary

According the Sheehan, when he initiated the tours people were skeptical. "What are you going to look at, bits of floating garbage?" was a common response. But the tours quickly became an important education and outreach program. Sheehan speaks about wildlife habitat, wildlife, natural and human history. Special tours are also given for members of the press and public officials, some of whom, including local mayors, had never been on the river. By 2003, some 16,000 people had participated in the tours.

Local businesses have also become involved. The Red Roof Inn in Secaucus started placing ecocruise brochures in its rooms. General manager Jim Mastrangelo began encouraging the hotel employees to take the boat trip so that they could better explain the tours to the guests. Mastrangelo noted that, "I think folks will be pleasantly surprised to know they can take a canoe out on a marsh that sits in the shadow of the Empire State Building."

In 1997, the Riverkeeper and Baykeeper programs began to re-introduce an historical artifact - the oyster - into the Hackensack River as an ally to assist in river cleanup. An adult oyster can filter 50 to 60 gallons of water a day and thus remove huge amounts of suspended sediments and other particulate matter. The reduction in suspended matter will allow more light to filter through the water, enabling plants to grow, with an increase in the oxygen supply and improvement in habitat for all marine life.

The work has been funded by grants from the Pew Charitable Trusts and the Victoria Foundation. Captain Sheehan and biologist Benjamin Longstreth have placed oyster seeds (oysters between three and five months old), in several waterways. These include the Hackensack and Navesink Rivers and Sandy Hook Bay. After each seed is measured and recorded, they are placed into tiered mesh net, tied it to a pole, and carefully lowered into the river. Every two weeks, the net is raised and the oyster's growth and mortality is tallied. The experiments are still preliminary. The entire program is expected to cost several million dollars and take ten or more years, and, as the scientists are quick to point out, edible oysters will not be available any time soon.

In October of 2006, the Meadowlands Commission was expected to approve the creation of an oyster reef in the lower Hackensack River. In addition to clearing suspended material from the water column, the accumulated oyster shells are expected to create a habitat for other marine animals. A similar program for the Passaic River is not considered feasible at this time due to the higher levels of pollution in that river.

The oysters will have work to do. According to Captain Sheehan silting is a major problem on the Hackensack River and one of the principle obstacles to increased recreational use. Most local marinas and the main channels are slowly being choked. The Army Corps of Engineers, citing low levels of commercial traffic, has not conducted maintenance dredging in recent years. Taking matters into their own hands, local marina owners are using homemade dredges to clear slips. This is unlawful and potentially damaging to the river ecosystem. At the beginning of the Riverkeeper program, Captain Sheehan held a meeting with Joe Seabo, the Corps of Engineer's Clean Water Act enforcement expert, and marina operators. The Corps of Engineers agreed that if the marina operators all agreed to put in applications for dredging, they would all be covered under a single permit for the dredging and silt disposal. The problem with the existing piecemeal dredging process is that each marina merely sends the dredge spoils either into the main channel or to the next marina.

Recognizing the importance of citizen involvement and public outreach, the Lower Passaic & Saddle River Alliance was created by the New Jersey DEP to serve as a Public Advisory committee on watershed management issues. All participants are volunteers and they include many ordinary citizens. There are also representatives from over 30 municipalities, community groups, businesses, and government agencies. One goal of the Alliance is to help the DEP identify and remove sources of pollution. The other focus is to help reconnect communities to the rivers and dispel the still widespread perception that the Passaic is too far gone to ever be returned to health.

The Alliance helps establish programs where organizations can adapt stream segments, conduct clean ups, and become stewards of the rivers. They also put people onto the rivers by organizing canoe and kayak events.

The importance of these grass roots citizen organizations has increased in direct proportion to the budget deficits in federal and state agencies. In the wake of budget and government cutbacks in the 1980s, environmental agencies throughout the country have come to rely on volunteer groups to collect samples, gather data, and perform basic monitoring functions.

In 1990, one early success was the result of a decision by the Passaic River Coalition to row the entire 80-mile length of the Passaic River and document environmental violations. The group delivered an impressive collection of maps and photographs to New Jersey's Environmental Prosecutor's office, which then initiated over a dozen enforcement actions. In 1993, the

Environmental Prosecutor's budget was cut in half and the office was forced to organize volunteer monitoring groups throughout the state. Said one of the prosecutors about the volunteers, "You'd be a fool not to work with them... These are things that we, as citizens, could not begin to pay for."

However, the use of volunteers did raise some questions especially regarding the reliability of the data that was being collected. Volunteers do not generally require much training to measure parameters such as water temperature, turbidity, and even oxygen concentrations. Both scientists and regulatory agencies question the dependability of the more complex determinations of such parameters as solvents, heavy metals, and other industrial contaminants.

To help with the quality control problems, the EPA began making grants to develop training materials and distribute information through newsletters and computer bulletin boards. (At the time, the internet was not yet readily available for public use.)

There were some deeper problems. Regulatory agencies were overloaded with data and already aware of problems that existed. There were also questions raised about who would (or should) control citizens groups. Some have filed lawsuits, gone to the press, and even approached violators on their own. Lawsuits have been brought against the very agencies that the groups are trying to assist, when it was thought that the agencies were failing to do an effective job.

A proven solution for the advocacy group has been to establish a core of professional environmental scientists and policy experts who would use the volunteers for supplement and support. This is the approach taken by the Baykeeper. "In the best of all possible worlds, we wouldn't be needed," says a spokesman for the organization. "But in reality, we are going to be needed for a long, long time."

Pleasure Boating

In 1975, there were only about 200 pleasure boats operating on the Hackensack. Membership and interest in local yacht clubs has increased as the river becomes cleaner. Yet problems remain.

Aside from the silting problem, boating is decreasing due to restrictions on the railroad lift bridges. In the past, boats always had the right of way. But then the bridge tenders began to "resist" opening on demand. The New Jersey Transit argued to the Coast Guard, who regulates moveable bridges, that they no longer needed 24 hour bridge tenders. Today a skeleton crew operates all the bridges and a half hour notice is needed so the crew can get to the specific bridge where they are needed. As a result, larger boats began moving out of rivers and it is impossible to get a bridge lift during rush hour. On the other hand, considering that thousands of passengers use the rail lines and how difficult it is to stop a fast moving train, perhaps it is time to give the railroad the right-of-way.

The author is aware of several instances when rescue workers have had to respond to distress calls from boaters. The Secaucus Fire Department's official history records that they were called out on June 15, 1978 to rescue three persons from an overturned sailboat. The department's rescue unit used its boat to tow the sailboat and crew back to the Harmon Cove marina. On October 22, 1981, the rescue unit responded to a call reporting a sinking boat and rescued four people.

Rescue activities have steadily increased on the Passaic and Hackensack rivers as recreational boating continues to grow in popularity and more boat ramps are added to the riverbanks. One of the largest efforts was collaboration between several fire and rescue departments in November of 2006. Joseph Rivera, a 27-year-old resident of Stanhope, New Jersey, was canoeing the Passaic River above the Great Falls. When his canoe capsized near Beattie Island in Little Falls, Rivera was unable to swim to safety. His body was recovered near the Great Falls hydroelectric plant 12 days after the accident.

Lyndhurst Township's water rescue team uses scuba-certified firefighters to conduct underwater searches during emergencies in both the Passaic and Hackensack rivers. The unit's only boat is kept in the town's fire station which is about a mile from the Passaic River. In the most recent effort to move rescue operations back to the rivers on a permanent basis, in January of 2007, the Township announced a plan for bond issue that would finance construction of a boathouse near the river and give the unit a permanent home.

Museums, Parks, and Floating Restaurants

Although now a part of the town of River Edge, the Zabriskie House at New Bridge Landing, the docks, and surrounding land are owned by the state and serve as a museum. In recent years the staff has helped to promote the river cleanup by sponsoring annual festivals. Visitors can examine exhibits on the river's history and the history of Bergen County in general. Military re-enactment groups demonstrate the drills and camp routines of the local Revolutionary War militias. Camp followers, the wives and girlfriends, demonstrate cooking and spinning. Local craftsmen sell their wares

and demonstrate their skills. Hot dogs, ice cream, and many shouting children lend the festivals a joyful mood and many organizations take advantage
of the festival to promote their conservation projects.

As these events became more popular they outgrew the limited facilities
at New Bridge Landing. The environmental festivals have since been moved
to the Meadowlands while the staff at New Bridge concentrates on historical
reenactments and museum open houses.

In 1998, the State Park Service upgraded the status of the Von Steuben
House so that the site had its own board of commissioners. Such a board
raises the awareness of elected officials by serving as the site's advocacy group
in the state government. A larger appropriation could now be spent on dredging the river and repairing the remaining wharves. A Friends of New Bridge
Landing has also been organized for the site. According to the Park Service's
rules, a "friends" organization is a non-profit citizens' group that promotes,
raises money for, and helps interpret a site.

The changes at the New Bridge site accompany a major shift in the inter-
pretative focus and the visitor experience. The site's major role in the American
Revolution was the strategic importance of the Hackensack River bridge. As
the Continental Army withdrew westward in the fall of 1776, the New Bridge
was the southernmost crossing of the Hackensack and as such was the most
direct and secure route to the safety of Pennsylvania. Had the British reached
New Bridge before the Americans made their crossing, the Continental
Army would have been trapped on the peninsula between the Hackensack
and Hudson Rivers. The park staff thus claims that the New Bridge was the
"bridge that saved a nation."

While watching the Army cross the bridge, Thomas Paine was inspired
to compose *The Crisis Number One*:

> These are the times that try men's souls. The summer soldier and
> the sunshine patriot will, in this crisis, shrink from the service
> of their country; but he that stands it now, deserves the love
> and thanks of man and woman. Tyranny, like hell, is not easily
> conquered; yet we have this consolation with us, that the harder
> the conflict, the more glorious the triumph. What we obtain too
> cheap, we esteem too lightly: it is dearness only that gives every
> thing its value.

If for no other reason, the New Bridge deserves to be preserved as a
monument.

Just a few miles downstream in Hackensack is the *USS Ling*. In 1972, the

Submarine Memorial Association was formed with the purpose of saving the *USS Ling* from being scrapped. By converting her into a floating museum they hoped to "perpetuate the memory of our shipmates who gave their lives in the pursuit of their duties while serving their country."

The *Ling* was towed to Hackensack and berthed at Borg Park. After being restored and outfitted with authentic gear, the submarine was opened to the public. She is a diesel-electric submarine of the *Balao* class that were built between 1943 and 1945. She was launched in 1945 by the Cramp Shipbuilding Company in Philadelphia. Commissioned in June 1945, she only made one patrol before the end of the Second World War. For the next 14 years she was inactive, part of the Atlantic Reserve Fleet. From 1962 to 1971, the Navy used her as a training ship for the Naval Reserve Submarine Division. Although the Ling did not actually go to sea, all aspects of submarine operations were simulated on board. The Navy donated the submarine to the memorial association in 1971. In 1988, she was made New Jersey's official Naval memorial. Over the years that followed additional exhibits were added to the facility. These included World War II era miniature submarines and a Vietnam era river patrol boat. Since opening to the public in 1973, the *USS Ling* has hosted more than 750,000 visitors.

The property where the submarine is berthed is owned by the North Jersey Media Group, parent company of the Bergen Record newspaper. The site had been leased to the Memorial Association for $1.00 per year. The Record's printing plant had been located on the river immediately north of the Ling, but when printing operations were moved to Morris County a large portion of the Record's building became vacant and the Media Group began considering selling the property.

The question of the *Ling's* future is complicated by the fact that she is upstream of the Court Street Bridge in Hackensack. Bergen County has discussed the possibility of replacing the 1908 swing bridge with a fixed span. This would trap the *Ling* at her current berth and has prompted the Coast Guard to warn against the fixed span. Although there were discussions of moving the submarine, the county changed its plans after it became obvious that moving the Ling would create a hardship for the museum. As of early 2007, the county sought bids for a new bridge that was expected to cost somewhere between $10 million and $11 million. The possible sale of the site has changed the situation, so that at the time of this writing there are proposals to remove the Ling from the Hackensack and bring her to Camden as part of the *USS New Jersey* Battleship Memorial. However, there have been no plans for funding the move.

There were other museums on the Hackensack River. An unusual museum was established just north of the Zabriskie house in New Milford in the early 1940s. The exhibits recreated the life of a Lenni-Lenape Indians. Even though the Lenape lived in New Jersey for thousands of years, few people knew much about their history. Mrs. Vivienne Paul and her father, Paselles Cole, began the village by constructing wigwams and holding weekly ceremonies and dances. Shinnecock Indians, who performed regularly at Jones Beach, came from Long Island to work and perform in the reconstructed settlement.

The Lenape village seems to have been a very small operation. One local resident remembers that there were only about 10 people in the village. Several of the Native Americans attended the dedication of the Steuben House in September 1939, including an "Indian Princess" and her "consort." There was talk of somehow coordinating these tourist attractions, but in the opinion of Kevin Wright, the Steuben House Museum curator, the Second World War diverted funds away from both the restoration of the Steuben House and the Lenape village. The village was subsequently abandoned.

Although the village seems to have been established with good intentions, its authenticity is open to debate. The "Indian Princess" was not only a Shinnecock, she was a trained dancer and a member of the faculty at Vasser College. The Lenape lived in small groups of extended families and did not have "princesses" as understood by Europeans, or even chiefs for that matter. Historian Kevin Wright goes on to state that his recollection of photographs is that the "Lenapes" wore the feathered headdresses and buffalo skins more appropriate to the Plains Indians.

Today there are no museums on the Passaic River. However, two of John P. Holland's submarines are on display at the Paterson Museum. Along with another New Jerseyman, Simon Lake, Holland is considered one of the two principle inventors of the modern submarine. The *Holland I* was the original vessel Holland used as a demonstration and test boat on the Passaic River. Fourteen feet long, and measuring four by three feet in cross-section, it is a boxy, 2.25-ton, riveted-iron boat with a one-man cockpit. A small steam engine (the boiler was on shore and connected to the boat by a long hose) powered the boat. In June of 1878, Holland submerged in this unlikely looking vessel for upwards of an hour in the Passaic River, just above the Great Falls. The other boat in the museum is the *Holland II*. She is also known as the *Fenian Ram*, after the name of the Irish nationalist group that financed her construction. The *Fenian Ram* is 31 feet long, six feet in beam, and seven feet high. Her hull of eleven-sixteenths inch thick iron gave the vessel "ramming power," never tested in combat, of an estimated 50 tons.

Although the *Holland I* was tested in full view of the public, Holland scuttled her in 14 feet of water above the Spruce Street Bridge. This was done obstinately to preserve secrecy. She was raised by a group of Paterson citizens in 1927 who presented her to the city. The *Fenian Ram*, on the other hand, was well known to a larger public. Construction of the *Fenian Ram* began in May of 1879 at the Delemeter Ironworks, at the foot of 13th Street in New York City. Although constructed in secret, her launch into the Hudson in May of 1881 attracted considerable press attention. On her test dives, the *Fenian Ram* was able to stay submerged for up to four hours and dive to a depth of 60 feet. The *Fenian Ram* was soon followed by the *Fenian Model*, a one ton, 16 feet long submarine. Both boats were transported by the Fenians to New Haven, Connecticut, a move not approved by an enraged Holland, who had not give his permission. Finally, in 1916, the *Fenian Ram* was taken back to New York and exhibited at Madison Square Garden, forming the centerpiece of an Irish charity bazaar aiding victims of the Easter Rising in 1916. The *Fenian Ram* never sailed again; she was purchased by Edward A. Browne of Paterson, who brought her back to that city, and placed on public display in West Side park. (A brief biography of Holland and discussion of his boats is found in Appendix E)

The development of riverside parks has been greatly facilitated by the New Jersey Green Acres program. Originally established in 1961 and now serving as the real estate arm of the Department of Environmental Protection, Green Acres funding has been used to preserve 120,000 acres or 2.5% of New Jersey's total area.

Several communities in the Lower Passaic River Basin received funding for watershed land acquisition that will increase opportunities for recreation by providing more public access to the Passaic River and its tributaries. The acquisitions are also expected to improve the overall environmental quality of the watersheds. A total of 4,120 preserved acres fall into this category. The communities that have received funding include; East Rutherford, Garfield, Lodi, and North Arlington (Bergen County), Montclair, East Orange, Bloomfield, Newark, and Nutley (Essex County), East Newark, Harrison, and Kearny (Hudson County), Clifton and Paterson (Passaic County.) Nonprofit organizations such as the Passaic River Coalition have received Green Acres funding as well.

The Great Falls of Paterson were designated a New Jersey State Park in 2004. Two years later in November of 2006, the state announced the winner of a design competition for the Great Falls State Park Master Plan. Mayor Jose Torres, Governor Jon Corzine, Representative William Pascrell, Jr., and

Paterson native, U.S. Senator Frank Lautenburg came to a ceremony at the Great Falls to unveil the 100 million dollar plan that would turn the area into "Paterson's new outdoor living room." The urban design firm Field Operations won the competition. Among the plan's components was a trail to link the falls to Overlook Park and other open spaces.

The Field Operations plan was selected over four others largely because it relied on enhancing what is already existed in place rather than introducing new construction. Mayor Torres emphasized the importance of the park in revitalizing the city center. "This Great Falls is the foundation from which Paterson's future will be built on." said the Mayor.

Merely preserving riverside and watershed land is often not sufficient for developing parks that can be enjoyed by the public. The three and a half mile Hackensack River Greenway was created on the east bank to bring people back to the river with walking trails, boat, and canoe access points.

Andreas Park was named for Maria W. Andreas, who first came to Teaneck with her husband in 1890 while searching for a summer home. Their son Frederic inherited the property and lived there until 1951. The historic house where they lived was built in 1760, and later expanded in 1840.

Frederic Andreas grew up to be one of Teaneck's civic leaders and it was his desire that after his retirement, people would continue to enjoy the area as he had. He deeded the property with the understanding that the mansion would be torn down and the park created. The Maria W. Andreas Memorial Park was dedicated on Memorial Day, 1952.

Three and a half miles of the Hackensack River Greenway are located in Andreas Park and at the time of this writing this is the section that comes closest to what the promoters hope to achieve. Eventually the Greenway's sponsors would like to create a path from Terhune Park (in the southwester corner of Teaneck) to New Bridge Landing. The Andreas Park section has a pedestrian walkway and nature trail. To provide a buffer between the Teaneck's developed areas and the river, native vegetation is being encouraged.

Other municipalities have built similar Greenway sections and work is continuing to coordinate these efforts and link them together. The Greenway is already used for walking tours, birding, and environmental education.

Combining interpretive signage with the walking paths is another way to enhance the visitor experience. A series of illustrated plaques along the Greenway entitled Hackensack River Stories was the creation of Richard Mills, an artist and printmaker who took a sabbatical from his position as Fine Arts Coordinator at the C.W. Post campus of Long Island University to create the work. After serving as an environmental educator, Mills became interested less in "representing the landscape" than "helping people read the landscape." After researching the history of the Hackensack River and talking to some of the elderly residents who remember what the river was like in earlier times, Mills created a series of collages. They illustrate not only boats and ships, but people swimming and fishing, along with native species such as cedars and cattails. The collages were positioned along the Greenway so that people might connect more deeply with the environment.

During the 1980s, there were three notable floating restaurants on the Hackensack. The first was on a converted Hudson River Dayline Excursion Boat. The Anritsu Supper Club had been berthed in Secaucus by the Meadowlands Parkway. The converted Dayline Excursion Boat was elegantly fitted with white-clothed tables, modern captain's chairs and highly polished wood, and the restaurant served American and continental dishes. The upper deck had a cocktail lounge and dancing, Tuesdays to Saturday. On January 21, 1988, the vessel sank at her moorings and the Secaucus Fire Department tried to save the vessel using pumps. She has since been towed from the river.

A 1931 ferryboat is moored in the Hackensack at a Carlstadt marina. The marinas owner, Bob Laukaitis, converted the vessel into an elegant club. The ferry began her career in 1931, running between Manhattan and Welfare Island. (Now renamed Roosevelt Island.) She became the *Drifters I*, a floating restaurant on the New Jersey side of the Hudson during the 1970s, but sank at her moorings in 1986. After being raised and towed to the Carlstadt Marina, she sat idle for several months. Then in 1987 a State Superior Court judge awarded her to Laukaitis in a dispute over the overdue docking fees.

Shovels and buckets were used to dig out the three foot deep carpet of mud that had covered the vessel's decks, and high pressure water hoses blasted away the accumulated weeds and barnacles. The entire renovation is estimated to take up to two years and cost $50,000. When completed, the 120 foot long ferry will be a members' only floating club. An elegant tiled bar is planned, a top deck swimming pool, and an apartment for her owner. The *Drifters II* was a converted fishing trawler moored in Hackensack off River Street. She too is gone from the river.

In Clifton, the *Passaic River Queen* was moored by River Road for use as a floating restaurant. Alex Komar brought the former Great Lakes passenger steamer to Clifton about 1970. She remained there for about four years before leaving her moorings and ending up downriver.

Public use of the Passaic River tidewater became easier with the 1997 completion of the New Jersey Performing Arts Center (NJPAC) in Newark. As part of the downtown revitalization that the center is expected to bring to Newark, a waterfront restoration with additional parkland is planned. Arrangements are also being made for a minor-league baseball stadium near the river.

In 1990, after the water company no longer needed the former Hackensack Water Company's pumping station in Oradell, the land and buildings were donated to Bergen County for use as a new park. The site had long been viewed by the historic preservation community for conversion into a museum. The 1880s era brick buildings were not just architecturally magnificent, but all of the original steam powered pumping equipment were still there and largely intact. The largest of the engines was a 1911 Allis-Chalmers triple-expansion, piston-type steam engine. (A triple expansion engine uses the exhaust steam from the first cylinder to power a second cylinder, and the exhaust from the second cylinder to power a third cylinder.) The same site also contained steam turbine powered pumps and electrically powered pumps. Aside from the industrial component of the site, the former water testing laboratories were to be converted into a river water monitoring facility and the two-football field sized settling tanks were going to be re-used as a reconstructed riverine habitat.

Courtesy Waterworks Conservancy

The 1911 Allis Chalmers triple expansion pumping engine stands in the rear of the Waterworks pump house. More modern turbine powered pumps are in the foreground.

The site was also historically significant because it was the site of many technological innovations in water purification and treatment technology.

These are detailed in Clifford W. Zink's book *The Hackensack Water Works*. At the time of this writing another book about the site is in preparation for future publication.

The county's Board of Freeholders did not agree that the site deserved preservation and led by County Executive William Schuber, wished to demolish the buildings and turn the entire 13-acre Van Buskirk Island into a "passive park." As a nod to the site's historic significance, they did propose leaving the Allis-Chalmers engine standing (rusting) in the open air.

In 1994, local residents, led by Maggie Harrer of Oradell, formed the Water Works Conservancy to create a museum and research center. "We save every place George Washington slept in," said Anthony Vouvalides, one of the Water Works directors. "By the same token, we should try to save the places that delivered clean water to citizens. This is what made New Jersey. This is not just an Oradell landmark, or a Bergen County landmark. It's a national landmark."

In 2002, the National Trust for Historic Preservation named the site to its annual list of the 11 most endangered historic sites in America. This was followed by being listed as one of America's Treasures by the organization, Save America's Treasures, a cooperative program of the White House, National Trust for Historic Preservation, and National Park Service.

Through a six-year effort that included intensive lobbying, a series of grant applications, petitions, news releases, and public outreach, the county government eventually, if reluctantly, came to see the value of preserving the site. By the summer of 1999, the Water Works Conservancy was able to lease the buildings. In July 2000, the Bergen County Freeholders voted to go forward with the museum plans. The site received a $575,000 grant from the NJ Historical Trust Fund which was matched by funds provided by the Hackensack Water Company to Bergen County, which provided a total $1.3 million to begin work on the site.

In June of 2003, NJ DEP Commissioner Bradley Campbell adopted the NJ Historic Advisory Board's Resolution that the Historic Water Works was of such historic importance to the State of NJ and the Nation that it must be preserved in its entirety. In August of 2003, Bergen County Executive Dennis McNerney signed an agreement with the State of New Jersey DEP that Bergen County would stabilize the site and prepare a full preservation proposal. And in 2006, Bergen County covered the buildings with a new slate roof and repaired a minor retaining wall. However, Bergen County has yet to prepare a full preservation proposal. The Water Works Conservancy continues to advocate full preservation of the site and is working to partner with

Bergen County to save this historic gem in the heart of the county.

The Water Works Conservancy opened new offices and a "vest pocket" museum at 383 Kinderkamack Road, Oradell, New Jersey to demonstrate the types of activities and exhibits that could occur on a larger scale at the historic site. The WWC has also created a new interactive website [http://www. hwwc.org/] which provides information regarding the site and educational programs.

Snake Hill, in Hudson County has already become a hugely popular park. After serving as the site of a trap-rock quarry, mental institution, and anchorage for a New Jersey Turnpike Bridge, in 1997 the park opened with playgrounds, ball fields, a boat launch, and nature trail. Ospreys have recently begun nesting near the new park.

This final chapter in our story is largely one of individuals who contribute their time and dedication to caring for the rivers and bay. In the future, hard choices will have to be made concerning recreation, development, public access, and pollution control measures. But the battle for cleaner, healthier rivers with the help of concerned citizens is being won. It is the most current chapter in the story and one I urge the reader to help write.

Photograph by Dr. Michael Passow

Kayakers explore the upper Hackensack River.

Appendix A: John Champe's Secret Mission

In the late summer of 1780, the American military was stunned by the revelation that General Benedict Arnold had tried to betray the key post of West Point. When this was unsuccessful, he`escaped to the British stronghold of New York. The incident caused a crisis among the Americans, because no one knew if Arnold was acting alone or if other officers were involved. It was soon discovered that Arnold was acting alone and that the Army was loyal and this in turn gave a valuable boost to morale. Arnold's failure was regarded as providential and proof that God was on the American side.

But another crisis quickly arose. Arnold was discovered because a British officer, Major John André, had been captured with the plans for West Point concealed in his boots and compromising documents on his person. André was a member of Sir Henry Clinton's staff with responsibilities for intelligence gathering. A likable, highly accomplished, and promising young man, John André was also a spy who had been captured behind enemy lines. Although the strict rules of warfare called for him to be hung, neither side wanted to see this happen.

Washington was determined to capture Benedict Arnold because in so doing he could spare the dashing Major André. One Major Lee formulated a daring plan for an American "deserter" to infiltrate a corps Arnold was raising in New York. At an opportune moment, the spy would seize the traitor and spirit him back to the American lines. For this dangerous mission, the Lee selected a 24 year old Virginian named John Champe.

The key to the plan was to make the desertion look convincing. Accordingly, at about eleven o'clock at night, Champe took a cloak, valise, and orderly book and rode from camp. The alarm was sounded for the "escaped" dragoon but Major Lee was able to issue conflicting orders and delay a pursuing party for about an hour.

Champe intended to make the British post at Paulus Hook but changed direction when he saw his pursuers beginning to close in. Heading down to the marshes and with his countrymen in hot pursuit (they, at least, were totally convinced of his desertion) he stopped to lash his valise to his shoulders, and draw his sword and then plunged through the reeds. Hearing his cries for help, the crew of a British galley fired on the Americans and drove them off. They then sent a boat for Champe and he was soon in New York.

Arnold was in the habit of taking nightly walks in his garden, the occasion of which Champe would use to his advantage. He planned to sneak through a loose board in the fence, grab Arnold and hustle him to the Hudson shore to a waiting boat.

But the day before the abduction, Arnold moved his headquarters to supervise the embarkation of the corps made up mostly of deserters, of which Champe was one. Unable to resume his real identity for some time, Champe ultimately was rewarded by Washington for the valiant effort.

From: Daniel Van Winkle, Old Bergen, History and Reminiscences, p. 121.

Appendix B: Whaling Ships of Newark

When the Stephens, Condit and Wright Whaling and Sealing Company began in 1835, they launched two ships - the *John Wells* and the *Columbus*. Both sailed in the summer of 1837 with crews of thirty men and boys in search of whales. Their quest led to the Gulf of Mexico, around Cape Horn, and finally into the Arctic Ocean. The *Columbus* struck an iceberg, but before she sank all hands were taken off to the *John Wells*. The ship returned to Newark with here hold full of 3,000 barrels of oil.

The *John Wells* made three more voyages from Newark and the master's log of the 1838-1839 voyage is still preserved at New Jersey Historical Society.

The industry was short lived; whaling grounds were too far distant and labor was too costly. The ship was sold to New Bedford investors who presumably had an easier time recruiting crews in Massachusetts.

Appendix C: Some Boy Trappers of the Hackensack

The late Edward Rutsch, one of New Jersey's foremost archaeologists and historical consultants, grew up near the Hackensack and spent many happy hours trapping muskrat in the marshes. He and his companions sold pelts to Sears-Roebuck, and sometimes reluctantly to older trappers who would bring them to market in New York, for which they would take a healthy mark-up.

Ed's father was in the textile business and from him Ed learned about the furriers in Manhattan's garment district. The boys decided to skip school and sell their pelts there. They emerged from the subway with bundles of pelts, wondering what to do first, when they were approached by a furrier who, spotting their bundles, offered 40 dollars. Not wanting to be hasty, they sought out other offers and finally returned to complete the deal.

The furrier not only bought the pelts, but he took the boys out to lunch. Introducing the boys to his colleagues, the excited man exclaimed, "I bought $8,000 worth of Russian sable this morning; this afternoon, I finally met some trappers from the Hackensack! And I bought muskrat for forty bucks."

Appendix D: The Brick Fleet

Schooners

- *John Schmults*
- *Fancy*
- *Ophelia*
- *Joseph Hammond*
- *Elizabeth Washburn*
- *Samuel Cunningham*
- *Philip Mehrof*
- *Stephan Underhill (*later renamed the *Annie Mehrof)*
- *William S. Peck*
- *William Low*
- *Robert Blair*
- *Magic*
- *Nicholas Mehrof*
- *Albert G. Lawson*
- *Peter Mehrof*

Masters

- Fred Christie
- John Christie
- Mike Brown
- John Orth
- Hank Money
- Walter Kizley
- Louis Bradbury
- George Mehrof
- John Fitzpatrick
- Patrick Fagan
- Peter Fagan

Note: The available records do not indicate which ships were commanded by which masters.

From Westervelt, Frances A., *History of Bergen County, New Jersey, 1630–1923, Vol. 1*, New York, Lewis Historical Publishing Company, 1923.

Hackensack Valley Brickyards as listed in *Within These Gates* by Daniel deNoyelles

Name of Company	Number of Machines
Charles E. Walsh, Hackensack, NJ	1
James W. Gillies, Hackensack, NJ	1
Edward Schmultz, Hackensack, NJ	2
M. B. & L. B. Gardner, Hackensack, NJ	1
M. & L. E. Gardner, Hackensack, NJ	1
I. & W. Felter, Little Ferry, NJ	4
Mehrhoff Brick Co., Little Ferry, NJ	5
N. Mehrhoff Co., Little Ferry, NJ	3
P. Mehrhoss Co., Little Ferry, NJ	5

Appendix E: John Holland and His Submarine Boats*

John Philip Holland was born at Liscannor Bay, County Clare, on the west coast of Ireland in February of 1841. The son of a coastguardsman, the small, bespectacled boy would not seem destined to profoundly change the face of the world's oceans. He became a schoolteacher and worked in different parts of Ireland from 1858 to 1873. It was during this time that he became interested in the work of earlier submarine inventors. He drew the plans for his first submarine in 1870, the same year that Jules Verne published *20,000 Leagues Under the Sea.*

In 1873, Holland emigrated to the United States and settled in Boston. He was invited by a Father Whalen to move to Paterson, New Jersey, to teach mathematics at St. John's Parochial School. Holland would often stay after school and use the blackboard in his classroom for working out the submarine design calculations. In 1875 Holland offered his plans to the U.S. Navy. They were rejected.

As an Irish patriot, Holland realized that a workable submarine could be used against Britain's navy in the cause of independence. Holland's brother was a member of an Irish nationalist group called the Fenians. It was through this connection that the Fenians came to finance experimental submarines.

The Fenian's involvement began after witnessing Holland's clockwork-powered model boat dive off the beach at Coney Island. Soon, money was available for Holland to construct a series of full size boats, beginning with the *Holland I.* She was followed by the *Fenian Ram* and *Fenian Model.*

Holland's most obvious contribution to submarine design was create streamlined hulls. His designs share more in common with modern nuclear submarines than the boats in either the First World War or the second. The uninformed visitor to the Paterson Museum might easily mistake the Fenian Ram for the latest oceanographic research submersible. Later in his career, when Holland was forced to collaborate with the US Navy's official engineers, he would become furious when seeing the boat's decks cluttered with equipment that ruined the streamlining and robbed her of underwater speed. Navy officers wanted "decks to strut upon" according to the disgusted inventor.

Holland's other major insight was that submarines should always maintain a slight positive buoyancy. The boat could be driven underwater by the force of the propellers and the angle of her diving planes, instead of passively sinking by flooding ballast tanks. If the engines should fail while operating in this manner, the boat would rise to the surface. This is a safety feature incorporated into several modern research submarines.

Although not as obvious to the casual observer, Holland also worked out many important details that made submarines practical. He designed devices that helped to control the vessel while underwater, regulate buoyancy, and even compensate for the sudden loss of weight when a torpedo was fired.

After falling out with the Fenians, Holland began working with Lieutenant Edmund L.G. Zalinski, the inventor of a pneumatic gun that hurled dynamite.** The result was the unsuccessful *Zalinski* boat of 1885-86. Holland had no opportunity to supervise construction, the boat was damaged in a launching accident, and the project was finally halted by a lack of funds.

Persistence and a small number of officers who believed in his ideas finally persuaded the Navy to give Holland official support. Holland's next boat, the *Plunger* (Hull #5) was launched in 1887. She was the U.S. Navy's first submarine. Although it was the JP Holland Torpedo Boat Company that was awarded a $150,000 contract to build the Plunger, the actual design was largely the work of Admiral George W. Melville. Melville was the chief of the Naval Bureau of Steam Engineering and had no experience with submarine design. The boat was a failure. It has been widely stated that the only time that the boat actually submerged was when she accidentally sank at the dock.

With $5,000 left over from the *Plunger* contract, Holland built his sixth and most impressive boat in 1898. The *Holland* (Hull #6) was 53 feet long, ten feet wide and displaced 75 tons while submerged. Her armament consisted of a torpedo tube and a pneumatic dynamite gun, both located at the bow. The *Holland* was also had a dual propulsion system. A gasoline motor powered her on the surface while charging electrical storage batteries, which powered the boat while submerged. The *Holland* was purchased by the U.S. Navy in 1900. Within a few months, the government ordered six more boats. Soon orders were coming in from the governments of Great Britain, Russia, and Japan.

By 1904, the self-taught inventor was relegated to the position of figurehead in his own company. Reorganized as the Electric Boat Company, it offered Holland a salary of $10,000 per year but no real duties. Holland was unable to leave the company and start another, because of litigation brought on by Electric Boat as well as difficulty in raising money.

Holland's success with the *Holland* in 1900 not only resulted in his own eventual displacement from active submarine design; it also put Simon Lake out of the submarine business. Lake was born in Pleasantville, New Jersey into a family of inventors. He started working on submarines a few years after Holland, but unlike the Irishman, he had no trouble with raising funds. Rejected by both bankers and the U.S. Navy, Lake turned to his aunt to finance his first boat. Simon Lake introduced a number of important innovations. His boats had periscopes at a time when Holland's were forced to surface in order to aim their weapons. Lake's *Argonaut* was the first modern submarine to use a snorkel and the first to operate on the open ocean. Like Holland, Lake had a group of supportive officers in the naval establishment. But when the government decided to buy Holland's boats exclusively, these officers were no longer able to offer Simon Lake any encouragement.

Holland's last two boats were designed for Japan during the Russo-Japanese War. According the *Dictionary of American Biography*, in 1910 he was awarded the Order of the Rising Sun for this work.

Having turned to aeronautics in his final years, Holland died in Newark in August of 1914. He did not live to see the effect of his inventions on naval warfare.

Possibly because the first ones were so small, all submarines, even today, are called boats.

**Dynamite is chemically too unstable to be placed into a projectile and fired from a conventional gun. Pneumatic guns could gently push the explosive out the barrel without setting it off.*

The material in this appendix came largely from the Paterson Museum, the Dictionary of American Biography, *Scribners, 1958, and* Down the Jersey Shore, *by Russell Roberts and Richard Youmans, Rutgers University Press, 1993.*

Appendix F: Destroyer Escorts Built at Federal Shipyards

Although Federal Shipbuilding Company's main yard was in Kearny, the company found itself short on space once the Navy began awarding contracts for new ships. Federal opened a second yard in Port Newark specifically to construct destroyers and destroyer escorts (DE.) The Port Newark's DE construction record as of 1945 is as follows:

DE#	Name	Commission Date
162	*Levy*	1943
163	*McConnell*	1943
164	*Osterhaus*	1943
165	*Parks*	1943
166	*Baron*	1943
167	*Acree*	1943
168	*Amick*	1943
169	*Atherton*	1943
170	*Booth*	1943
171	*Carroll*	1943
172	*Cooner*	1943
173	*Eldridge*	1943
174	*Marts*	delivered to Brazil; commissioned as the *Bocaina*
175		delivered to Brazil; commissioned as the *Bertioga*
176	*Micka*	1943
177		delivered to Brazil; commissioned as the *Bauru*
178		delivered to Brazil; commissioned as the *Beberibe*
179		delivered to Brazil; commissioned as the *Bracui*
180	*Trumpeter*	1943
181	*Straub*	1943
182	*Gustafson*	1943
183	*Samuel S. Miles*	1943
184	*Wesson*	1943

185	*Riddle*	1943
186	*Swearer*	1943
187	*Stern*	1943
188	*O'Neill*	1943
189	*Bronstein*	1943
190	*Baker*	1943
191	*Coffman*	1943
192	*Eisner*	1944
193	*Garfield Thomas*	1944
194	*Wingfield*	1944
195	*Thornhill*	1944
196	*Rinehart*	1944
197	*Roche*	1944

All of the above DE's featured diesel-electric tandem motor drives; long hulls and 3-inch guns.

Specifications for these DE's: Light Displacement--1,240 tons; Full Load--1,520 tons; LOA--306'; Beam--36'10"; HP--6,000; Main Battery--3-3"/50; Torpedo Tubes--3-21" Triple; Crew--220

438	*Corbesier*	1944
439	*Conklin*	1944
440	*McCoy Reynolds*	1944
441	*Wm. Seiverling*	1944
442	*Ulvert M. Moore*	1944
443	*K.C. Campbell*	1944
444	*Goss*	1944
445	*Grady*	1944
446	*Charles Brannon*	1944
447	*Albert T. Harris*	1944
448	*Cross*	1945
449	*Hanna*	1945
450	*Jos. E. Connolly*	1945
508	*Gilligan*	1944
509	*Formoe*	1944
510	*Heyliger*	1945

All of the above DE's featured geared-turbine drives and 5-inch guns. Specifications for these DE's: Light Displacement--1,275 tons; Full Load--

unknown; LOA-306'; Beam--36'10"; HP--12,000; Main Battery--2-5"/38; Torpedo Tubes--3-21" Triple; Crew--220

The federal government placed additional DE orders with Federal, but these contracts were cancelled when the Allies won full control of the Atlantic Ocean and the threat of U-Boat attacks lessened considerably. Federal also constructed some larger landing craft, but it unclear which yard actually handled this activity.

These statistics were provided by:

Paul W. Schopp
Staff Historian
A.D. Marble & Co.
Conshohocken, PA 19428

Appendix G: Traffic on the Passaic River 1899 to 1904

1899 - 1,962,462 tons
1900 - 2,037,363 tons
1901 - 2,009,356 tons

1902 - 2,494,312 tons
1903 - 2,356,511 tons
1904 - 2,567,942 tons

Two of the principle freight companies operating boats on the Passaic River were the Passaic River Towing Line and the Merchants Express & Transportation Company.

Preliminary Report of the Inland Waterways Commission, *Washington, Government Printing Office, 1908.*

Glossary

Beakhead: A structure extending forward from the bow of a ship. Its resemblence to a bird's beak gave it this name. Sails are not attached to the beakhead.

Beam: The width of a vessel at the widest point in the hull

Bollard: A short vertical post on a dock or pier where mooring lines can be secured

Boom: The horizontal spar to which the bottom edge of a sail is attached.

Bowsprit: A spar extending forward from the bow of a sailing vessel.

Bow: The front of a vessel.

Brig: A square-rigged ship with two masts. Most brigs have a small number of fore-and-aft sails but these do not provide the principle propulsion.

Cat: A sailing vessel without head sails, i.e., sails carried forward of the foremast. A catboat is a fore-and-aft rigged boat with one sail behind her single mast. A cat schooner has no sails forward of the foremast.

Deadrise: A measure of the flatness of the bottom of a vessel's hull. Deadrise is the distance between the keel and the point where the hull's side begins to become vertical. The smaller the deadrise, the flatter the vessel's bottom. A flat bottom scow, for instance, has no deadrise.

Draft or Draught: When a vessel is floating, the distance between the waterline and the keel. The smaller a vessel's draft the shallower the water in which it can operate.

Foredeck: The deck ahead of the foremast and covering the area behind the bow.

Foremast: On a vessel with two or more masts, the mast closest to the bow.

Gaff: A spar used to raise the top, rear corner of a fore-and-aft sail. Although not widely used today, a gaff allowed a much larger sail area than is possible with a triangular sail.

Head Sails: Sails carried in a position where they are over the bow. *See also* "Jib".

Jib: A triangular sail set in front of the foremast. *See also* head sail.

Keel: Sometimes referred to as the "backbone" of a ship. On a large vessel the keel is a strong structure running at the very bottom of the ship between the bow and the stern. Even when a vessel lacks this structure the line traced by the lowest point of the hull as it runs from bow to stern is sometimes called the keel.

Lee Board: A flat board, usually made of several planks, which is attached to the side of a sailing vessel and pivoted so it can be lowered into the water. This acts like a keel and provides lateral resistance when sailing into the wind.

Lighter: A small vessel used in lighterage service. The name came about because taking off cargo made the ship lighter. Sometimes this was done because a fully loaded ship was too low in the water to pass over sandbars at the entrance to a harbor.

Lighterage: Cargo movements within a port. Usually this term applies to the movement of cargoes from anchored ships to shore. In the Port of New York "lighterage" also referred to movements of cargoes from riverside railroad terminals to other areas in the harbor where there was no railroad service or where service was only available from a competing railroad.

Mainmast: The largest mast on a sailing vessel. When all the masts are the same size the mainmast is usually the second mast from the bow.

Mainsail: The largest sail attached to the mainmast. Often this sail provides the principle propulsion for a sailing vessel.

Quarter-deck: An elevated deck over a vessel's stern, usually measuring one-quarter of the vessel's total length. This deck was traditionally where the officers watched over the ship.

Rocker: The curve from bow to stern along the bottom of the hull.

Schooner: A fore-and-aft rigged vessel with two or more masts. Traditionally the schooner's masts are all approximately the same height.

Scow: Any flat bottomed boat.

Sheer: The line formed where the side of the hull meets the deck.

Sloop: A small sailing vessel having a fore-and-aft rig.

Spar: Any pole, mast, gaff, or other straight, slender piece of wood to which any part of a sail is attached.

Stern: The rear of a vessel.

Thwart: Anything extending from one side of a ship or boat to the other. Usually used to describe a seat in a small boat.

Tons or tonnage: Originally a measure of the number of "tuns" or casks that a ship could carry. It is a measure of the volume of the ship's hold. Today ship designers define a "ton" as either 100 cubic feet or 2.83 cubic meters. Deadweight tonnage is a term used in modern times to define the volume (not the weight) a ship can carry.

Tumblehome: A description of the inward curve formed when a ship's decks are narrower than the widest part of the hull, especially when the hull is widest near the waterline.

Sources

1984 Annual Report of the Hackensack Meadowlands Development Commission, Hackensack Meadowlands Development Commission, Lyndhurst, NJ, 1984.

"22-Car Freight Trains Plunges Into the Passaic River," *New York Times,* October 7, 1970, p. 93.

"73 Polluters Agree to Spend $37M on Passaic River Study," Diskin, Colleen, *The Record,* May 9, 2007, p. A-3.

"5,000 Passengers Delayed," *New York Times,* March 20, 1901, p. 5.

Adams, Arthur, personal communication.

American Lloyd's Universal Register of Shipping, 15 June to 31 May, 1867, Charles Vogt, Printer, New York, 1867.

"An Important Project," *New York Times,* March 31, 1873, p. 8.

"An Incident in Bergen County", *Papers and Proceedings of the Bergen County Historical Society,* Rev. John C. Voorhis, no. 10, 1914-1915.

Archives of the State of NJ, *Documents Relating to the Colonial History of the State of New Jersey, Vol. XXVIII, Extracts from American Newspapers, Relating to New Jersey Vol. IX 1772-1773,* Paterson, The Call Printing and Publishing Co., 1916.

"Army Deepening River Lane to Kearny," *New York Times,* July 1, 1973, p. 48.

Atchsin, Robert and Perazio, Philip, *Phase IA Cultural Resources Investigation of the Tunnel Outlet & Workshaft Locations for the Passaic RiverBasin Flood Control Tunnel, Hudson, Essex and Passaic Counties, New Jersey,* Kittatinny Archaeological Resources, Stroudsburg, PA, 1995.

Altshuler, Jeanee, *Dumont Heritage,* Mayor & Council of the Borough of Dumont, Dumont, NJ, 1969.

Anderson Family, Collection of the.

A Basin Wide Approach to Dredged Material Management in New York/New Jersey Harbor, Thomas H. Wakeman, Department of Port Commerce, Port Authority of New York and New Jersey, 2001.

Barry, Kevin, Editor, *New Jersey 1992 State Wide Water Quality Inventory Report*, New Jersey Department of Environmental Protection and Energy, Trenton, NJ, 1993.

Becker, Donald, *Indian Place Names in New Jersey*, Phillips – Campbell Publishing Co., Cedar Grove, NJ, 1964.

Bergen County Democrat, September 8, 1905.

Ibid., May 15, 1858.

Ibid., June 26th 1858.

Ibid., August 7th, 1858.

Ibid., August 21, 1858.

"Big Trash Heap to Become Urban Park," Jacobs, Andrew, *New York Times*, May 13, 2003.

Bill of Sale for the sloop "Union of Hackensack", dated October 18, 1794, Bergen County Historical Society.

"The Blind Lighthouse of the Passaic," *Newark Sunday Call*, July 4, 1915.

"Boats Jammed Into a Draw," *New York Times*, March 16, 1881, p. 8.

Boatnerd website, http://www.boatnerd.com/pictures/fleet/algocen.htm

Bogert, Frederick, *Bergen County, New Jersey History and Heritage, Vol. 3.*, Bergen County Board of Chosen Freeholders, Hackensack, NJ, 1983.

"Boisterous Crew Reveals Rum Ship," *New York Times*, May 4, 1928, p. 10.

Brooks, Christopher J., *Passaic Valley Sewerage Commissioners' Education and Outreach Program*, Passaic Valley Sewerage Commissioners, 600 Wilson Avenue, Newark, NJ, 2006.

Brydon, Norman F. *The Passaic River, Past, Present and Future*, Rutgers University Press, 1974.

Bunker, J., *Harbor and Haven: An Illustrated History of the Port of New York*, Windsor Publications, Northridge, CA, 1979.

"Canoe has Experts at Sea", May, Timothy D., *The Record*, February, 3, 1997.

Carse, Robert, *Towline - The Story of American Tugboats*, W.W. Norton & Co., 1969.

Cawley, James & Margaret, *Exploring the Little Rivers of New Jersey*, Princeton University Press, Princeton, 1942.

"City and Suburban News," *New York Times*, October 21, 1891, p. 3.

Clark, Edmund S., "Death List of a Day," *New York Times*, May 30, 1907, p. 7.

Clayton, Woodford W., *History of Bergen & Passaic Counties, New Jersey*, Everts & Pek, Philadelphia, 1882.

"Cleaning up a River," Fallon, Scott, *The Record*, April 26, 2007, p. L-1.

Coates, Joann, *Trade Networks in the Monksville Area*. Paper presented to the Archeological Society of New Jersey, October, 1985.

Cole, Howard, personal communication.

Collections of the New Jersey Historical Society, Vol. VI, New Jersey Historical Society, Newark, NJ 1864.

Colonial New Jersey Newspaper Extracts

"Color Manufacturers Buy Industrial Plant in Newark," *New York Times*, December 26, 1927, p. 38.

Conniff, James, *The Energy People, A History of PSE&G*, Public Service Electric and Gas, Newark, NJ, 1978.

"Crews Down to Five," *New York Times*, March 23, 1973, p. 100.

Cultural Resource Investigation of Ten Sites in the Hackensack Meadowlands, Prepared for: U.S. Army Corps of Engineers New York District, February 2006 (revised August 2006).

Cunningham, John T., "Games People Played: Sports in New Jersey History," *New Jersey History*, Vol. 103, numbers 3-4, Fall/Winter 1985, p. 1.

Cunningham, John T., *Railroading in New Jersey*, Associated Railroads of New Jersey, 1951.

Cunningham, John T., *Railroads in New Jersey: the Formative Years*, Afton Publishing Co, Andover, NJ, 1998.

Cunningham, John T. and Cummings, Charles F., *Remembering Essex: A Pictoral History of Essex County*, New Jersey, Donning Company Publishers, Virginia Beach, VA, 1995.

DeGraeve, G. M., *Contaminant Assessment and Reduction Program (CARP) Overview As related to Contaminants Being Discharged to the Passaic River*, Great Lakes Environmental Center, 739 Hastings Street, Traverse City, MI, 2006.

"Delays on the Erie," Maddy, J.H., *New York Times*, May 6, 1910.

"The Development of the Kearny Meadows, Hudson County New Jersey", Michael A. McGowan and Mark J. Zdepski, JZM Geology Flemington, NJ, Presented at the Drew Symposium for Industrial Archaeology, Drew University, 1998.

The Development of Transportation in New Jersey, New Jersey Department of Transportation, Office of Information Services, Trenton, NJ, 1975.

DeVita, Robert, *Passaic Valley Sewerage Commissioners' Passaic River/Newark Bay Restoration Program*, Passaic Valley Sewerage Commissioners, 600 Wilson Avenue, Newark, NJ, 2006.

Donnelley's Industrial Directory, New York District 1928 - 29, Reuben H. Donnelley Corp, New York, 1928.

Draft Geochemical Evaluation, Lower Passaic River Restoration Project, Malcolm Pirnie, Inc., March, 2006.

Dunlop's Pennsylvania Packet, No. 133, May 9, 1774.

"Early Evolution of the Sloops of the Hudson River", *American Neptune*, Paul E. Fontenoy, Vol. 54, no. 3, Summer 1994.

Elliott-Shaw, Catherine and Cost, Sharon, *On the Lower Passaic River - the New Jersey Green Acres Program has allowed the Land Preservation within the Lower Passaic River Watershed*, NJDEP, Green Acres Program, Trenton, NJ, 2006.

"Employment Forecast for Northern New Jersey is Bright with a Lot of Highs," Pinto, Jennefer, *The Record*, Sunday February 4, 2007, p. J-1.

"Environmentalists Sue over Newark Bay Study," Spencer, Peter N., *Newhouse News Service*, March 11, 2004.

Ewald, Diary of Cpt. Johann, German Light Infantry.

Eric Stern, USEPA, personal communication.

Fabend, Firth Haring, *A Dutch Family in the Middle Colonies, 1660-1800*, copyright 1991 by Firth Haring Fabend.

"Federal Shipyard has Begun to Hire Women as Replacements", *New York Times*, October 18, 1942, p. S10.

"The Final Century of the Wampum Industry in Bergen County", *Papers and Proceedings of the Bergen County Historical Society*, Frances A. Westervelt 1915-1916.

Fogarty, Catherine M., O'Connor, John E. and Cummings, Charles F., *Bergen County: a Pictorial History*, Donning Company, Norfolk, VA, 1985.

Folsom, *Municipalities of Essex*, Lewis Historical Publishing Co., New York, 1925.

Frazer, Perry, D. "September is the Month for Railbird Shooting," *New York Times*, September 1, 1912, p. SM15.

Garvey, Edward A.;, Accardi-Dey, AmyMarie; Atmadja, Juliana; Biteman, Susanne; Desai, Manali; Ezeagu, Adrian; Gbondo-Tugbawa, Solomon; How, Cindy; McDonald, Shane; Peake, John; Zamek, Erika; and Zeiner, Carolyn, *A Basin Wide Approach to dredged material management in New York, New Jersey Harbor, Recent Findings on the Extent of Contamination in the Lower Passaic River*, Malcolm Pirnie, Inc., Fair Lawn, NJ, 2006

Goudsward, Jack, personal communication.

"Great Falls Master Plan Announced Wednesday," Lara, Elizabeth, *Herald News*, November 22, 2006.

Greiff, Constance, personal communication.

Hackensack Meadowlands Development Commission, Master Land Use Plan. Hackensack Meadowlands Development Commission, Lyndhurst, NJ, 1973.

"Hackensack River Rolls on as of Old, but Scenery Has Changed With Traffic," Hays, Daniel, *New York Times*, February 20, 1972, p. 98.

Hackensack River Guardian, Sept. 1985, Vol. 1, no. 2, Hackensack River Coalition.

Hackensack Water Company News, #083, August 5, 1993.

Harcron, Robert W., and Tliesing, Mary Anne, *The Hackensack Meadowlands District*, USEPA, Region 11, New York, NY.

Haynes, William S., *American Chemical Industry, Background & Beginnings*, Vol. I, D. Van Nostrand & Co., New York, 1954, p. 183.

"High Gale Makes Trouble in the Bay," *New York Times*, February 21, 1909, p. 5.

History of Paterson and Its Relations with the World, by the Senior Class of the State Normal School at Paterson, NJ, Hudson Dispatch Printers, Union City, NJ, 1932.

"HMDC is Now the New Jersey Meadowlands Commission", New Jersey Meadowlands Commission, NJMC Press Release, August 27, 2001.

Iannuzzi, Timothy J., Editor, *A Common Tragedy: History of an Urban River*, Amhearst Scientific Publishers, 2002.

Iannuzzi, T. J.; Huntley S. L.; Schmidt, C. W.; Finley, B. L.; McNutt, R. P.; and Burton, S. J.; "Combined sewer overflows (CSOs) as sources of sediment contamination in the lower Passaic River," *Chemosphere*, Volume 34, Issue 2 , January 1997, pp. 213-231.

"In New Jersey," *New York Times*, August 7, 1914, p. 18.

Jackson, Charles, Brickmaking Exhibit at the 1985 Hackensack River Festival.

John Philip Holland 1841 - 1914, The Paterson Museum, Paterson, NJ.

Johns, Al, Personal Communication.

Johnson, James, P., *New Jersey History of Ingenuity and Invention*, Windsor Publications, Northridge, CA, 1987.

Kalata, Barbara, N., *A Hundred Years, A Hundred Miles, New Jersey's Morris Canal*, Morristown, Morris County Historical Society, 1983.

Kearny Museum Commission, personal communication.

Koehler, Frances C., *Three Hundred Years, the Story of the Hackensack Valley, Its Settlement and Growth*, 1940.

Krzminski, Thaddeus, personal communication.

Kummel, Henry B., State Geologist, *The Clays and Clay Industry of New Jersey*, Geological Survey of N.J., Trenton, N.J., 1904.

Lane, Wheaton J. *From Indian Trail to Iron Horse*, Princeton University Press, Princeton, NJ, 1939.

Larry Robertson, Historian, personal communication.

Lee, James, *Tales the Boatmen Told*, Canal Press Inc., 1977.

Levitt, James H., *For Want of Trade, Shipping and the New Jersey Ports, 1680 to 1783*, New Jersey Historical Society, Newark, NJ, 1981.

Lieby, Adrian C., Wichman, Nancy, *The Hackensack Water Company 1869-1969*, Bergen County Historical Society, River Edge, NJ, 1969.

Leiby, Adrian C. *The Revolutionary War in the Hackensack Valley*, Rutgers University Press, 1962.

Little Ferry Municipal website, http://www.littleferrynj.org/page2.html

Lucas, Walter Arndt, *From the Hills to the Hudson*, The Cornwall Press Inc., 1944.

Mankiewicz, Paul S. and McDonnell, Todd, *Coupling Ecological Restoration with Bioremediation to Target Dioxin Mineralization, Metal and Hydrocarbon Removal in the Passaic River*, The Gaia Institute, Bronx, NY, 2006.

Marshall, Stephen G. and Marshall, Tammy A., *An Environmental History of the Harrison Reach of the Lower Passaic River, 1666-2006*, New Jersey Meadowlands Commission, 1 DeKorte Park Plaza, Lyndhurst, NJ, 2006.

Meyers, William S., Ph.D., Editor, *The Story of New Jersey*, Lewis Historical Publishing Co., New York, 1945.

"A Mile of Trains Stalled," *New York Times*, May 5, 1910, p. 6.

Minutes of the Provincial Congress of the State of New Jersey, Day & Naar, Trenton, NJ, 1879.

Morrison, John H., *History of American Steam Navigation*, W.F. Sametz & Co., 1903.

"Motor Boats and Cruising," *New York Times*, June 8, 1947, p. S7.

The Municipalities of Essex County 1666-1924, edited by Joseph Fulford Folson, Vol 1, 1925, Lewis Historical Publishing Co., New York, 1925.

Munoz, Gabriela R.; Panero, Marta A.; and Valle, Sandra; *Dioxin Inputs from Contaminated Land Sites along the Passaic River*, Harbor Project, New York Academy of Sciences, 2 East 63rd Street, New York, NY, 2006.

Murphy, Palmer J, *Paterson and Passaic County, An Illustrated History*, Windsor Publications, Northridge, CA, 1987.

Musser, James, Musser Historic Research, personal communication.

Naval Documents of the American Revolution, United States Naval Institute Press, Annapolis, MD.

"Navy Takes Over Kearny Shipyard," *New York Times*, January 1, 1949, p. 27.

"Newark Bay," *New York Times*, July 24, 1868, p. 8.

Newark Evening News, July 27th, 1893.

"New Bridge", *Papers & Proceedings of the Bergen County Historical Society, 1906-1907.*

New Jersey State Papers, Vol. VI, no. 63.

New Jersey 1992 State Water Quality Inventory Report, New Jersey Department of Environmental Protection and Energy, Trenton, NJ, 1993.

"New Transports Biggest Ever Built Here; Liken to a 'Small City on the Move'," *New York Times,* October 31, 1943, p. 51.

The New York Gazette and Weekly Mercury, February 7, 1774.

Ibid., April 7, 1777.

Ibid., November 27, 1780.

New York Times, June 1, 1861, p. 8.

"Oysters Hackensack", Fallon, Scott, *The Record,* Thursday October 5, 2006, p. L1

Passaic River Basin News, Spring-Winter 1998.

"The Passaic River As It Was of Old," *Newark Sunday Call,* June 11, 1905, p. B1.

Paterson Intelligencer, January 16, 1828.

Ibid., May 7, 1828.

Ibid., July 16, 1828.

Ibid., August 20, 1828.

Ibid., August 27, 1828

Pence, Anne, Ph.D. dissertation, *Dominant Forces in an Estuarine Complex with Multiple Tributaries and Free Connections to the Open Ocean with Application to Sediment Transport,* Department of Civil, Environmental, and Ocean Engineering, Stevens Institute of Technology, 2004.

The Port of New York, N.Y. and N.J., Port Series No.5, Government Printing Office, 1978.

"Raid Newark Distillery," New York Times, February 27, 1932, p. 22.

"The Ramapo Works", North Jersey Highlander, Jack Chard, Vol. XVII, No. 2, 1982.

Ransome, James, *Vanishing Ironworks of the Ramapos*, Rutgers University Press, 1966.

Read, Phillip, *Images of Clifton*, Arcadia Books, Charlestown, SC, 2001.

"Return of the Oyster," Traster, Tina, *Bergen Record*, September 27, 1997.

"The Ridgefield Regatta," *New York Times*, September 28, 1873, p. 5.

"Rights of Navigation," Putney, Jr., Freeman, *New York Times*, February 8, 1907, p. 8.

"River rescue team hopes bond plan is floated," Gavin, John A., *The Record*, Sunday, February 4, 2007.

"River Trip Industrial Index of Newark," Brennan-Carr, Gertrude, *Newark Call*, November 1, 1936.

Robinson, Archibald, *Diaries and Sketches in America*, edited by H.M. Lydenberg, reprinted in *Bulletin of the New York Public Library*, Vol. XXXVII, 1933.

Rutsch, Edward, personal communication.

Ryerson, Phylis, personal communication.

"Sale of Shipyard Draws Union Fire," *New York Times*, April 24, 1948, p. 31.

Schoepf, J.D., *Travels in the Confederation*, Vol. I, 1911.

"Scooped Alligator in Crab Net", *New York Times*, August 30, 1903, p. 12.

Scott, William W., *History of Passaic and Its Environs*, Lewis Historical Publishing Co., New York, 1922.

"Searchers pull missing man's body from Passaic River," Crouse, Douglass, *The Record*, Saturday, November 25, 2006.

Sheehan, Captain Bill, personal communication.

"Ship Hits Rail Bridge, Halting New Jersey Lines," *New York Times*, December 2, 1994, p. B4.

"A Shipwright of 1812", *Sunday News*, December 30, 1883, p. 2.

Siegel, Alan, A., *Out of Our Past, A History of Irvington, New Jersey*, Irvington Centennial Committee, Irvington, NJ, 1974.

Sekoni, Tosin A. and Friedman, Bruce S., *The Impact of the Municipal Stormwater Regulations on the Quality of the Passaic River*, New Jersey Department of Environmental Protection, Trenton, NJ, 2006.

Smith, Leon A. *The Story of New Milford, N.J., Birthplace of Bergen County*, Borough of New Milford, NJ, 1964.

Society for Establishing Useful Manufacturers, Paterson, NJ, 1829.

"Steamer Wrecks Bridge in Jersey," *New York Times*, February 4, 1946, p. 24.

The Steuben House, New Jersey Dept. of Environmental Protection, Division of Parks and Forestry, Trenton, NJ, 1989.

"Stirring the Waters, Some Fear Deepening the Harbor will Dredge Up Pollution," Pearce, Jeremy, *New York Times*, August 24, 2003, p. NJ1.

"Strike Cripples Kearny Shipyard; 6,000 Quit Over 5 Men," *New York Times*, October 15, 1943, p. 1.

Taylor, Milfred, *The History of Teaneck*, Teaneck American Revolution Bicentennial Committee, Teaneck, NJ, 1977.

"Testifies He Bought Ship Job For $500," *New York Times*, May 25, 1943, p. 17.

Townsend, Thomas. *The Home Afloat, or Boy Trappers of the Hackensack*, Athenia Publishing Co., Athenia, NJ, 1908.

Toxic Crab Outreach in the Newark Bay Complex: Working with Local Liaisons to Communicate the Dangers of Eating Contaminated Crabs, Kerry Kirk Pflugh, Lynette Lurig and Harold Nebling, New Jersey Department of Environmental Protection, 401 East State Street, Trenton, NJ., 2006.

"Trains Delayed in Jersey," *New York Times*," August 5, 1947, p. 12.

US EPA Weequahic Lake website, http://epa.gov/region2/water/lakes/we-equahic.htm

"USS Ling needs a new home," Alvarado, Monsy, *The Record*, January 24, 2007.

USS Ling SS297, Leward Publications, Annapolis, MD, 1979.

"Volunteers aid environmental agencies," Tomsho, Robert, *Wall Street Journal*. (Eastern edition), July 27, 1993, p. B1.

"Waterworks is at Center of a Battle In New Jersey," Newman, Maria, *New York Times*, June 7, 2002. p. B1.

Weiss, Harry B., and Weiss Grace M., *Early Sports and Pastimes in New Jersey*, The Past Times Press, Trenton, NJ, 1960.

Westervelt, Frances A., *History of Bergen County, New Jersey, 1630-1923*, New York, Lewis Historical Publishing Company, Inc., Vol. 1, 1923.

Whitehead, John, LL.D., *The Passaic Valley in Three Centuries*, New Jersey Geneological Company, New York, NY, 1901.

"Wind Jammers of the Hackensack", Eugene Bird, *Papers and Proceedings of the Bergen County Historical Society*, No. 11, 1915-1916.

Winfield, *History of Hudson County*, Kennard & Hay, New York, 1874.

"With His Art, One Can Find a River's History on a Sign," Marsh, Margo, *New York Times*, September 10, 2000, p. NJ12.

Woodford, Clayton W., *History of Bergen and Passaic Counties New Jersey*, Everts & Pek, Philadelphia, PA, 1882.

World Dredging Mining & Construction, December 2005, pp. 1 and 3.

Wright, Kevin, Curator, New Bridge Landing State Historic Site, personal communication.

Writings of George Washington from the Original Manuscript Sources, 1745-1799, John C. Fitzpatrick, Editor. Library of Congress Collection.

Yeager, Henry J. "By Steamboat Across New Jersey," *New Jersey History*, Vol LXXXVII, no. 2, Summer 1969, p. 105.

Index

C

D

O

Occidental Chemical *see Diamond Alkali Corporation*
Old Bridge, 30, 31, 35, 60, 103
Oradell Reservoir, 134-36, 194
Oradell, town of, 6, 69, 125-26, 131-32, 192-93, 206-08
Outwater Militia, 47-48, 51
Overpeck Creek, 31-32, 69, 89, 112

P

Paramus, 14, 99
Passaic (city of), 4, 15, 31, 67, 76, 78, 80-82, 98, 151, 153
Passaic Valley Sewerage Commission, 173-76, 179, 185
Paterson, 6, 15, 31, 36, 53, 55-56, 59, 67-69, 78, 81, 88, 107, 116, 127, 136-38, 141, 174, 177, 202-04, 215
Paterson and Hudson River Railroad, 54, 67-70
Paulus Hook, 9, 31-33, 35, 41, 49, 102, 209
Pennsylvania Railroad, 78, 92, 94, 103, 146
Periauger, 19, 20-22, 26, 29, 53, 84, 89
Petroleum, 96, 154, 168-69, 171
Pirate(s), 24, 37, 38
Plank Road, 37, 103, 116-17, 142
Prohibition, 142-43, 162, 181

Q

Queen's College *see Rutgers University*

R

Railroads *see individual railroad names*
Reclamation, 18, 111-12, 114-16, 189
Refugees *see Loyalists*
River and Harbor Acts, 93, 151-52
River Edge, 4, 13-14, 60, 99, 101-02, 131, 199
Rockaway (Long Island), 60, 130
Rowing, 11, 49, 110, 121-25, 128
Rumrunner *see prohibition*
Rutgers University, 75-76, 178, 183, 188
Rutherford, 17, 37, 69, 114-15, 203

About the Author

Kevin Olsen is a member of Montclair State University's Passaic River Institute. He is a native of northern New Jersey and at one time or another has paddled up, floated down, or sailed over every important water body in the region. He is a former officer of the North Jersey Highlands Historical Society. He has been a volunteer at Wayne Township's Van Riper Hopper House Museum's Archaeological  Research Laboratory and a docent at the Dey Mansion Museum. During a brief time as a professional field archaeologist he worked on sites in the Delaware Water Gap, lower Manhattan, and at the Monksville Reservoir in Ringwood, New Jersey.

He has a B.S. in chemistry from New Hampshire's Plymouth State University and a M.S. in chemistry from New Jersey's Montclair State University. He is currently employed as an instrumentation specialist on the support staff of Montclair State's Chemistry and Biochemistry Department.

His past publications on local history have appeared in the *North Jersey Highlander*, the *American Neptune*, and the *Encyclopedia of New Jersey*. His papers about the history of chemistry have appeared in the *Bulletin for the History of Chemistry* and the *Indicator*, News Magazine of the North Jersey Section of the American Chemical Society.